5th Workshop on Innovative Use of NLP for Building Educational Applications 2010

Held at NAACL HLT 2010

Los Angeles, California, USA
5 June 2010

ISBN: 978-1-61738-679-4

Printed from e-media with permission by:

Curran Associates, Inc.
57 Morehouse Lane
Red Hook, NY 12571

Some format issues inherent in the e-media version may also appear in this print version.

Printed by Curran Associates, Inc. (2010)

Association for Computational Linguistics
209 N. Eighth Street
Stroudsburg, Pennsylvania 18360

Phone: 1-570-476-8006
Fax: 1-570-476-0860

acl@aclweb.org

Additional copies of this publication are available from:

Curran Associates, Inc.
57 Morehouse Lane
Red Hook, NY 12571 USA
Phone: 845-758-0400
Fax: 845-758-2634
Email: curran@proceedings.com
Web: www.proceedings.com

Introduction

NLP researchers are now building educational applications across a number of areas, including automated evaluation of student writing and speaking, rich grammatical error detection with an increasing focus on English language learning, tools to support student reading, and intelligent tutoring.

This workshop is the fifth in a series, specifically related to Building NLP Applications for Education, that began at NAACL/HLT (2003), and continued at ACL 2005 (Ann Arbor), ACL/HLT 2008 (Columbus), NAACL/HLT 2009 (Boulder), and now at NAACL/HLT 2010 (Los Angeles). Research in this area continues to grow, and there is ever-increasing interest and practical application which was evidenced this year, again, by an even larger number of submissions.

We received a record 28 submissions and accepted 13 papers, two of which include demos. All of the papers are published in these proceedings. Each paper was carefully reviewed by two members of the Program Committee. We selected reviewers most appropriate for each paper so as to give more helpful feedback and comments. This workshop offers an opportunity to present and publish work that is highly relevant to NAACL, but is also highly specialized, and so this workshop is often a more appropriate venue for such work. While the field is growing, we do recognize that there is a core group of institutions and researchers who work in this area. That said, we continue to have a very strong policy to deal with conflicts of interest. First, reviewers were not assigned any papers to evaluate if the paper had an author from their institution. Second, with respect to the organizing committee, authors of papers where there was a conflict of interest recused themselves from the discussion.

The papers accepted to this workshop were selected on the basis of several factors: the strength of the research, the novelty of the approach or domain, and the appropriateness for this workshop. The final set of papers fall under several main themes which we show below in the order of the workshop program.

Technology designed to support reading comprehension:

- Readability Assessment for Text Simplification (Aluisio, Specia, Gasperin and Scarton)
- Enhancing Authentic Web Pages for Language Learners (Meurers, Ziai, Amaral, Boyd, Dimitrov, Metcalf and Ott)
- AutoTutor: a piece of cake for teachers (Quixal, Preu, Garca-Narbona and Boullosa)

Learner error detection and annotation:

- Annotating ESL Errors: Challenges and Rewards (Rozovskaya and Roth)
- Search right and thou shalt find ... Using Web Queries for Learner Error Detection (Gamon and Leacock)
- Rethinking Grammatical Error Annotation and Evaluation with the Amazon Mechanical Turk (Tetreault, Filatova and Chodorow)

Classroom assessment and instruction:

- Predicting Cloze Task Quality for Vocabulary Training (Skory and Eskenazi)
- Generating Quantifiers and Negation to Explain Homework Testing (Perry and Shan)
- Leveraging Hidden Dialogue State to Select Tutorial Moves (Boyer, Phillips, Ha, Wallis, Vouk and Lester)

Evaluation of Noisy Data:

- Towards Using Structural Events To Assess Non-native Speech (Lei Chen, Joel Tetreault and Xiaoming Xi)
- A Human-Computer Collaboration Approach to Improve Accuracy of an Automated English Scoring System (Jee Eun Kim and Kong Joo Lee)
- Towards Identifying Unresolved Discussions in Student Online Forums (Jihie Kim, Jia Li and Taehwan Kim)
- Off-topic essay detection using short prompt texts (Louis and Higgins)

We wish to thank everyone who showed interest and submitted a paper, all of the authors for their contributions, the members of the Program Committee for their thoughtful reviews, and everyone who attended this workshop. All of these factors contribute to a truly rich and successful event!

Joel Tetreault, Educational Testing Service
Jill Burstein, Educational Testing Service
Claudia Leacock, Butler-Hill Group

Organizers:

Joel Tetreault, Educational Testing Service
Jill Burstein, Educational Testing Service
Claudia Leacock, Butler Hill Group

Program Committee:

Delphine Bernhard, LIMSI-CNRS, France
Jared Bernstein, Pearson, USA
Martin Chodorow, Hunter College, CUNY, USA
Barbara Di Eugenio, University of Illinois at Chicago, USA
Markus Dickinson, Indiana University, USA
William B. Dolan, Microsoft, USA
Maxine Eskenazi, Carnegie Mellon University, USA
Peter Foltz, Pearson, USA
Jennifer Foster, Dublin City University, Ireland
Annette Frank, University of Heidelberg, Germany
Michael Gamon, Microsoft, USA
Caroline Gasperin, University of Sao Paolo, Brazil
Iryna Gurevych, University of Darmstadt, Germany
Na-Rae Han, University of Pittsburgh, USA
Trude Heift, Simon Frasier University, Canada
Derrick Higgins, ETS, USA
Emi Izumi, NICT, Japan
Pamela Jordan, University of Pittsburgh, USA
Ola Knutsson, KTH Nada, Sweden
John Lee, City University of Hong Kong, China
Diane Litman, University of Pittsburgh, USA
Detmar Meurers, University of Tubingen, Germany
Lisa Michaud, Saint Anselm College, USA
Ani Nenkova, University of Pennsylvania, USA
Mari Ostendorf, University of Washington, USA
Ted Pedersen, University of Minnesota, USA
Mihai Rotaru, TextKernel, the Netherlands
Dan Roth, UIUC, USA
Mathias Schulze, University of Waterloo, Canada
Stephanie Seneff, MIT, USA
Richard Sproat, Oregon Graduate Institute, USA
Jana Sukkarieh, ETS, USA
Svetlana Stoyanchev, Open University, UK
Nai-Lung Tsao, National Central University, Taiwan

Pete Whitelock, Oxford University Press, UK
David Wible, National Central University, Taiwan
Magdalena Wolska, Saarbruken University, Germany

Table of Contents

Readability Assessment for Text Simplification
Sandra Aluisio, Lucia Specia, Caroline Gasperin and Carolina Scarton 1

Enhancing Authentic Web Pages for Language Learners
Detmar Meurers, Ramon Ziai, Luiz Amaral, Adriane Boyd, Aleksandar Dimitrov, Vanessa Metcalf and Niels Ott 10

AutoLearn's authoring tool: a piece of cake for teachers
Martí Quixal, Susanne Preuß, David García-Narbona and Beto Boullosa 19

Annotating ESL Errors: Challenges and Rewards
Alla Rozovskaya and Dan Roth 28

Search right and thou shalt find ... Using Web Queries for Learner Error Detection
Michael Gamon and Claudia Leacock 37

Rethinking Grammatical Error Annotation and Evaluation with the Amazon Mechanical Turk
Joel Tetreault, Elena Filatova and Martin Chodorow 45

Predicting Cloze Task Quality for Vocabulary Training
Adam Skory and Maxine Eskenazi 49

Generating Quantifiers and Negation to Explain Homework Testing
Jason Perry and Chung-chieh Shan 57

Leveraging Hidden Dialogue State to Select Tutorial Moves
Kristy Boyer, Rob Phillips, Eun Young Ha, Michael Wallis, Mladen Vouk and James Lester . . . 66

Towards Using Structural Events To Assess Non-native Speech
Lei Chen, Joel Tetreault and Xiaoming Xi 74

A Human-Computer Collaboration Approach to Improve Accuracy of an Automated English Scoring System
Jee Eun Kim and Kong Joo Lee 80

Towards Identifying Unresolved Discussions in Student Online Forums
Jihie Kim, Jia Li and Taehwan Kim 84

Off-topic essay detection using short prompt texts
Annie Louis and Derrick Higgins 92

Workshop Program

Saturday, June 5, 2010

9:00–9:15 Opening Remarks

9:15–9:40 *Readability Assessment for Text Simplification*
Sandra Aluisio, Lucia Specia, Caroline Gasperin and Carolina Scarton

9:40–10:05 *Enhancing Authentic Web Pages for Language Learners*
Detmar Meurers, Ramon Ziai, Luiz Amaral, Adriane Boyd, Aleksandar Dimitrov, Vanessa Metcalf and Niels Ott

10:05–10:30 *AutoLearn's authoring tool: a piece of cake for teachers*
Martí Quixal, Susanne Preuß, David García-Narbona and Beto Boullosa

10:30–11:00 **Break**

11:00–11:25 *Annotating ESL Errors: Challenges and Rewards*
Alla Rozovskaya and Dan Roth

11:25–11:50 *Search right and thou shalt find ... Using Web Queries for Learner Error Detection*
Michael Gamon and Claudia Leacock

11:50–12:10 *Rethinking Grammatical Error Annotation and Evaluation with the Amazon Mechanical Turk*
Joel Tetreault, Elena Filatova and Martin Chodorow

12:10–1:45 **Lunch**

1:45–2:10 *Predicting Cloze Task Quality for Vocabulary Training*
Adam Skory and Maxine Eskenazi

2:10–2:35 *Generating Quantifiers and Negation to Explain Homework Testing*
Jason Perry and Chung-chieh Shan

2:35–3:00 *Leveraging Hidden Dialogue State to Select Tutorial Moves*
Kristy Boyer, Rob Phillips, Eun Young Ha, Michael Wallis, Mladen Vouk and James Lester

3:00–3:30 **Break**

3:30–3:55 *Towards Using Structural Events To Assess Non-native Speech*
Lei Chen, Joel Tetreault and Xiaoming Xi

3:55–4:15 *A Human-Computer Collaboration Approach to Improve Accuracy of an Automated English Scoring System*
Jee Eun Kim and Kong Joo Lee

4:15–4:40 *Towards Identifying Unresolved Discussions in Student Online Forums*
Jihie Kim, Jia Li and Taehwan Kim

4:40–5:00 *Off-topic essay detection using short prompt texts*
Annie Louis and Derrick Higgins

Readability Assessment for Text Simplification

Sandra Aluisio[1], Lucia Specia[2], Caroline Gasperin[1] and Carolina Scarton[1]

[1]Center of Computational Linguistics (NILC)
University of São Paulo
São Carlos - SP, Brazil
{sandra,cgasperin}@icmc.usp.br,
carol.scarton@gmail.com

[2]Research Group in Computational Linguistics
University of Wolverhampton
Wolverhampton, UK
L.Specia@wlv.ac.uk

Abstract

We describe a readability assessment approach to support the process of text simplification for poor literacy readers. Given an input text, the goal is to predict its readability level, which corresponds to the literacy level that is expected from the target reader: rudimentary, basic or advanced. We complement features traditionally used for readability assessment with a number of new features, and experiment with alternative ways to model this problem using machine learning methods, namely classification, regression and ranking. The best resulting model is embedded in an authoring tool for Text Simplification.

1 Introduction

In Brazil, the National Indicator of Functional Literacy (INAF) index has been computed annually since 2001 to measure the levels of literacy of the Brazilian population. The 2009 report presented a worrying scenario: 7% of the individuals are illiterate; 21% are literate at the rudimentary level; 47% are literate at the basic level; only 25% are literate at the advanced level (INAF, 2009). These literacy levels are defined as:

(1) Illiterate: individuals who cannot perform simple tasks such as reading words and phrases;

(2) Rudimentary: individuals who can find explicit information in short and familiar texts (such as an advertisement or a short letter);

(3) Basic: individuals who are functionally literate, i.e., they can read and understand texts of average length, and find information even when it is necessary to make some inference; and

(4) Advanced: fully literate individuals, who can read longer texts, relating their parts, comparing and interpreting information, distinguish fact from opinion, make inferences and synthesize.

In order to promote digital inclusion and accessibility for people with low levels of literacy, particularly to documents available on the web, it is important to provide text in a simple and easy-to-read way. This is a requirement of the Web Content Accessibility Guidelines 2.0's principle of comprehensibility and accessibility of Web content[1]. It states that for texts which demand reading skills more advanced than that of individuals with lower secondary education, one should offer an alternative version of the same content suitable for those individuals. While readability formulas for English have a long history – 200 formulas have been reported from 1920 to 1980s (Dubay, 2004) – the only tool available for Portuguese is an adaptation of the *Flesch Reading Ease* index. It evaluates the complexity of texts in a 4-level scale corresponding to grade levels (Martins et al., 1996).

In the PorSimples project (Aluísio et al., 2008) we develop text adaptation methods (via text simplification and elaboration approaches) to improve the comprehensibility of texts published on government websites or by renowned news agencies, which are expected to be relevant to a large audience with various literacy levels. The project provides automatic simplification tools to aid (1) poorly literate readers to understand online content – a browser plug-in for automatically simplifying websites – and (2) authors producing texts for this audience – an authoring tool for guiding the creation of simplified versions of texts.

This paper focuses on a readability assessment approach to assist the simplification process in the authoring tool, SIMPLIFICA. The current version of SIMPLIFICA offers simplification operations addressing a number of lexical and syntactic phenomena to make the text more readable. The au-

[1] http://www.w3.org/TR/WCAG20/

Proceedings of the NAACL HLT 2010 Fifth Workshop on Innovative Use of NLP for Building Educational Applications, pages 1–9,
Los Angeles, California, June 2010.

thor has the freedom to choose when and whether to apply the available simplification operations, a decision based on the level of complexity of the current text and on the target reader.

A method for automatically identifying such level of complexity is therefore of great value. With our readability assessment tool, the author is able to automatically check the complexity/readability level of the original text, as well as modified versions of such text produced as he/she applies simplification operations offered by SIMPLIFICA, until the text reaches the expected level, adequate for the target reader.

In this paper we present such readability assessment tool, developed as part of the PorSimples project, and discuss its application within the authoring tool. Different from previous work, the tool does not model text difficulty according to linear grade levels (e.g., Heilman et al., 2008), but instead maps the text into the three levels of literacy defined by INAF: rudimentary, basic or advanced. Moreover, it uses a more comprehensive set of features, different learning techniques and targets a new language and application, as we discuss in Section 4. More specifically, we address the following research questions:

1. Given some training material, is it possible to detect the complexity level of Portuguese texts, which corresponds to the different literacy levels defined by INAF?
2. What is the best way to model this problem and which features are relevant?

We experiment with nominal, ordinal and interval-based modeling techniques and exploit a number of the cognitively motivated features proposed by Coh-Metrix 2.0 (Graesser et al., 2004) and adapted to Portuguese (called Coh-Metrix-PORT), along with a set of new features, including syntactic features to capture simplification operations and n-gram language model features.

In the remainder of this paper, we first provide some background information on the need for a readability assessment tool within our text simplification system (Section 2) and discuss prior work on readability assessment (Section 3), to then present our features and modeling techniques (Section 4) and the experiments performed to answer our research questions (Section 5).

2. Text Simplification in PorSimples

Text Simplification (TS) aims to maximize reading comprehension of written texts through their simplification. Simplification usually involves substituting complex by simpler words and breaking down and changing the syntax of complex, long sentences (Max, 2006; Siddharthan, 2003).

To meet the needs of people with different levels of literacy, in the PorSimples project we propose two types of simplification: *natural* and *strong*. The first type results in texts adequate for people with a basic literacy level and the second, rudimentary level. The difference between these two is the degree of application of simplification operations to complex sentences. In strong simplification, operations are applied to all complex syntactic phenomena present in the text in order to make it as simple as possible, while in natural simplification these operations are applied selectively, only when the resulting text remains "natural". One example of original text (a), along with its natural (b) and strong (c) manual simplifications, is given in Table 1.

(a)	The cinema theaters around the world were showing a production by director Joe Dante in which a shoal of piranhas escaped from a military laboratory and attacked participants of an aquatic show. (...) More than 20 people were bitten by palometas (Serrasalmus spilopleura, a species of piranhas) that live in the waters of the Sanchuri dam.
(b)	The cinema theaters around the world were showing a production by director Joe Dante. In the production a shoal of piranhas escaped from a military laboratory and attacked participants of an aquatic show. (…) More than 20 people were bitten by palometas that live in the waters of the Sanchuri dam. Palometas are Serrasalmus spilopleura, a species of piranhas.
(c)	The cinema theaters around the world were showing a movie by director Joe Dante. In the movie a shoal of piranhas escaped from a military laboratory. The shoal of piranhas attacked participants of an aquatic show. (...). Palometas have bitten more than 20 people. Palometas live in the waters of the Sanchuri dam. Palometas are Serrasalmus spilopleura, a species of piranhas.

Table 1: Example of original and simplified texts

The association between these two types of simplification and the literacy levels was identified by means of a corpus study. We have manually built a corpus of simplified texts at both natural and strong levels and analyzed their linguistic structures according to the description of the two literacy levels. We verified that strong simplified sentences are more adequate for rudimentary level readers, and natural ones for basic level readers. This claim is supported by several studies which relate capabilities and performance of the working memory with reading levels (Siddharthan, 2003; McNamara et al., 2002).

2.1 The Rule-based Simplification System

The association between simplification operations and the syntactic phenomena they address is implemented within a rule-based syntactic simplification system (Candido Jr. et al., 2009). This system is able to identify complex syntactic phenomena in a sentence and perform the appropriate operations to simplify each phenomenon.

The simplification rules follow a manual for syntactic simplification in Portuguese also developed in PorSimples. They cover syntactic constructions such as apposition, relative clauses, coordination and subordination, which had already been addressed by previous work on text simplification (Siddharthan, 2003). Additionally, they address the transformation of sentences from passive into active voice, normalization of sentences into the Subject-Verb-Object order, and simplification of adverbial phrases. The simplification operations available are: sentence splitting, changing particular discourse markers by simpler ones, transforming passive into active voice, inverting the order of clauses, converting to subject-verb-object order, relocating long adverbial phrases.

2.2 The SIMPLIFICA Tool

The rule-based simplification system is part of SIMPLIFICA, an authoring tool for writers to adapt original texts into simplified texts. Within SIMPLIFICA, the author plays an active role in generating natural or strong simplified texts by accepting or rejecting the simplifications offered by the system on a sentence basis and post-editing them if necessary.

Despite the ability to make such choices at the sentence level, it is not straightforward for the author to judge the complexity level of the *text as whole* in order to decide whether it is ready for a certain audience. This is the main motivation for the development of a readability assessment tool.

The readability assessment tool automatically detects the level of complexity of a text at any moment of the authoring process, and therefore guides the author towards producing the adequate simplification level according to the type of reader. It classifies a text in one of three levels: rudimentary, basic or advanced.

Figure 1 shows the interface of SIMPLIFICA, where the complexity level of the current text as given by the readability assessment tool is shown at the bottom, in red (in this case, "*Nível Pleno*", which corresponds to *advanced*). To update the readability assessment of a text the author can choose "*Nível de Inteligibilidade*" (r*eadability level*) at any moment.

The text shown in Figure 1 is composed of 13 sentences, 218 words. The lexical simplification module (not shown in the Figure 1) finds 10 candidate words for simplification in this text, and the syntactic simplification module selects 10 sentences to be simplified (highlighted in gray).

When the author selects a highlighted sentence, he/she is presented with all possible simplifications proposed by the rule-based system for this sentence. Figure 2 shows the options for the first sentence in Figure 1. The first two options cover non-finite clause and adverbial adjuncts, respectively, while the third option covers both phenomena in one single step. The original sentence is also given as an option.

It is possible that certain suggestions of automatic simplifications result in ungrammatical or inadequate sentences (mainly due to parsing errors). The author can choose not to use such suggestions as well as manually edit the original or automatically simplified versions. The impact of the author's choice on the *overall* readability level of the text is not always clear to the author. The goal of the readability assessment function is to provide such information.

Simplified texts are usually longer than the original ones, due to sentence splittings and repetition of information to connect such sentences. We acknowledge that low literacy readers prefer short texts, but in this tool the shortening of the text is a responsibility of the author. Our focus is on the linguistic structure of the texts; the length of the text actually is a feature considered by our readability assessment system.

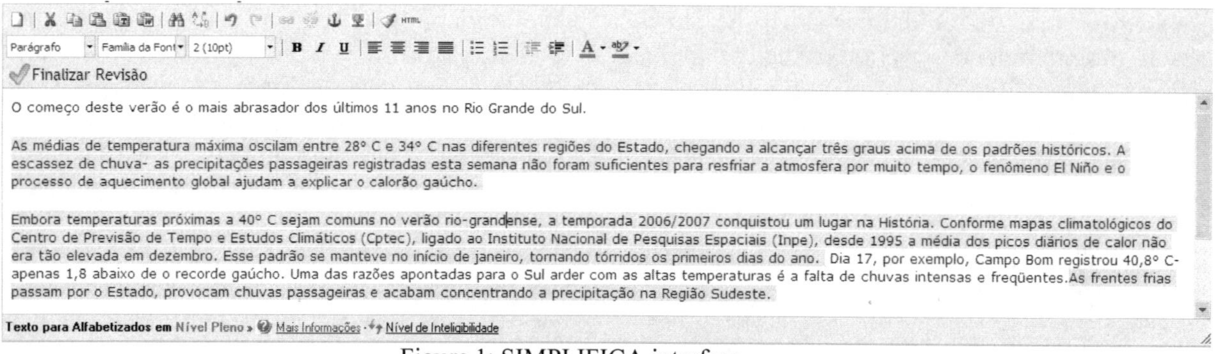

Figure 1: SIMPLIFICA interface

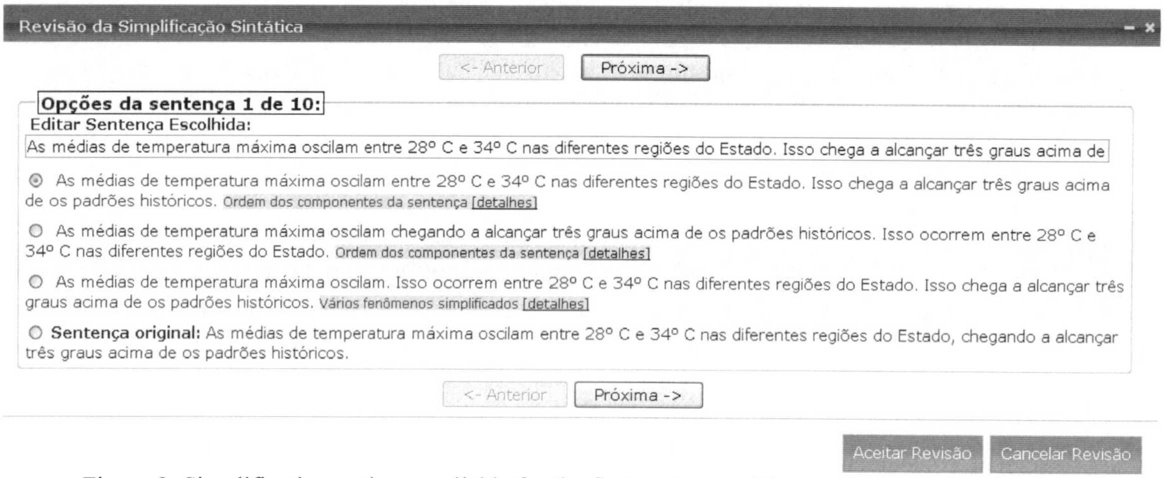

Figure 2. Simplification options available for the first sentence of the text presented in Figure 1

3. Readability Assessment

Recent work on readability assessment for the English language focus on: (i) the **feature set** used to capture the various aspects of readability, to evaluate the contribution of lexical, syntactic, semantic and discursive features; (ii) the **audience** of the texts the readability measurement is intended to; (iii) the **genre** effects on the calculation of text difficult; (iv) the type of **learning technique** which is more appropriate: those producing nominal, ordinal or interval scales of measurement, and (v) providing an **application** for the automatic assessment of reading difficulty.

Pitler and Nenkova (2008) propose a unified framework composed of vocabulary, syntactic, elements of lexical cohesion, entity coherence and discourse relations to measure text quality, which resembles the composition of rubrics in the area of essay scoring (Burstein et al., 2003).

The following studies address readability assessment for specific audiences: learners of English as second language (Schwarm and Ostendorf, 2005; Heilman et al., 2007), people with intellectual disabilities (Feng et al., 2009), and people with cognitive impairment caused by Alzheimer (Roark at al, 2007).

Sheehan et al. (2007) focus on models for literary and expository texts, given that traditional metrics like Flesch-Kincaid Level score tend to overpredict the difficulty of literary texts and underpredict the difficulty of expository texts.

Heilman et al. (2008) investigate an appropriate scale of measurement for reading difficulty – nominal, ordinal, or interval – by comparing the effectiveness of statistical models for each type of data. Petersen and Ostendorf (2009) use classification and regression techniques to predict a readability score.

Miltsakali and Troutt (2007; 2008) propose an automatic tool to evaluate reading difficulty of Web texts in real time, addressing teenagers and adults with low literacy levels. Using machine learning, Glöckner et al. (2006) present a tool for automatically rating the readability of German texts using several linguistic information sources and a global readability score similar to the *Flesch Reading Ease*.

4. A Tool for Readability Assessment

In this section we present our approach to readability assessment. It differs from previous work in the following aspects: (i) it uses a feature set with cognitively-motivated metrics and a number of additional features to provide a better explanation of the complexity of a text; (ii) it targets a new audience: people with different literacy levels; (iii) it investigates different statistical models for non-linear data scales: the levels of literacy defined by INAF, (iv) it focus on a new application: the use of readability assessment for text simplification systems; and (v) it is aimed at Portuguese.

4.1 Features for Assessing Readability

Our feature set (Table 2) consists of 3 groups of features. The first group contains cognitively-motivated features (features 1-42), derived from the Coh-Metrix-PORT tool (see Section 4.1.1). The second group contains features that reflect the incidence of particular syntactic constructions which we target in our text simplification system (features 43-49). The third group (the remaining features in Table 2) contains features derived from n-gram language models built considering unigrams, bigrams and trigrams probability and perplexity plus out-of-vocabulary rate scores. We later refer to a set of *basic features*, which consist of simple counts that do not require any linguistic tool or external resources to be computed. This set corresponds to features 1-3 and 9-11.

4.1.1 Coh-Metrix-Port

The Coh-Metrix tool was developed to compute features potentially relevant to the comprehension of English texts through a number of measures informed by linguistics, psychology and cognitive studies. The main aspects covered by the measures are cohesion and coherence (Graesser et al., 2004).

Coh-Metrix 2.0, the free version of the tool, contains 60 readability metrics. The Coh-Metrix-PORT tool (Scarton et al., 2009) computes similar metrics for texts in Brazilian Portuguese. The major challenge to create such tool is the lack of some of the necessary linguistic resources. The following metrics are currently available in the tool (we refer to Table 2 for details):

1. Readability metric: feature 12.
2. Words and textual information:
   - Basic counts: features 1 to 11.

1	Number of words
2	Number of sentences
3	Number of paragraphs
4	Number of verbs
5	Number of nouns
6	Number of adjectives
7	Number of adverbs
8	Number of pronouns
9	Average number of words per sentence
10	Average number of sentences per paragraph
11	Average number of syllables per word
12	*Flesch* index for Portuguese
13	Incidence of content words
14	Incidence of functional words
15	Raw Frequency of content words
16	Minimal frequency of content words
17	Average number of verb hypernyms
18	Incidence of NPs
19	Number of NP modifiers
20	Number of words before the main verb
21	Number of high level constituents
22	Number of personal pronouns
23	Type-token ratio
24	Pronoun-NP ratio
25	Number of "e" (and)
26	Number of "ou" (or)
27	Number of "se" (if)
28	Number of negations
29	Number of logic operators
30	Number of connectives
31	Number of positive additive connectives
32	Number of negative additive connectives
33	Number of positive temporal connectives
34	Number of negative temporal connectives
35	Number of positive causal connectives
36	Number of negative causal connectives
37	Number of positive logic connectives
38	Number of negative logic connectives
39	Verb ambiguity ratio
40	Noun ambiguity ratio
41	Adverb ambiguity ratio
42	Adjective ambiguity ratio
43	Incidence of clauses
44	Incidence of adverbial phrases
45	Incidence of apposition
46	Incidence of passive voice
47	Incidence of relative clauses
48	Incidence of coordination
49	Incidence of subordination
50	Out-of-vocabulary words
51	LM probability of unigrams
52	LM perplexity of unigrams
53	LM perplexity of unigrams, without line break
54	LM probability of bigrams
55	LM perplexity of bigrams
56	LM perplexity of bigrams, without line break
57	LM probability of trigrams
58	LM perplexity of trigrams
59	LM perplexity of trigrams, without line break

Table 2. Feature set

- Frequencies: features 15 to 16.
- Hypernymy: feature 17.

3. Syntactic information:
   - Constituents: features 18 to 20.
   - Pronouns: feature 22
   - Types and Tokens: features 23 to 24.
   - Connectives: features 30 to 38.
4. Logical operators: features 25 to 29.

The following resources for Portuguese were used: the MXPOST POS tagger (Ratnaparkhi, 1996), a word frequency list compiled from a 700 million-token corpus[2], a tool to identify reduced noun phrases (Oliveira et al., 2006), a list of connectives classified as positives/negatives and according to cohesion type (causal, temporal, additive or logical), a list of logical operators and WordNet.Br (Dias-da-Silva et al., 2008).

In this paper we include seven new metrics to Coh-Metrix-PORT: features 13, 14, 21, and 39 to 42. We used TEP[3] (Dias-da-Silva et al., 2003) to obtain the number of senses of words (and thus their ambiguity level), and the *Palavras* parser (Bick, 2000) to identify the higher level constituents. The remaining metrics were computed based on the POS tags.

According to a report on the performance of each Coh-Metrix-PORT metric (Scarton et al., 2009), no individual feature provides sufficient indication to measure text complexity, and therefore the need to exploit their combination, and also to combine them with the other types of features described in this section.

4.1.2 Language-model Features

Language model features were derived from a large corpus composed of a sample of the Brazilian newspaper *Folha de São Paulo* containing issues from 12 months taken at random from 1994 to 2005. The corpus contains 96,868 texts and 26,425,483 tokens. SRILM (Stolcke, 2002), a standard language modelling toolkit, was used to produce the language model features.

4.2 Learning Techniques

Given that the boundaries of literacy level classes are one of the subjects of our study, we exploit three different types of models in order to check which of them can better distinguish among the three literacy levels. We therefore experiment with three types of machine learning algorithms: a standard classifier, an ordinal (ranking) classifier and a regressor. Each algorithm assumes different relations among the groups: the classifier assumes no relation, the ordinal classifier assumes that the groups are ordered, and the regressor assumes that the groups are continuous.

As classifier we use the Support Vector Machines (SVM) implementation in the Weka[4] toolkit (SMO). As ordinal classifier we use a meta classifier in Weka which takes SMO as the base classification algorithm and performs pairwise classifications (OrdinalClassClassifier). For regression we use the SVM regression implementation in Weka (SMO-reg). We use the linear versions of the algorithms for classification, ordinal classification and regression, and also experiment with a radial basis function (RBF) kernel for regression.

5. Experiments

5.1 Corpora

In order to train (and test) the different machine learning algorithms to automatically identify the readability level of the texts we make use of manually simplified corpora created in the PorSimples project. Seven corpora covering our three literacy levels (advanced, basic and rudimentary) and two different genres were compiled. The first corpus is composed of general news articles from the Brazilian newspaper *Zero Hora* (*ZH original*). These articles were manually simplified by a linguist, expert in text simplification, according to the two levels of simplification: natural (*ZH natural*) and strong (*ZH strong*). The remaining corpora are composed of popular science articles from different sources: (a) the *Caderno Ciência* section of the Brazilian newspaper *Folha de São Paulo*, a mainstream newspaper in Brazil (*CC original*) and a manually simplified version of this corpus using the natural (*CC natural*) and strong (*CC strong*) levels; and (b) advanced level texts from a popular science magazine called *Ciência Hoje* (*CH*). Table 3 shows a few statistics about these seven corpora.

5.2 Feature Analysis

As a simple way to check the contribution of different features to our three literacy levels, we com-

[2] http://www2.lael.pucsp.br/corpora/bp/index.htm
[3] http://www.nilc.icmc.usp.br/tep2/index.htm
[4] http://www.cs.waikato.ac.nz/ml/weka/

Corpus	Doc	Sent	Words	Avg. words per text (std. deviation)	Avg. words p. sentence
ZH original	104	2184	46190	444.1 (133.7)	21.1
ZH natural	104	3234	47296	454.7 (134.2)	14.6
ZH strong	104	3668	47938	460.9 (137.5)	13.0
CC original	50	882	20263	405.2 (175.6)	22.9
CC natural	50	975	19603	392.0 (176.0)	20.1
CC strong	50	1454	20518	410.3 (169.6)	14.1
CH	130	3624	95866	737.4 (226.1)	26.4

Table 3. Corpus statistics

puted the (absolute) Pearson correlation between our features and the expected literacy level for the two sets of corpora that contain versions of the three classes of interest (original, natural and strong). Table 4 lists the most highly correlated features.

	Feature	Corr.
1	Words per sentence	**0.693**
2	Incidence of apposition	0.688
3	Incidence of clauses	0.614
4	Flesch index	0.580
5	Words before main verb	0.516
6	Sentences per paragraph	0.509
7	Incidence of relative clauses	0.417
8	Syllables per word	0.414
9	Number of positive additive connectives	0.397
10	Number of negative causal connectives	0.388

Table 4: Correlation between features and literacy levels

Among the top features are mostly basic and syntactic features representing the number of appositive and relative clauses and clauses in general, and also features from Coh-Metrix-PORT. This shows that traditional cognitively-motivated features can be complemented with more superficial features for readability assessment.

5.3 Predicting Complexity Levels

As previously discussed, the goal is to predict the complexity level of a text as original, naturally or strongly simplified, which correspond to the three literacy levels of INAF: rudimentary, basic and advanced level.

Tables 5-7 show the results of our experiments using 10-fold cross-validation and standard classification (Table 5), ordinal classification (Table 6) and regression (Table 7), in terms of F-measure (F), Pearson correlation with true score (Corr.) and mean absolute error (MAE). Results using our complete feature set (All) and different subsets of it are shown so that we can analyze the performance of each group of features. We also experiment with the Flesch index on its own as a feature.

Features	Class	F	Corr.	MAE
All	original	**0.913**	**0.84**	**0.276**
	natural	**0.483**		
	strong	**0.732**		
Language Model	original	0.669	0.25	0.381
	natural	0.025		
	strong	0.221		
Basic	original	0.846	0.76	0.302
	natural	0.149		
	strong	0.707		
Syntactic	original	0.891	0.82	0.285
	natural	0.32		
	strong	0.74		
Coh-Metrix-PORT	original	0.873	0.79	0.290
	natural	0.381		
	strong	0.712		
Flesch	original	0.751	0.52	0.348
	natural	0.152		
	strong	0.546		

Table 5: Standard Classification

Features	Class	F	Corr.	MAE
All	original	**0.904**	**0.83**	**0.163**
	natural	0.484		
	strong	**0.731**		
Language Model	original	0.634	0.49	0.344
	natural	**0.497**		
	strong	0.05		
Basic	original	0.83	0.73	0.231
	natural	0.334		
	strong	0.637		
Syntactic	original	0.891	0.81	0.180
	natural	0.382		
	strong	0.714		
Coh-Metrix-PORT	original	0.878	0.8	0.183
	natural	0.432		
	strong	0.709		
Flesch	original	0.746	0.56	0.310
	natural	0.489		
	strong	0		

Table 6: Ordinal classification

The results of the standard and ordinal classification are comparable in terms of F-measure and correlation, but the mean absolute error is lower for the ordinal classification. This indicates that ordinal classification is more adequate to handle our classes, similarly to the results found in (Heilman et al., 2008). Results also show that distinguishing between natural and strong simplifications is a harder problem than distinguishing between these and original texts. This was expected, since these two levels of simplification share many features. However, the average performance achieved is considered satisfactory.

Concerning the regression model (Table 7), the RBF kernel reaches the best correlation scores among all models. However, its mean error rates are above the ones found for classification. A linear SVM (not shown here) achieves very poor results across all metrics.

Features	Corr.	MAE
All	**0.8502**	**0.3478**
Language Model	0.6245	0.5448
Basic	0.7266	0.4538
Syntactic	0.8063	0.3878
Coh-Metrix-PORT	0.8051	0.3895
Flesch	0.5772	0.5492

Table 7: Regression with RBF kernel

With respect to the different feature sets, we can observe that the combination of all features consistently yields better results according to all metrics across all our models. The performances obtained with the subsets of features vary considerably from model to model, which shows that the combination of features is more robust across different learning techniques. Considering each feature set independently, the syntactic features, followed by Coh-Metrix-PORT, achieve the best correlation scores, while the language model features performed the poorest.

These results show that it is possible to predict with satisfactory accuracy the readability level of texts according to our three classes of interest: original, naturally simplified and strongly simplified texts. Given such results we embedded the classification model (Table 5) as a tool for readability assessment into our text simplification authoring system. The linear classification is our simplest model, has achieved the highest F-measure and its correlation scores are comparable to those of the other models.

6. Conclusions

We have experimented with different machine learning algorithms and features in order to verify whether it was possible to automatically distinguish among the three readability levels: original texts aimed at advanced readers, naturally simplified texts aimed at people with basic literacy level, and strongly simplified texts aimed at people with rudimentary literacy level. All algorithms achieved satisfactory performance with the combination of all features and we embedded the simplest model into our authoring tool.

As future work, we plan to investigate the contribution of deeper cognitive features to this problem, more specifically, semantic, co-reference and mental model dimensions metrics. Having this capacity for readability assessment is useful not only to inform authors preparing simplified material about the complexity of the current material, but also to guide automatic simplification systems to produce simplifications with the adequate level of complexity according to the target user.

The authoring tool, as well as its text simplification and readability assessment systems, can be used not only for improving text accessibility, but also for educational purposes: the author can prepare texts that are adequate according to the level of the reader and it will also allow them to improve their reading skills.

References

Sandra M. Aluísio, Lucia Specia, Thiago A. S. Pardo, Erick G. Maziero, Renata P. M. Fortes (2008). Towards Brazilian Portuguese Automatic Text Simplification Systems. In the *Proceedings of the 8th ACM Symposium on Document Engineering*, pp. 240-248.

Eckhard Bick (2000). *The Parsing System "Palavras": Automatic Grammatical Analysis of Portuguese in a Constraint Grammar Framework.* PhD Thesis. University of Århus, Denmark.

Jill Burstein, Martin Chodorow and Claudia Leacock (2003). CriterionSM Online Essay Evaluation: An Application for Automated Evaluation of Student Essays. In the *Proceedings of the Fifteenth Annual Conference on Innovative Applications of Artificial Intelligence*, Acapulco, Mexico.

Arnaldo Candido Jr., Erick Maziero, Caroline Gasperin, Thiago A. S. Pardo, Lucia Specia, and Sandra M. Aluisio (2009). Supporting the Adaptation of Texts for Poor Literacy Readers: a Text Simplification Editor for Brazilian Portuguese. In *NAACL-HLT Workshop on Innovative Use of NLP for Building Educational Applications*, pages 34–42, Boulder'.

Helena de M. Caseli, Tiago de F. Pereira, Lúcia Specia, Thiago A. S. Pardo, Caroline Gasperin and Sandra Maria Aluísio (2009). Building a Brazilian Portuguese Parallel Corpus of Original and Simplified Texts. In the *Proceedings of CICLing*.

Max Coltheart (1981). The MRC psycholinguistic database. In *Quartely Jounal of Experimental Psychology*, 33A, pages 497-505.

Scott Deerwester, Susan T. Dumais, George W. Furnas, Thomas K. Landauer e Richard Harshman (1990). Indexing By Latent Semantic Analysis. In *Journal of the American Society For Information Science*, V. 41, pages 391-407.

Bento C. Dias-da-Silva and Helio R. Moraes (2003). A construção de um thesaurus eletrônico para o português do Brasil. In *ALFA- Revista de Lingüística*, V.

47, N. 2, pages 101-115.
Bento C Dias-da-Silva, Ariani Di Felippo and Maria das Graças V. Nunes (2008). The automatic mapping of Princeton WordNet lexical conceptual relations onto the Brazilian Portuguese WordNet database. In *Proceedings of the 6th LREC*, Marrakech, Morocco.
William H. DuBay (2004). *The principles of readability*. Costa Mesa, CA: Impact Information: http://www.impact-information.com/impactinfo/readability02.pdf
Christiane Fellbaum (1998). *WordNet: An electronic lexical database*. Cambridge, MA: MIT Press.
Lijun Feng, Noémie Elhadad and Matt Huenerfauth (2009). Cognitively Motivated Features for Readability Assessment. *In the Proceedings of EACL 2009*, pages 229-237.
Ingo Glöckner, Sven Hartrumpf, Hermann Helbig, Johannes Leveling and Rainer Osswald (2006b). An architecture for rating and controlling text readability. In *Proceedings of KONVENS 2006*, pages 32-35. Konstanz, Germany.
Arthur C. Graesser, Danielle S. McNamara, Max M. Louwerse and Zhiqiang Cai (2004). Coh-Metrix: Analysis of text on cohesion and language. In *Behavioral Research Methods, Instruments, and Computers*, V. 36, pages 193-202.
Ronald K. Hambleton, H. Swaminathan and H. Jane Rogers (1991). *Fundamentals of item response theory*. Newbury Park, CA: Sage Press.
Michael Heilman, Kevyn Collins-Thompson, Jamie Callan and Max Eskenazi (2007). Combining lexical and grammatical features to improve readability measures for first and second language texts. In the *Proceedings of NAACL HLT 2007*, pages 460-467.
Michael Heilman, Kevyn Collins-Thompson and Maxine Eskenazi (2008). An Analysis of Statistical Models and Features for Reading Difficulty Prediction. *In Proceedings of the 3rd Workshop on Innovative Use of NLP for Building Educational Applications*, pages 71-79.
INAF (2009). Instituto P. Montenegro and Ação Educativa. *INAF Brasil - Indicador de Alfabetismo Funcional - 2009*. Available online at http://www. ibope.com.br/ipm/relatorios/relatorio_inaf_2009.pdf
Teresa B. F. Martins, Claudete M. Ghiraldelo, Maria das Graças V. Nunes e Osvaldo N. de Oliveira Jr. (1996). *Readability formulas applied to textbooks in brazilian portuguese*. ICMC Technical Report, N. 28, 11p.
Aurélien Max (2006). Writing for Language-impaired Readers. In *Proceedings of CICLing*, pages 567-570.
Danielle McNamara, Max Louwerse, and Art Graesser, 2002. Coh-Metrix: Automated cohesion and coherence scores to predict text readability and facilitate comprehension. Grant proposal. http://cohmetrix. memphis.edu/cohmetrixpr/publications.html
Eleni Miltsakaki and Audrey Troutt (2007). Read-X: Automatic Evaluation of Reading Difficulty of Web Text. In the *Proceedings of E-Learn 2007*, Quebec, Canada.
Eleni Miltsakaki and Audrey Troutt (2008). Real Time Web Text Classification and Analysis of Reading Difficulty. In the *Proceedings of the 3rd Workshop on Innovative Use of NLP for Building Educational Applications*, Columbus, OH.
Cláudia Oliveira, Maria C. Freitas, Violeta Quental, Cícero N. dos Santos, Renato P. L. and Lucas Souza (2006). A Set of NP-extraction rules for Portuguese: defining and learning. In *7th Workshop on Computational Processing of Written and Spoken Portuguese*, Itatiaia, Brazil.
Sarah E. Petersen and Mari Ostendorf (2009). *A machine learning approach to reading level assessment*. Computer Speech and Language 23, 89-106.
Emily Pitler and Ani Nenkova (2008). Revisiting readability: A unified framework for predicting text quality. In *Proceedings of EMNLP, 2008*.
Adwait Ratnaparkhi (1996). A Maximum Entropy Part-of-Speech Tagger. In *Proceedings of the First Empirical Methods in Natural Language Processing* Conference, pages133-142.
Brian Roark, Margaret Mitchell and Kristy Hollingshead (2007). Syntactic complexity measures for detecting mild cognitive impairment. In the *Proceedings of the Workshop on BioNLP 2007: Biological, Translational, and Clinical Language Processing*, Prague, Czech Republic.
Caroline E. Scarton, Daniel M. Almeida, Sandra M. Aluísio (2009). Análise da Inteligibilidade de textos via ferramentas de Processamento de Língua Natural: adaptando as métricas do Coh-Metrix para o Português. In *Proceedings of STIL-2009*, São Carlos, Brazil.
Sarah E. Schwarm and Mari Ostendorf (2005). Reading Level Assessment Using Support Vector Machines and Statistical Language Models. In the *Proceedings of the 43rd Annual Meeting of the ACL*, pp 523–530.
Kathleen M. Sheehan, Irene Kostin and Yoko Futagi (2007). Reading Level Assessment for Literary and Expository Texts. In D. S. McNamara and J. G. Trafton (Eds.), *Proceedings of the 29th Annual Cognitive Science Society*, page 1853. Austin, TX: Cognitive Science Society.
Advaith Siddharthan (2003). *Syntactic Simplification and Text Cohesion*. PhD Thesis. University of Cambridge.
Andreas Stolcke. *SRILM -- an extensible language modeling toolkit*. In Proceedings of the International Conference on Spoken Language Processing, 2002.

Enhancing Authentic Web Pages for Language Learners

Detmar Meurers[1], Ramon Ziai[1],
Luiz Amaral[2], Adriane Boyd[3], Aleksandar Dimitrov[1], Vanessa Metcalf[3], Niels Ott[1]
[1] Universität Tübingen
[2] University of Massachusetts Amherst
[3] The Ohio State University

Abstract

Second language acquisition research since the 90s has emphasized the importance of supporting awareness of language categories and forms, and input enhancement techniques have been proposed to make target language features more salient for the learner.

We present an NLP architecture and web-based implementation providing automatic visual input enhancement for web pages. Learners freely choose the web pages they want to read and the system displays an enhanced version of the pages. The current system supports visual input enhancement for several language patterns known to be problematic for English language learners, as well as fill-in-the-blank and clickable versions of such pages supporting some learner interaction.

1 Introduction

A significant body of research into the effectiveness of meaning-focused communicative approaches to foreign language teaching has shown that input alone is not sufficient to acquire a foreign language, especially for older learners (cf., e.g., Lightbown and Spada, 1999). Recognizing the important role of consciousness in second-language learning (Schmidt, 1990), learners have been argued to benefit from (Long, 1991) or even require (Lightbown, 1998) a so-called *focus on form* to overcome incomplete or incorrect knowledge of specific forms or regularities. Focus on form is understood to be "an occasional shift of attention to linguistic code features" (Long and Robinson, 1998, p. 23).

In an effort to combine communicative and structuralist approaches to second language teaching, Rutherford and Sharwood Smith (1985) argued for the use of consciousness raising strategies drawing the learner's attention to specific language properties. Sharwood Smith (1993, p. 176) coined the term *input enhancement* to refer to strategies highlighting the salience of language categories and forms.

Building on this foundational research in second language acquisition and foreign language teaching, in this paper we present an NLP architecture and a system for automatic visual input enhancement of web pages freely selected by language learners. We focus on learners of English as a Second Language (ESL), and the language patterns enhanced by the system include some of the well-established difficulties: determiners and prepositions, the distinction between gerunds and *to*-infinitives, *wh*-question formation, tense in conditionals, and phrasal verbs.

In our approach, learners can choose any web page they like, either by using an ordinary search-engine interface to search for one or by entering the URL of the page they want to enhance. In contrast to textbooks and other pre-prepared materials, allowing the learner to choose up-to-date web pages on any topic they are interested in and enhancing the page while keeping it intact (with its links, multimedia, and other components working) clearly has a positive effect on learner motivation. Input enhanced web pages also are attractive for people outside a traditional school setting, such as in the voluntary, self-motivated pursuit of knowledge often referred to as lifelong learning. The latter can be particularly relevant for adult immigrants, who are

Proceedings of the NAACL HLT 2010 Fifth Workshop on Innovative Use of NLP for Building Educational Applications, pages 10–18,
Los Angeles, California, June 2010.

already functionally living in the second language environment, but often stagnate in their second language acquisition and lack access or motivation to engage in language classes or other explicit language learning activities. Nevertheless, they do use the web to obtain information that is language-based and thus can be enhanced to also support language acquisition while satisfying information needs.

In terms of paper organization, in section 2 we first present the system architecture and in 2.1 the language phenomena handled, before considering the issues involved in evaluating the approach in 2.2. The context of our work and related approaches are discussed in section 3, and we conclude and discuss several avenues for future research in section 4.

2 The Approach

The WERTi system (*Working with English Real Texts interactively*) we developed follows a client-server paradigm where the server is responsible for fetching the web page and enriching it with annotations, and the client then receives the annotated web page and transforms it into an enhanced version. The client here is a standard web browser, so on the learner's side no additional software is needed.

The system currently supports three types of input enhancement: i) color highlighting of the pattern or selected parts thereof, ii) a version of the page supporting identification of the pattern through clicking and automatic color feedback, and iii) a version supporting practice, such as a fill-in-the-blank version of the page with automatic color feedback.

The overall architecture is shown in Figure 1. Essentially, the automated input enhancement process consists of the following steps:

1. Fetch the page.
2. Find the natural language text portions in it.
3. Identify the targeted language pattern.
4. Annotate the web page, marking up the language patterns identified in the previous step.
5. Transform the annotated web page into the output by visually enhancing the targeted pattern or by generating interaction possibilities.

Steps 1–4 take place on the server side, whereas step 5 happens in the learner's browser.[1] As NLP is only involved in step 3, we here focus on that step.

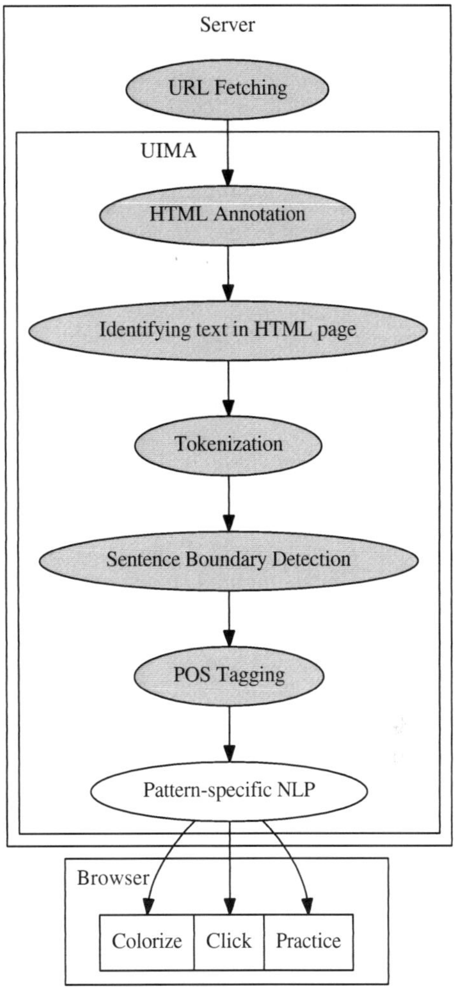

Figure 1: Overall WERTi architecture. Grey components are the same for all patterns and activities, cf. section 2.1.

While the first prototype of the WERTi system[2] presented at CALICO (Amaral, Metcalf and Meurers, 2006) and EUROCALL (Metcalf and Meurers, 2006) was implemented in Python, the current system is Java-based, with all NLP being integrated in the UIMA framework (Ferrucci and Lally, 2004). UIMA is an architecture for the management and analysis of unstructured information such as text, which is built on the idea of referential annotation and can be seen as an NLP analysis counterpart to current stand-off encoding standards for annotated corpora (cf., e.g., Ide et al. 2000). The input

[1] As an alternative to the server-based fetching of web pages, we are developing a Firefox plugin, leaving only the NLP up to the server. This increases compatibility with web pages using dynamically generated contents and special session handling.

[2] `http://purl.org/icall/werti-v1`

can be monotonically enriched while passing from one NLP component to the next, using a flexible data repository common to all components (Götz and Suhre, 2004). Such annotation-based processing is particularly useful in the WERTi context, where keeping the original text intact is essential for displaying it in enhanced form.

A second benefit of using the UIMA framework is that it supports a flexible combination of individual NLP components into larger processing pipelines. To obtain a flexible approach to input enhancement in WERTi, we need to be able to identify and analyze phenomena from different levels of linguistic analysis. For example, lexical classes can be identified by a POS tagger, whereas other patterns to be enhanced require at least shallow syntactic chunking. The more diverse the set of phenomena, the less feasible it is to handle all of them within a single processing strategy or formalism. Using the UIMA framework, we can re-use the same basic processing (e.g., tokenizing, POS tagging) for all phenomena and still be able to branch into pattern-specific NLP in a demand-driven way. Given that NLP components in UIMA include self-describing meta-information, the processing pipeline to be run can dynamically be obtained from the module configuration instead of being hard-wired into the core system. The resulting extensible, plugin-like architecture seems particularly well-suited for the task of visual input enhancement of a wide range of heterogeneous language properties.

Complementing the above arguments for the UIMA-based architecture of the current WERTi system, a detailed discussion of the advantages of an annotation-based, demand-driven NLP architecture for Intelligent Computer-Assisted Language Learning can be found in Amaral, Meurers, and Ziai (To Appear), where it is employed in an Intelligent Language Tutoring System.

2.1 Implemented Modules

The modules implemented in the current system handle a number of phenomena commonly judged as difficult for second language learners of English. In the following we briefly characterize each module, describing the nature of the language pattern, the required NLP, and the input enhancement results, which will be referred to as *activities*.

Lexical classes

Lexical classes are the most basic kind of linguistic category we use for input enhancement. The inventory of lexical categories to be used and which ones to focus on should be informed by second language acquisition research and foreign language teaching needs. The current system focuses on functional elements such as prepositions and determiners given that they are considered to be particularly difficult for learners of English (cf. De Felice, 2008 and references therein).

We identify these functional elements using the LingPipe POS tagger (`http://alias-i.com/lingpipe`) employing the Brown tagset (Francis and Kucera, 1979). As we show in section 2.2, the tagger reliably identifies prepositions and determiners in native English texts such as those expected for input enhancement.

The input enhancement used for lexical classes is the default set of activities provided by WERTi. In the simplest case, *Color*, all automatically identified instances in the web page are highlighted by coloring them; no learner interaction is required. This is illustrated by Figure 2, which shows the result of enhancing prepositions in a web page from the British

Figure 2: Screenshot of color activity for prepositions, cf. `http://purl.org/icall/werti-color-ex`

newspaper The Guardian.[3]

In this and the following screenshots, links already present in the original web page appear in light blue (e.g., *Vauban in Germany*). This raises an important issue for future research, namely how to determine the best visual input enhancement for a particular linguistic pattern given a specific web page with its existing visual design features (e.g., boldfacing in the text or particular colors used to indicate links), which includes the option of removing or altering some of those original visual design features.

A more interactive activity type is *Click*, where the learner during reading can attempt to identify instances of the targeted language form by clicking on it. Correctly identified instances are colored green by the system, incorrect guesses red.

Thirdly, input can be turned into *Practice* activities, where in its simplest form, WERTi turns web pages into fill-in-the-blank activities and provides immediate color coded feedback for the forms entered by the learner. The system currently accepts only the form used in the original text as correct. In principle, alternatives (e.g., other prepositions) can also be grammatical and appropriate. The question for which cases equivalence classes of target answers can automatically be determined is an interesting question for future research.[4]

Gerunds vs. *to*-infinitives

Deciding when a verb is required to be realized as a *to*-infinitive and when as a gerund *-ing* form can be difficult for ESL learners. Current school grammars teach students to look for certain lexical clues that reliably indicate which form to choose. Examples of such clues are prepositions such as *after* and *of*, which can only be followed by a gerund.

In our NLP approach to this language pattern, we use Constraint Grammar rules (Karlsson et al., 1995) on top of POS tagging, which allow for straightforward formulation of local disambiguation rules such as: "If an *-ing* form immediately follows the preposition *by*, select the gerund reading." Standard POS tagsets for English contain a single tag for all *-ing* forms. In order to identify gerunds only, we introduce all possible readings for all *-ing* forms and wrote 101 CG rules to locally disambiguate them. The *to*-infinitives, on the other hand, are relatively easy to identify based on the surface form and require almost no disambiguation.

For the implementation of the Constraint Grammar rules, we used the freely available CG3 system.[5] While simple local disambiguation rules are sufficient for the pattern discussed here, through iterative application of rules, Constraint Grammar can identify a wide range of phenomena without the need to provide a full grammatical analysis.

The *Color* activity resulting from input enhancement is similar to that for lexical classes described above, but the system here enhances both verb forms and clue phrases. Figure 3 shows the system highlighting gerunds in orange, infinitives in purple, and clue phrases in blue.

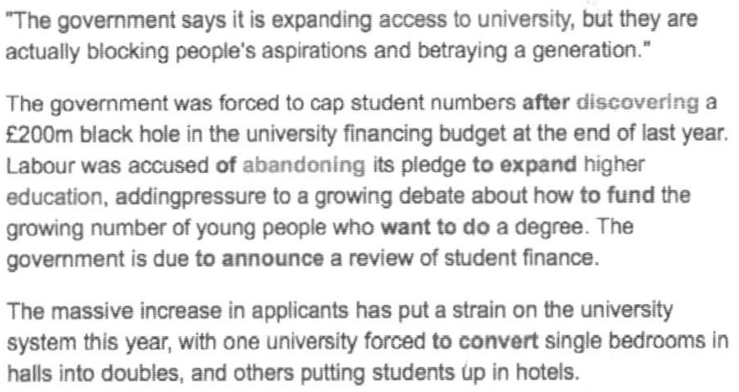
"The government says it is expanding access to university, but they are actually blocking people's aspirations and betraying a generation."

The government was forced to cap student numbers **after discovering** a £200m black hole in the university financing budget at the end of last year. Labour was accused **of abandoning** its pledge **to expand** higher education, addingpressure to a growing debate about how **to fund** the growing number of young people who **want to do** a degree. The government is due **to announce** a review of student finance.

The massive increase in applicants has put a strain on the university system this year, with one university forced **to convert** single bedrooms in halls into doubles, and others putting students up in hotels.

Figure 3: Color activity for gerunds vs. *to*-infinitives, cf. `http://purl.org/icall/werti-color-ex2`

For the *Click* activity, the web page is shown with colored gerund and *to*-infinitival forms and the learner can click on the corresponding clue phrases.

For the *Practice* activity, the learner is presented with a fill-in-the-black version of the web page, as in the screenshot in Figure 4. For each blank, the learner needs to enter the gerund or *to*-infinitival form of the base form shown in parentheses.

Wh-questions

Question formation in English, with its particular word order, constitutes a well-known challenge for second language learners and has received significant attention in the second language acquisi-

[3]Given the nature of the input enhancement using colors, the highlighting in the figure is only visible in a color printout.

[4]The issue bears some resemblance to the task of identifying paraphrases (Androutsopoulos and Malakasiotis, 2009) or classes of learner answers which differ in form but are equivalent in terms of meaning (Bailey and Meurers, 2008).

[5]`http://beta.visl.sdu.dk/cg3.html`

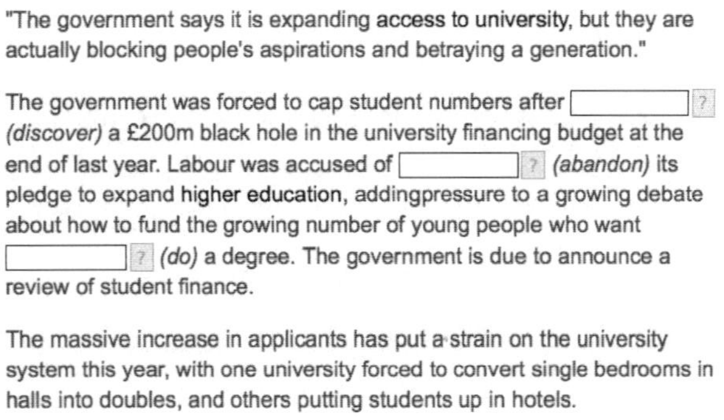
"The government says it is expanding access to university, but they are actually blocking people's aspirations and betraying a generation."

The government was forced to cap student numbers after [ ] ? *(discover)* a £200m black hole in the university financing budget at the end of last year. Labour was accused of [ ] ? *(abandon)* its pledge to expand higher education, addingpressure to a growing debate about how to fund the growing number of young people who want [ ] ? *(do)* a degree. The government is due to announce a review of student finance.

The massive increase in applicants has put a strain on the university system this year, with one university forced to convert single bedrooms in halls into doubles, and others putting students up in hotels.

Figure 4: Practice activity for gerunds vs. *to*-infinitives, cf. `http://purl.org/icall/werti-cloze-ex`

tion literature (cf., e.g., White et al., 1991; Spada and Lightbown, 1993). Example (1) illustrates the use of *do*-support and subject-aux inversion in *wh*-questions as two aspects challenging learners.

(1) *What* do **you** think it takes to be successful?

In order to identify the *wh*-question patterns, we employ a set of 126 hand-written Constraint Grammar rules. The respective *wh*-word acts as the lexical clue to the question as a whole, and the rules then identify the subject and verb phrase based on the POS and lexical information of the local context.

Aside from the *Color* activity highlighting the relevant parts of a *wh*-question, we adapted the other activity types to this more complex language pattern. The *Click* activity prompts learners to click on either the subject or the verb phrase of the question. The *Practice* activity presents the words of a *wh*-question in random order and requires the learner to rearrange them into the correct one.

Conditionals

English has five types of conditionals that are used for discussing hypothetical situations and possible outcomes. The tenses used in the different conditional types vary with respect to the certainty of the outcome as expressed by the speaker/writer. For example, one class of conditionals expresses high certainty and uses present tense in the *if*-clause and future in the main clause, as in example (2).

(2) **If** the rain *continues*, we *will* return home.

The recognition of conditionals is approached using a combination of shallow and deep methods. We first look for lexical triggers of a conditional, such as the word *if* at the beginning of a sentence. This first pass serves as a filter to the next, more expensive processing step, full parsing of the candidate sentences using Bikel's statistical parser (Bikel, 2002). The parse trees are then traversed to identify and mark the verb forms and the trigger word.

For the input enhancement, we color all relevant parts of a conditional, namely the trigger and the verb forms. The *Click* activity for conditionals requires the learner to click on exactly these parts. The *Practice* activity prompts users to classify the conditional instances into the different classes.

Phrasal verbs

Another challenging pattern for English language learners are phrasal verbs consisting of a verb and either a preposition, an adverb or both. The meaning of a phrasal verb often differs considerably from that of the underlying verb, as in (3) compared to (4).

(3) He *switched* the glasses without her noticing.

(4) He *switched off* the light before he went to bed.

This distinction is difficult for ESL learners, who often confuse phrasal and non-phrasal uses.

Since this is a lexical phenomenon, we approached the identification of phrasal verbs via a database lookup in a large online collection of verbs known to occur in phrasal form.[6] In order to find out about noun phrases and modifying adverbs possibly occurring in between the verb and its particles, we run a chunker and use this information in specifying a filter for such intervening elements.

The visual input enhancement activities targeting phrasal verbs are the same as for lexical classes, with the difference that for the *Practice* activity, learners have to fill in only the particle, not the particle and the main verb, since otherwise the missing contents may be too difficult to reconstruct. Moreover, we want the activity to focus on distinguishing phrasal from non-phrasal uses, not verb meaning in general.

2.2 Evaluation issues

The success of a visual input enhancement approach such as the one presented in this paper depends on a number of factors, each of which can in principle

[6]`http://www.usingenglish.com/reference/phrasal-verbs`

be evaluated. The fundamental but as far as we are aware unanswered question in second language acquisition research is for which language categories, forms, and patterns input enhancement can be effective. As Lee and Huang (2008) show, the study of visual input enhancement sorely needs more experimental studies. With the help of the WERTi system, which systematically produces visual input enhancement for a range of language properties, it becomes possible to conduct experiments in a real-life foreign language teaching setting to test learning outcomes[7] with and without visual input enhancement under a wide range of parameters. Relevant parameters include the linguistic nature of the language property to be enhanced as well as the nature of the input enhancement to be used, be it highlighting through colors or fonts, engagement in different types of activities such as clicking, entering fill-in-the-blank information, reordering language material, etc.

A factor closely related to our focus in this paper is the impact of the quality of the NLP analysis.[8] For a quantitative evaluation of the NLP, one significant problem is the mismatch between the phenomena focused on in second language learning and the available gold standards where these phenomena are actually annotated. For example, standard corpora such as the Penn Treebank contain almost no questions and thus do not constitute a useful gold standard for *wh*-question identification. Another problem is that some grammatical distinctions taught to language learners are disputed in the linguistic literature. For example, Huddleston and Pullum (2002, p. 1120) eliminate the distinction between gerunds and present participles, combining them into a class called "gerund-participle". And in corpus annotation practice, gerunds are not identified as a class by the tagsets used to annotate large corpora, making it unclear what gold standard our gerund identification component should be evaluated against.

While the lack of available gold standards means that a quantitative evaluation of all WERTi modules is beyond the scope of this paper, the determiner and preposition classes focused on in the lexical classes module can be identified using the standard CLAWS-7 or Brown tagsets, for which gold-standard corpora are available. We thus decided to evaluate this WERTi module against the BNC Sampler Corpus (Burnard, 1999), which contains a variety of genres, making it particularly appropriate for evaluating a tool such as WERTi, which learners are expected to use with a wide range of web pages as input. The BNC Sampler corpus is annotated with the fine-grained CLAWS-7 tagset[9] where, e.g., prepositions are distinguished from subordinating conjunctions. By mapping the relevant POS tags from the CLAWS-7 tagset to the Brown tagset used by the LingPipe tagger as integrated in WERTi, it becomes possible to evaluate WERTi's performance for the specific lexical classes focused on for input enhancement, prepositions and determiners. For prepositions, precision was 95.07% and recall 90.52% while for determiners, precision was 97.06% with a recall of 94.07%.

The performance of the POS tagger on this reference corpus thus seems to be sufficient as basis for visual input enhancement, but the crucial question naturally remains whether identification of the target patterns is reliable in the web pages that language learners happen to choose. For a more precise quantitative study, it will thus be important to try the system out with real-life users in order to identify a set of web pages which can constitute an adequate test set. Interestingly, which web pages the users choose depends on the search engine front-end we provide for them. As discussed under outlook in section 4, we are exploring the option to implicitly guide them towards web pages containing enough instances of the relevant language patterns in text at the appropriate reading difficulty.

3 Context and related work

Contextualizing our work, one can view the automatic visual input enhancement approach presented here as an enrichment of Data-Driven Learning (DDL). Where DDL has been characterized as an "attempt to cut out the middleman [the teacher] as far as possible and to give the learner direct access to the data" (Boulton 2009, p. 82, citing Tim Johns), in visual input enhancement the learner stays in con-

[7] Naturally, online measures of noticing, such as eye tracking or Event-Related Potentials (ERP) would also be relevant.

[8] The processing time for the NLP analysis as other relevant aspect is negligible for most of the activities presented here.

[9] `http://www.natcorp.ox.ac.uk/docs/c7spec.html`

trol, but the NLP uses 'teacher knowledge' about relevant and difficult language properties to make those more prominent and noticeable for the learner.

In the context of Intelligent Computer-Assisted Language Learning (ICALL), NLP has received most attention in connection with Intelligent Language Tutoring Systems, where NLP is used to analyze learner data and provide individual feedback on that basis (cf. Heift and Schulze, 2007). Demands on such NLP are high given that it needs to be able to handle learner language and provide high-quality feedback for any sentence entered by the learner.

In contrast, visual input enhancement makes use of NLP analysis of authentic, native-speaker text and thus applies the tools to the native language they were originally designed and optimized for. Such NLP use, which we will refer to as Authentic Text ICALL (ATICALL), also does not need to be able to correctly identify and manipulate all instances of a language pattern for which input enhancement is intended. Success can be incremental in the sense that any visual input enhancement can be beneficial, so that one can focus on enhancing those instances which can be reliably identified in a text. In other words, for ATICALL, precision of the NLP tools is more important than recall. It is not necessary to identify and enhance all instances of a given pattern as long as the instances we do identify are in fact correct, i.e., true positives. As the point of our system is to enhance the reading experience by raising language awareness, pattern occurrences we do not identify are not harmful to the overall goal.[10]

We next turn to a discussion of some interesting approaches in two closely related fields, exercise generation and reading support tools.

3.1 Exercise Generation

Exercise generation is widely studied in CALL research and some of the work relates directly to the input enhancement approach presented in this paper. For instance, Antoniadis et al. (2004) describe the plans of the MIRTO project to support "gap-filling" and "lexical spotting" exercises in combination with a corpus database. However, MIRTO seems to focus on a general architecture supporting instructor-determined activity design. Visual input enhancement or language awareness are not mentioned. The VISL project (Bick, 2005) offers games and visual presentations in order to foster knowledge of syntactic forms and rules, and its KillerFiller tool can create slot-filler exercises from texts. However, KillerFiller uses corpora and databases as the text base and it presents sentences in isolation in a testing setup. In contrast to such exercise generation systems, we aim at enhancing the reader's second language input using the described web-based mash-up approach.

3.2 Reading Support Tools

Another branch of related approaches consists of tools supporting the reading of texts in a foreign language. For example, the Glosser-RuG project (Nerbonne et al., 1998) supports reading of French texts for Dutch learners with an online, context-dependent dictionary, as well as morphological analysis and examples of word use in corpora. A similar system, focusing on multi-word lexemes, was developed in the COMPASS project (Breidt and Feldweg, 1997). More recently, the ALPHEIOS project[11] has produced a system that can look up words in a lexicon and provide aligned translations. While such lexicon-based tools are certainly useful to learners, they rely on the learner asking for help instead of enhancing specific structures from the start and thus clearly differ from our approach.

Finally, the REAP project[12] supports learners in searching for texts that are well-suited for providing vocabulary and reading practice (Heilman et al., 2008). While it differs in focus from the visual input enhancement paradigm underlying our approach, it shares with it the emphasis on providing the learner with authentic text in support of language learning.

4 Conclusion and Outlook

In this paper we presented an NLP architecture and a concrete system for the enhancement of authentic web pages in order to support language awareness in ESL learners. The NLP architecture is flexible enough to integrate any processing approach that lends itself to the treatment of the language phe-

[10]While identifying all instances of a pattern indeed is not crucial in this context, representativeness remains relevant to some degree. Where only a skewed subset of a pattern is highlighted, learners may not properly conceptualize the pattern.

[11]`http://alpheios.net`

[12]`http://reap.cs.cmu.edu`

nomenon in question, without confining the developer to a particular formalism. The WERTi system illustrates this with five language patterns typically considered difficult for ESL learners: lexical classes, gerunds vs. *to*-infinitives, *wh*-questions, conditionals and phrasal verbs.

Looking ahead, we already mentioned the fundamental open question where input enhancement can be effective in section 2.2. A system such as WERTi, systematically producing visual input enhancement, can help explore this question under a wide range of parameters in a real-life language teaching setting. A more specific future research issue is the automatic computation of equivalence classes of target forms sketched in section 2.1. Not yet mentioned but readily apparent is the goal to integrate more language patterns known to be difficult for language learners into WERTi (e.g., active/passive, tense and aspect distinctions, relative clauses), and to explore the approach for other languages, such as German.

A final important avenue for future research concerns the starting point of the system, the step where learners search for a web page they are interested in and select it for presentation with input enhancement. Enhancing of patterns presupposes that the pages contain instances of the pattern. The less frequent the pattern, the less likely we are to find enough instances of it in web pages returned by the standard web search engines typically used by learners to find pages of interest to them. The issue is related to research on providing learners with texts at the right level of reading difficulty (Petersen, 2007; Miltsakaki and Troutt, 2008), but the focus for us is on ensuring that texts which include instances of the specific language pattern targeted by a given input enhancement are ranked high in the search results. Ott (2009) presents a search engine prototype which, in addition to the content-focused document-term information and traditional readability measures, supports indexing based on a more general notion of a text model into which the patterns relevant to input enhancement can be integrated – an idea we are exploring further (Ott and Meurers, Submitted).

Acknowledgments

We benefited from the feedback we received at CALICO 06, EUROCALL 06, and the ICALL course[13] at ESSLLI 09, where we discussed our work on the Python-based WERTi prototype. We would like to thank Chris Hill and Kathy Corl for their enthusiasm and encouragement. We are grateful to Magdalena Leshtanska, Emma Li, Iliana Simova, Maria Tchalakova and Tatiana Vodolazova for their good ideas and WERTi module contributions in the context of a seminar at the University of Tübingen in Summer 2008. Last but not least, the paper benefited from two helpful workshop reviews.

References

Luiz Amaral, Vanessa Metcalf, and Detmar Meurers. 2006. Language awareness through re-use of NLP technology. Presentation at the CALICO Workshop on *NLP in CALL – Computational and Linguistic Challenges*, May 17, 2006. University of Hawaii. http://purl.org/dm/handouts/calico06-amaral-metcalf-meurers.pdf.

Luiz Amaral, Detmar Meurers, and Ramon Ziai. To Appear. Analyzing learner language: Towards a flexible NLP architecture for intelligent language tutors. *Computer-Assisted Language Learning*. http://purl.org/dm/papers/amaral-meurers-ziai-10.html.

Ion Androutsopoulos and Prodromos Malakasiotis. 2009. A survey of paraphrasing and textual entailment methods. Technical report, NLP Group, Informatics Dept., Athens University of Economics and Business, Greece. http://arxiv.org/abs/0912.3747.

Georges Antoniadis, Sandra Echinard, Olivier Kraif, Thomas Lebarbé, Mathieux Loiseau, and Claude Ponton. 2004. NLP-based scripting for CALL activities. In *Proceedings of the COLING Workshop on eLearning for CL and CL for eLearning*, Geneva.

Stacey Bailey and Detmar Meurers. 2008. Diagnosing meaning errors in short answers to reading comprehension questions. In (Tetreault et al., 2008), pages 107–115.

Eckhard Bick. 2005. Grammar for fun: IT-based grammar learning with VISL. In P. Juel, editor, *CALL for the Nordic Languages*, pages 49–64. Samfundslitteratur, Copenhagen.

Daniel M. Bikel. 2002. Design of a multi-lingual, parallel-processing statistical parsing engine. In *Proceedings of the Second Int. Conference on Human Language Technology Research*, San Francisco.

Alex Boulton. 2009. Data-driven learning: Reasonable fears and rational reassurance. *Indian Journal of Applied Linguistics*, 35(1):81–106.

[13] http://purl.org/dm/09/esslli/

Elisabeth Breidt and Helmut Feldweg. 1997. Accessing foreign languages with COMPASS. *Machine Translation*, 12(1–2):153–174.

L. Burnard, 1999. *Users Reference Guide for the BNC Sampler*. Available on the BNC Sampler CD.

Rachele De Felice. 2008. *Automatic Error Detection in Non-native English*. Ph.D. thesis, St Catherine's College, University of Oxford.

Catherine Doughty and J. Williams, editors. 1998. *Focus on form in classroom second language acquisition*. Cambridge University Press, Cambridge.

David Ferrucci and Adam Lally. 2004. UIMA: an architectural approach to unstructured information processing in the corporate research environment. *Natural Language Engineering*, 10(3–4):327–348.

W. Nelson Francis and Henry Kucera, 1979. *Brown corpus manual*. Dept. of Linguistics, Brown University.

Thilo Götz and Oliver Suhre. 2004. Design and implementation of the UIMA Common Analysis System. *IBM Systems Journal*, 43(3):476–489.

Trude Heift and Mathias Schulze. 2007. *Errors and Intelligence in Computer-Assisted Language Learning: Parsers and Pedagogues*. Routledge.

Michael Heilman, Le Zhao, Juan Pino, and Maxine Eskenazi. 2008. Retrieval of reading materials for vocabulary and reading practice. In (Tetreault et al., 2008), pages 80–88.

Rodney Huddleston and Geoffrey K. Pullum. 2002. *The Cambridge Grammar of the English Language*. Cambridge University Press.

Nancy Ide, Patrice Bonhomme, and Laurent Romary. 2000. XCES: An XML-based encoding standard for linguistic corpora. In *Proceedings of the 2nd Int. Conference on Language Resources and Evaluation*.

Tim Johns. 1994. From printout to handout: Grammar and vocabulary teaching in the context of data-driven learning. In T. Odlin, editor, *Perspectives on Pedagogical Grammar*, pages 293–313. CUP, Cambridge.

Fred Karlsson, Atro Voutilainen, Juha Heikkilä, and Arto Anttila, editors. 1995. *Constraint Grammar: A Language-Independent System for Parsing Unrestricted Text*. Mouton de Gruyter, Berlin, New York.

Sang-Ki Lee and Hung-Tzu Huang. 2008. Visual input enhancement and grammar learning: A meta-analytic review. *Studies in Second Language Acquisition*, 30:307–331.

Patsy M. Lightbown and Nina Spada. 1999. *How languages are learned*. Oxford University Press, Oxford.

Patsy M. Lightbown. 1998. The importance of timing in focus on form. In (Doughty and Williams, 1998), pages 177–196.

Michael H. Long and Peter Robinson. 1998. Focus on form: Theory, research, and practice. In (Doughty and Williams, 1998), pages 15–41.

M. H. Long. 1991. Focus on form: A design feature in language teaching methodology. In K. De Bot, C. Kramsch, and R. Ginsberg, editors, *Foreign language research in cross-cultural perspective*, pages 39–52. John Benjamins, Amsterdam.

Vanessa Metcalf and Detmar Meurers. 2006. Generating web-based English preposition exercises from real-world texts. Presentation at EUROCALL, Sept. 7, 2006. Granada, Spain. `http://purl.org/dm/handouts/eurocall06-metcalf-meurers.pdf`.

Eleni Miltsakaki and Audrey Troutt. 2008. Real time web text classification and analysis of reading difficulty. In (Tetreault et al., 2008), pages 89–97.

John Nerbonne, Duco Dokter, and Petra Smit. 1998. Morphological processing and computer-assisted language learning. *Computer Assisted Language Learning*, 11(5):543–559.

Niels Ott and Detmar Meurers. Submitted. Information retrieval for education: Making search engines language aware. `http://purl.org/dm/papers/ott-meurers-10.html`.

Niels Ott. 2009. Information retrieval for language learning: An exploration of text difficulty measures. Master's thesis, International Studies in Computational Linguistics, University of Tübingen.

Sarah E. Petersen. 2007. *Natural Language Processing Tools for Reading Level Assessment and Text Simplification for Bilingual Education*. Ph.D. thesis, University of Washington.

William E. Rutherford and Michael Sharwood Smith. 1985. Consciousness-raising and universal grammar. *Applied Linguistics*, 6(2):274–282.

Richard W. Schmidt. 1990. The role of consciousness in second language learning. *Applied Linguistics*, 11:206–226.

Michael Sharwood Smith. 1993. Input enhancement in instructed SLA: Theoretical bases. *Studies in Second Language Acquisition*, 15:165–179.

Nina Spada and Patsy M. Lightbown. 1993. Instruction and the development of questions in l2 classrooms. *Studies in Second Language Acquisition*, 15:205–224.

Joel Tetreault, Jill Burstein, and Rachele De Felice, editors. 2008. *Proceedings of the Third Workshop on Innovative Use of NLP for Building Educational Applications*. ACL, Columbus, Ohio, June.

Lydia White, Nina Spada, Patsy M. Lightbown, and Leila Ranta. 1991. Input enhancement and L2 question formation. *Applied Linguistics*, 12(4):416–432.

AutoLearn's authoring tool: a piece of cake for teachers

Martí Quixal[1], Susanne Preuß[3], David García-Narbona[2], Jose R. Boullosa[2]

[1] Voice and Language Group,
[2] Advanced Development Group
Barcelona Media Centre d'Innovació
Diagonal, 177, E-08018 Barcelona, Spain
{marti.quixal,david.garcian,
beto.boullosa}@barcelonamedia.org

[3] GFAI
Martin-Luther-Str. 14
Saarbrücken, Germany
susannep@iai.uni-sb.de

Abstract

This paper[1] presents AutoLearn's authoring tool: AutoTutor, a software solution that enables teachers (content creators) to develop language learning activities including automatic feedback generation without the need of being a programmer. The software has been designed and implemented on the basis of processing pipelines developed in previous work. A group of teachers has been trained to use the technology and the accompanying methodology, and has used materials created by them in their courses in real instruction settings, which served as an initial evaluation.

The paper is structured in four sections: Section 1 introduces and contextualizes the research work. Section 2 describes the solution, its architecture and its components, and specifically the way the NLP resources are created automatically with teacher input. Section 3 describes and analyses a case study using the tool to create and test a language learning activity. Finally Section 4 concludes with remarks on the work done and connections to related work, and with future work.

1 Introduction

Over the past four decades there have been several hundreds of CALL (Computer-Aided Language Learning) projects, often linked to CALL practice (Levy 1997), and within the last twenty years a considerable number of them focused on the use of NLP in the context of CALL (Amaral and Meurers, in preparation). Despite this, there is an appalling absence of parser-based CALL in real instruction settings, which has been partially attributed to a certain negligence of the pedagogical needs (Amaral and Meurers, in preparation). In contrast, projects and systems that were pedagogically informed succeeded, yielded and are yielding interesting results, and are evolving for over a decade now (Nagata 2002; Nagata 2009; Heift 2001; Heift 2003; Heift 2005; Amaral and Meurers, in preparation). According to Amaral and Meurers successful projects were able to restrict learner production in terms of NLP complexity by limiting the scope of the learning activities to language-oriented (as opposed to communicative-oriented) or translation exercises, or by providing feedback on formal aspects of language in content oriented activities, always under pedagogical considerations –focus on form.

Our proposal is a step forward in this direction in two ways: a) it allows for feedback generation focusing both on formal and content (communicative-oriented) aspects of language learning activities, and b) it provides teachers with a tool and a methodology –both evolving– for them to gain autonomy in the creation of parser-based CALL activities –which by the way has a long tradition in CALL (Levy 1997, chap. 2). The goal is to shape language technologies to the needs of the teachers, and truly ready-to-hand.

1.1 Related work and research context

The extent to which pedagogues appreciate and require autonomy in the design and creation of CALL activities can be traced in the historical

[1] Research funded by the Lifelong Learning Programme 2007-2013 (AUTOLEARN, 2007-3625/001-001).

Proceedings of the NAACL HLT 2010 Fifth Workshop on Innovative Use of NLP for Building Educational Applications, pages 19–27,
Los Angeles, California, June 2010. ©2010 Association for Computational Linguistics

overview offered by (Levy 1997, 16, 17, 19, 23 and 38). Moreover, parallel research shows that the integration of CALL in the learning context is critical to ensure the success of whatever materials are offered to learners (Levy 1997, 200-203; Polisca 2006).

AutoTutor goes beyond tools such as Hot Potatoes, eXelearning or JClic[2] in that it offers the possibility of authoring NLP-based CALL activities. It is also more ambitious than other authoring tools developed for the creation of activities in intelligent tutoring systems. Chen and Tokuda (2003) and Rösener (2009) present authoring tools for translation exercises, where expected learner input is much more controlled (by the sentence in the source language).

Heift and Toole (2002) present Tutor Assistant, which enables to create activities such as build-a-sentence, drag-and-drop and fill-in-the-blank. An important difference between AutoTutor and Tutor Assistant is that the latter is a bit more restrictive in terms of the linguistic objects that can be used. It also presents a lighter complexity in the modelling of the underlying correction modules. However, the system underlying Tutor Assistant provides with more complex student adaptation functionalities (Heift 2003) and would be complementary in terms of overall system functionalities.

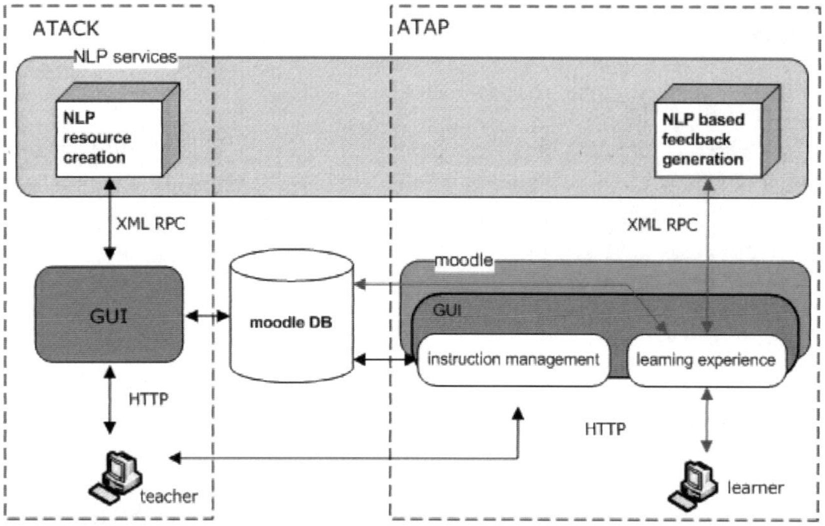

Figure 1. AutoTutor software architecture.

2 AutoTutor: AutoLearn's authoring software

AutoTutor is a web-based software solution to assist non-NLP experts in the creation of language learning activities using NLP-intensive processing techniques. The process includes a simplified specification of the means to automatically create the resources used to analyse learner input for each exercise. The goal is to use computational devices to analyse learner production and to be able to go beyond "yes-or-no" answers providing additional feedback focused both on form and content.

This research work is framed within the AutoLearn project, a follow up of the ALLES project (Schmidt et al., 2004, Quixal et al., 2006). AutoLearn's aim was to exploit in a larger scale a subset of the technologies developed in ALLES in real instruction settings. Estrada et al. (2009) describe how, in AutoLearn's first evaluation phase, the topics of the activities were not attractive enough for learners and how learner activity decreased within the same learning unit across exercises. Both observations –together with what it has been shown with respect to the integration of independent language learning, see above – impelled us to develop AutoTutor, which allows teachers to create their own learning units.

As reflected in Figure 1, AutoTutor consists primarily of two pieces of software: AutoTutor Activity Creation Kit (ATACK) and AutoTutor Activity Player (ATAP). ATACK, an authoring

[2] http://hotpot.uvic.ca/, http://sourceforge.net/apps/trac/exe/wiki, http://clic.xtec.cat/es/jclic/index.htm.

tool, provides teachers with the ability to create parser-based CALL exercises and define the corresponding exercise specifications for the generation of automated feedback. ATAP allows teachers to insert, track and manage those exercises in Moodle (http://moodle.org), giving learners the possibility to visualize and answer them. Both ATACK and ATAP share a common infrastructure of NLP services which provides the basic methods for generating, storing and using NLP tools. Access to those methods is made through XML-RPC calls.

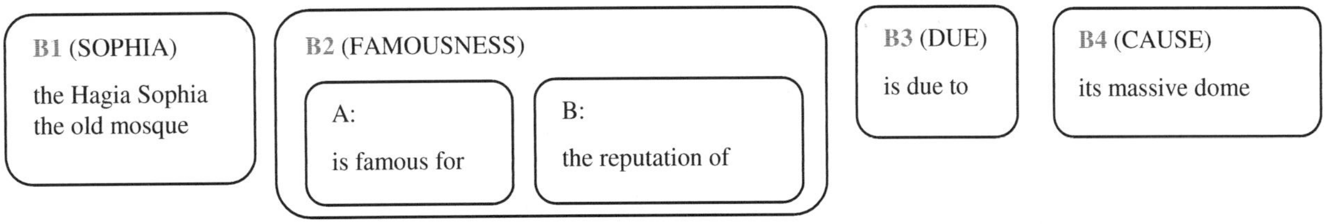

Figure 2 Blocks as specified in AutoTutor GUI.

2.1 AutoTutor Activity Creation Kit

ATACK is divided in two components: a GUI that allows content creators to enter the text, questions and instructions to be presented to learners in order to elicit answers from them; and an NLP resource creation module that automatically generates the resources that will be used for the automated feedback. Through the GUI, teachers are also able to define a set of expected correct answers for each question, and, optionally, specific customized feedback and sample answers.

To encode linguistic and conceptual variation in the expected answers, teachers are required to turn them into linguistic patterns using blocks. Blocks represent abstract concepts, and contain the concrete chunks linked to those concepts. Within a block one can define alternative linguistic structures representing the same concept. By combining and ordering blocks, teachers can define the sequences of text that correspond to the expected correct answers –i.e., they can provide the seeds for answer modelling.

Modelling answers

Given an exercise where learners are required to answer the question "From an architecture point of view, what makes Hagia Sophia in Istanbul so famous according to its Wikipedia entry?", the following answers would be accepted:

1. {The Hagia Sophia/The old mosque} is famous for its massive dome.
2. The reputation of {the Hagia Sophia/the old mosque} is due to its massive dome.

To model these possible answers, one would use four blocks (see Figure 2) corresponding to WHO (*Hagia Sophia*), WHAT (*Famousness*), and WHY (*Dome*), and complementary linguistic expressions such as "is due to". Thus, the possible correct block sequences would be (indices corresponding to Figure 2):

a) B1 B2.A B4
b) B2.B B1 B3 B4

Block B1 is an example of interchangeable alternatives (*the Hagia Sophia* or *the old mosque*), which do not require any further condition to apply. In contrast, block B2 is an instance of a syntactic variation of the concept. *Famousness* can be expressed through an adjective or through a verb (in our example), but each of the choices requires a different sentence structure.

Alternative texts in a block with no variants (as in B1) exploit the paradigmatic properties of language, while alternative texts in a block with two variants as in B2 account for its syntagmatic properties, reflected in the block sequences. Interestingly, this sort of splitting of a sentence into blocks is information-driven and simplifies the linguistic expertise needed for the exercise specifications.

2.2 Automatic generation of exercise-specific NLP-resources

Figure 3 shows how the teacher's input is converted into NLP-components. Predefined system components present plain borders, and the resulting ones present hyphenised borders. The figure also reflects the need for answer and error modelling resources.

NLP resource generation process

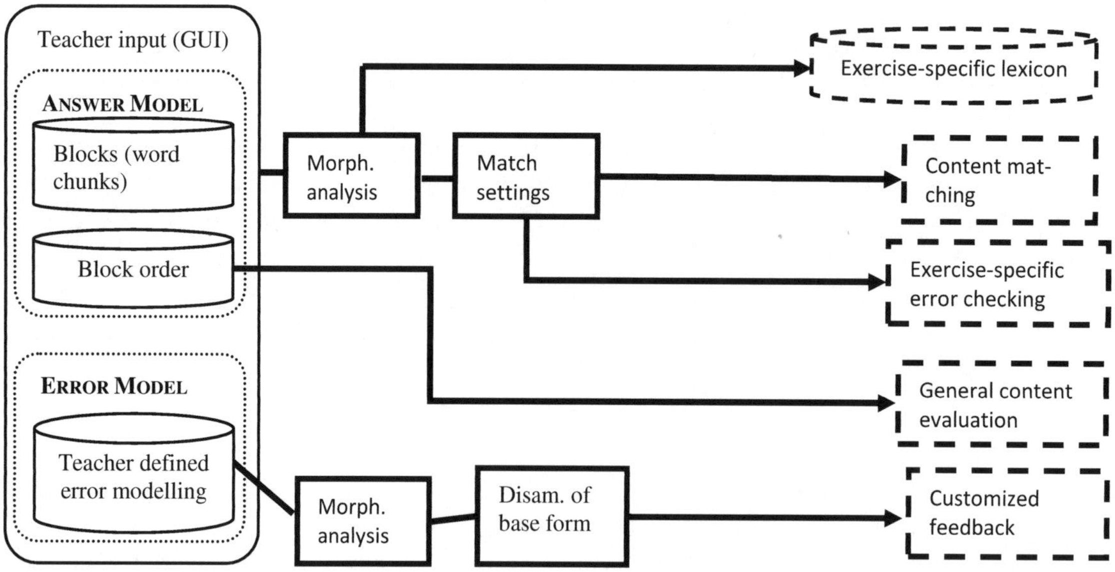

Figure 3. Processing schema and components of the customizable NLP resources of ATACK

The generation of the NLP resources is possible through the processing of the teacher's input with three modules: the morphological analysis module performs a lexicon lookup and determines unknown words that are entered into the exercise-specific lexicon; the disambiguation of base form module, disambiguates base forms, e.g. "better" is disambiguated between verb and adjective depending on the context in preparation of customized feedback.

The last and most important module in the architecture is the match settings component, which determines the linguistic features and structures to be used by the content matching and the exercise-specific error checking modules (see Figure 4). Using relaxation techniques, the parsing of learner input is flexible enough to recognize structures including incorrect word forms and incorrect, missing or additional items such as determiners, prepositions or digits, or even longish chunks of text with no correspondence the specified answers. The match settings component contains rules that later on trigger the input for the exercise-specific error checking.

The match settings component consists of KURD rules (Carl et al. 1998). Thus it can be modified and extended by a computational linguist any time without the need of a programmer.

Once the exercise's questions and expected answers have been defined, ATACK allows for the generation of the NLP resources needed for the automatic correction of that exercise. The right-hand side of Figure 3 shows which the generated resources are:

- An *exercise-specific lexicon* to handle unknown words
- A *content matching module* based on the KURD formalism to define several linguistically-motivated layers with different levels of relaxation (using word, lemma, and grammatical features) for determining the matching between the learner input and the expected answers
- A *customized feedback module* for teacher-defined exercise-specific feedback
- An *exercise-specific error checking module* for context-dependent errors linked to language aspects in the expected answers
- A *general content evaluation component* that checks whether the analysis performed by the content matching module conforms to the specified block orders

2.3 AutoTutor Activity Player (ATAP)

With ATAP learners have access to the contents enhanced with automatic tutoring previously created by teachers. ATAP consists of a) a client GUI for learners, integrated in Moodle, to answer exercises and track their own activity; b) a client GUI for teachers, also integrated in Moodle, used to manage and track learning resources and learner activity; and c) a backend module, integrated into the AutoTutor NLP Services Infrastructure, responsible for parsing the learner's input and generating feedback messages.

Figure 4 describes the two steps involved in the NLP-based feedback generation: the NLP components created through ATACK –in hyphenised rectangles– are combined with general built-in NLP-based correction modules.

2.4 The feedback generation software

Feedback is provided to learners in two steps, which is reflected in Figure 4 by the two parts, the upper and lower part, called General Checking and Exercise Specific Checking respectively. The former consists in the application of standard spell and grammar checkers. The latter consists in the application of the NLP resources automatically generated with the teacher's input.

Content matching module

The text chunks (blocks) that the teacher has entered into ATACK's GUI are converted into KURD rules. KURD provides with sophisticated linguistically-oriented matching and action operators. These operators are used to model (predictable) learner text. The content matching module is designed to be able to parse learners input with different degrees of correctness combining both relaxation techniques and mal-rules. For instance, it detects the presence of both correct and incorrect word forms, but it also detects incorrect words belonging to a range of closed or open word classes –mainly prepositions, determiners, modal verbs and digits– which can be used to issue a corresponding linguistically motivated error messages like "Preposition wrong in this context", in a context where the preposition is determined by the relevant communicative situation.

Error types that are more complex to handle in technical terms involve mismatches between the amount of expected elements and the actual amount of informational elements in the learner's answer. Such mismatches arise on the grammatical level if a composite verb form is used instead of a simple one, or when items such as determiners or commas are missing or redundant. The system also accounts for additional modifiers and other words interspersed in the learner's answer.

The matching strategy uses underspecified empty slots to fit in textual material in between the correct linguistic structures. Missing words are handled by a layer of matching in which certain elements, mainly grammatical function words such as determiners or auxiliary verbs, are optional.

Incorrect word choice in open and closed word classes is handled by matching on more abstract linguistic features instead of lexeme features.

The interaction between KURD-based linguistically-driven triggers in the content matching module and the rules in the exercise-specific error checking (see below) module allows for specific mal-rule based error correction.

Customized feedback

Teachers can create specific error messages for simple linguistic patterns (containing errors or searching for missing items) ranging from one or two word structures to more complex word-based linguistic structures. Technically, error patterns are

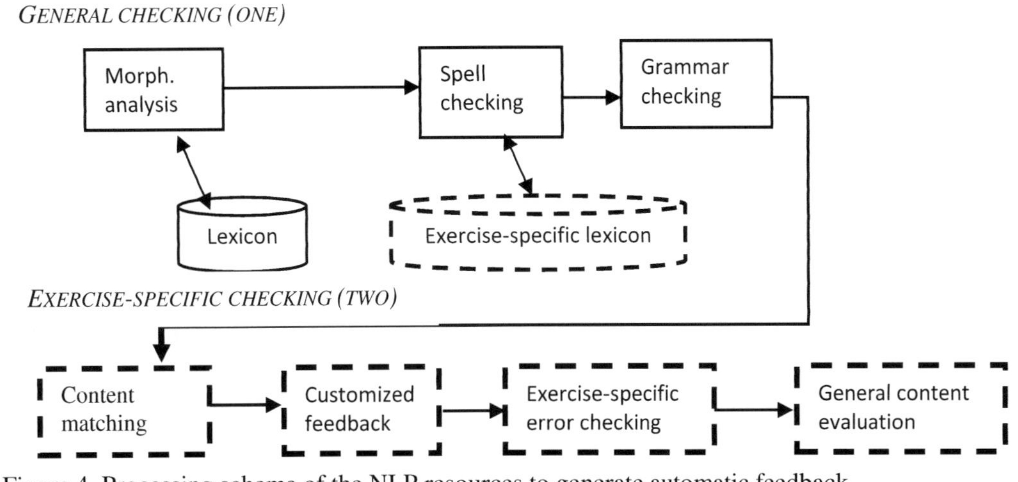

Figure 4. Processing schema of the NLP resources to generate automatic feedback.

implemented as KURD rules linked to a specific error message. These rules have preference over the rules applied by any other later module.

Exercise-specific error checking

Teachers do not encode all the exercise-specific errors themselves because a set of KURD rules for the detection of prototypical errors is encoded –this module uses the triggers set by the content matching component. Exercise-specific linguistic errors handled in this module have in common that they result in sentences that are likely to be wrong either from a formal (but context-dependent) point of view or from an informational point of view.

General content evaluation

Since the contents are specified by the blocks created by teachers, the evaluation has a final step in which the system checks whether the learner's answer contains all the necessary information that belongs to a valid block sequence.

This module checks for correct order in information blocks, for blending structures (mixtures of two possible correct structures), missing information and extra words (which do not always imply an error). The messages generated with this component pertain to the level of completeness and adequacy of the answer in terms of content.

3 Usage and evaluation

AutoTutor has been used by a group of seven content creators –university and school teachers– for a period of three months. They developed over 20 activities for learning units on topics such as business and finance, sustainable production and consumption, and new technologies. Those activities contain listening and reading comprehension activities, short-text writing activities, enabling tasks on composition writing aspects, etc. whose answers must be expressed in relatively free answers consisting of one sentence. In November 2009, these activities were used in real instruction settings with approximately 600 learners of English and German. Furthermore, an evaluation of both teacher and learner satisfaction and system performance was carried out.

We briefly describe the process of creating the materials by one of the (secondary school) teachers participating in the content creation process and evaluate the results of system performance in one activity created by this same teacher.

3.1 Content creation: training and practice

To start the process teachers received a 4-hour training course (in two sessions) where they were taught how to plan, pedagogically speaking, a learning sequence including activities to be corrected using automatically generated feedback. We required them to develop autonomous learning units if possible. And we invited them to get hold of any available technology or platform functionality to implement their ideas (and partially offered support to them too), convinced that technology had to be a means rather than a goal in itself. The course also included an overview of NLP techniques and a specific course on the mechanics of ATACK (the authoring tool) and ATAP (the activity management and deployment tool).

During this training we learned that most teachers do not plan how activities will be assessed: that is, they often do not think of the concrete answers to the possible questions they will pose to learners. They do not need to, since they have all the knowledge required to correct learner production any place, any time in their heads (the learner, the activity and the expert model) no matter if the learner production is written or oral. This is crucial since it requires a change in normal working routine.

After the initial training they created learning materials. During creation we interacted with them to make sure that they were not designing activities whose answers were simply impossible to model. For instance, the secondary school teacher who prepared the activity on sustainable production and consumption provided us with a listening comprehension activity including questions such as:

1) *Which is your attitude concerning responsible consumption? How do you deal with recycling? Do you think yours is an ecological home? Are you doing your best to reduce your ecological footprint? Make a list with 10 things you could do at home to reduce, reuse o recycle waste at home.*

All these things were asked in one sole instruction, to be answered in one sole text area. We then talked to the teacher and argued with her the kinds of things that could be modelled using simple one-sentence answers. We ended up reducing the input provided to learners to perform the activity to one video (initially a text and a video) and prompting learners with the following three questions:

1) *Explain in your words what the ecological footprint is.*
2) *What should be the role of retailers according to Timo Mäkelä?*
3) *Why should producers and service providers use the Ecolabel?*

Similar interventions were done in other activities created by other content creators. But some of them were able to create activities which could be used almost straightforwardly.

3.2 System evaluation

The materials created by teachers were then used in their courses. In the setting that we analyse learners of English as a second language were Catalan and Spanish native speakers between 15 and 17 years old that attended a regular first year of *Batxillerat* (first course for those preparing to enter university studies). They had all been learning English for more than five years, and according to their teacher their CEF level was between A2 and B1. They were all digital literates and they all used the computer on a weekly basis for their studies or leisure (80% daily).

We analyse briefly the results obtained for two of the questions in one of the activities created by the school teacher who authored the learning unit on sustainable production and consumption, namely questions 1) and 2) above. This learning unit was offered to a group of 25 learners.

Overall system performance

Table 1 reflects the number of attempts performed by learners trying to answer the two questions evaluated here: correct, partially correct and incorrect answers are almost equally distributed (around 30% each) and non-evaluated answers are roughly 10%. In non-evaluated answers we include basically answers where learners made a bad use of the system (e.g., answers in a language other than the one learned) or answers which were exactly the same as the previous one for two attempts in a row, which can interpreted in several ways (misunderstanding of the feedback, usability problems with the interface, problems with pop-up windows, etc.) that fall out of the scope of the current analysis.

Table 2 and Table 3 show the number of messages issued by the system for correct, partially correct and incorrect answers for each of the two questions analyzed. The tables distinguish between Form Messages and Content Messages, and Real Form Errors and Real Content Errors –a crucial distinction given our claim that using AutoTutor more open questions could be tackled.[3]

QST	CORR.	PART.	INCORR.	INV.	TOT
1ST	36	23	12	2	**73**
2ND	14	29	36	21	**100**
ALL	**50 (29%)**	**52(30%)**	**48(28%)**	**23(13%)**	**173**

Table 1. Correct, partially correct and incorrect answers.

Table 2 and Table 3 show that the contrast between issued feedback messages (most commonly error messages, but sometimes rather pieces of advice or suggestions) and real problems found in the answers is generally balanced in formal problems (31:15, 8:7 and 41:39 for Table 2; and 6:8, 29:18, and 20:21 for Table 3) independently of the correctness of the answer.

On the contrary, the contrast between issued messages and content problems is much more unbalanced in correct and partially correct answers (139:71 and 84:42 for Table 2; and 45:20 and 110:57 for Table 3) and more balanced for incorrect answers (30:18 for Table 2; and 93:77 for Table 3).

	MESSAGES		REAL ERRORS	
	Form	**Cont**	**Form**	**Cont**
CORRECT ANSWERS	31	139	15	71
PARTIALLY CORRECT	8	84	7	42
INCORRECT ANSWERS	41	30	39	18
TOTAL ANSWERS	80	253	61	131

Table 2. Messages issued vs. real errors for question 1 in the answers produced by learners.

	MESSAGES		REAL ERRORS	
	Form	**Cont**	**Form**	**Cont**
CORRECT ANSWERS	6	45	8	20
PARTIALLY CORRECT	29	110	18	57
INCORRECT ANSWERS	20	93	21	77
TOTAL ANSWERS	55	248	47	154

Table 3. Messages issued vs. real errors for question 2 in the answers produced by learners.

This indicates that generally speaking the system behaved more confidently in the detection of formal errors than in the detection of content errors.

[3] A proper evaluation would require manual correction of the activities by a number of teachers and the corresponding evaluation process.

System feedback analysis

To analyze the system's feedback we looked into the answers and the feedback proposed by the system and annotated each answer with one or more of the tags corresponding to a possible cause of misbehaviour. The possible causes and its absolute frequency are listed in Table 4.

The less frequent ones are bad use of the system on the learner side, bad guidance (misleading the learner to an improper answer or to a more complex way of getting to it), connection failure, and message drawing attention on form when the error was on content.

MISBEHAVIOUR	QUESTION 1	QUESTION 2
CONN-FAIL	1	0
BAD-USE	1	1
FRM-INSTOF-CONT	2	1
BAD-GUIDE	4	2
OOV	11	13
WRNG-DIAG	11	20
FRM-STRICT	33	20
ARTIF-SEP	0	61
SPECS-POOR	1	62

Table 4. Frequent sources of system errors.

The most frequent causes of system misbehaviour are *out-of-vocabulary words*, *wrong diagnoses*, and corrections too *restrictive* with respect to *form*.

Two interesting causes of misbehaviour and in fact the most frequent ones were *artificial separation* and *poor specifications*. The former refers to the system dividing answer parts into smaller parts (and therefore generation of a larger number of issued messages). For instance in a sentence like (as an answer to question 2)

> *The* ***retailers*** *need to make sure that* ***whatever*** *they label* ***or they put*** *in shelf is understandable to consumers.*[4]

the system would generate six different feedback messages informing that some words were not expected (even if correct) and some were found but not in the expected location or form.

In this same sentence above we find examples of too *poor specifications*, where, for instance, it was not foreseen that *retailers* was used in the answer. These two kinds of errors reflect the flaws of the current system: artificial separation reflects a lack of generalization capacity of the underlying parser, and poor specifications reflect the incompleteness of the information provided by novice users, teachers acting as material designers.

4 Concluding remarks

This paper describes software that provides non-NLP experts with a means to utilize and customize NLP-intensive resources using an authoring tool for language instruction activities. Its usability and usefulness have been tested in real instruction settings and are currently being evaluated and analyzed. Initial analyses show that the technology and methodology proposed allow teachers to create contents including automatic generation feedback without the need of being neither a programmer nor an NLP expert.

Moreover, system performance shows a reasonable confidence in error detection given the immaturity of the tool and of its users –following Shneiderman and Plaisant's terminology (2006). There is room for improvement in the way to reduce false positives related with poor specifications. It is quite some work for exercise designers to foresee a reasonable range of linguistic alternatives for each answer. One could further support them in the design of materials with added functionalities –using strategies such as shallow semantic parsing, as in (Bailey and Meurers, 2008), or adding functionalities on the user interface that allow teachers to easily feed exercise models or specific feedback messages using learner answers.

The architecture presented allows for portability into other languages (English and German already available), with a relative simplicity provided that the lexicon for the language exists and contains basic morpho-syntactic information. Moreover, having developed it as a Moodle extension makes it available to a wide community of teachers and learners. The modularity of ATACK and ATAP makes them easy to integrate in other Learning Management Systems.

In the longer term we plan to improve AutoTutor's configurability so that its behaviour can be defined following pedagogical criteria. One of the aspects to be improved is that a computational linguist is needed to add new global error types to be handled or new linguistic phenomena to be considered in terms of block order. If such a system is used by wider audiences, then statistically driven techniques might be employed gradually, probably

[4] One of the expected possible answers was "They need to make sure that whatever they label and whatever they put in the shelves is understood by consumers".

in combination with symbolic techniques –the usage of the tool will provide with invaluable learner corpora. In the meantime AutoTutor provides with a means to have automatic correction and feedback generation for those areas and text genres where corpus or native speaker text is scarce, and experiments show it could be realistically used in real instruction settings.

Acknowledgments

We want to thank the secondary school teachers who enthusiastically volunteered in the creation and usage of AutoLearn materials: Eli Garrabou (Fundació Llor), Mònica Castanyer, Montse Padareda (Fundació GEM) and Anna Campillo (Escola Sant Gervasi). We also want to thank their learners, who took the time and made the effort to go through them. We also thank two anonymous reviewers for their useful comments.

References

Amaral, Luiz A., and Detmar Meurers. On Using Intelligent Computer-Assisted Language Learning in Real-Life Foreign Language Teaching and Learning (Submitted).

Bailey, Stacey and Detmar Meurers (2008) Diagnosing meaning errors in short answers to reading comprehension question. In Proceedings of the Third ACL Workshop on Innovative Use of NLP for Building Educational Applications, pages 107–115, Columbus, Ohio, USA, June 2008.

Carl, Michael, and Antje Schmidt-Wigger (1998). Shallow Post Morphological Processing with KURD. In Proceedings of NeMLaP'98, Sydney.

Chen, Liang and Naoyuki Tokuda (2003) A New Template-Template-enhanced ICALL System for a Second Language Composition Course. CALICO Journal, Vol. 20, No. 3: May 2003.

Estrada, M., R. Navarro-Prieto, M. Quixal (2009) Combined evaluation of a virtual learning environment: use of qualitative methods and log interpretation to evaluate a computer mediated language course. In Proceedings of International Conference on Education and New Learning Technologies, EDULEARN 09. Barcelona (Spain), 6th-8th July, 2009.

Heift, Trude. 2001. Intelligent Language Tutoring Systems for Grammar Practice. Zeitschrift für Interkulturellen Fremdsprachenunterricht 6, no. 2. http://www.ualberta.ca/~german/ejournal/ heift2.htm.

———. 2003. Multiple learner errors and meaningful feedback: A challenge for ICALL systems. CALICO Journal 20, no. 3: 533-548.

———. 2005. Corrective Feedback and Learner Uptake in CALL. ReCALL Journal 17, no. 1: 32-46.

Heift, Trude, and Mathias Schulze. 2007. Errors and Intelligence in Computer-Assisted Language Learning: Parsers and Pedagogues. New York: Routledge.

Levy, Michael. 1997. Computer-Assisted Language Learning. Context and Conceptualization. Oxford: Oxford University Press.

Nagata, Noriko. 2002. BANZAI: An Application of Natural Language Processingto Web based Language Learning. CALICO Journal 19, no. 3: 583-599.

———. 2009. Robo-Sensei's NLP-Based Error Detection and Feedback Generation. CALICO Journal 26, no. 3: 562-579.

Polisca, Elena. 2006. Facilitating the Learning Process: An Evaluation of the Use and Benefits of a Virtual Learning Environment (VLE)-enhanced Independent Language-learning Program (ILLP). CALICO Journal 23, no.3: 499-51.

Quixal, M., T. Badia, B. Boullosa, L. Díaz, and A. Ruggia. (2006). Strategies for the Generation of Individualised Feedback in Distance Language Learning. In Proceedings of the Workshop on Language-Enabled Technology and Development and Evaluation of Robust Spoken Dialogue Systems of ECAI 2006. Riva del Garda, Italy, Sept. 2006.

Rösener, C.: "A linguistic intelligent system for technology enhanced learning in vocational training – the ILLU project". In Cress, U.; Dimitrova, V.; Specht, M. (Eds.): Learning in the Synergy of Multiple Disciplines. 4th European Conference on Technology Enhanced Learning, EC-TEL 2009 Nice, France, Sept. 29 – Oct. 2, 2009. Lecture Notes in Computer Science. Programming and Software Engineering, Vol. 5794, 2009, XVIII, p. 813, Springer, Berlin.

Schmidt, P., S. Garnier, M. Sharwood, T. Badia, L. Díaz, M. Quixal, A. Ruggia, A. S. Valderrabanos, A. J. Cruz, E. Torrejon, C. Rico, J. Jimenez. (2004) ALLES: Integrating NLP in ICALL Applications. In Proceedings of Fourth International Conference on Language Resources and Evaluation. Lisbon, vol. VI p. 1888-1891. ISBN: 2-9517408-1-6.

Shneiderman, B. and C. Plaisant. (2006) Strategies for evaluating information visualization tools: multi-dimensional in-depth long-term case studies. BELIV '06: Proceedings of the 2006 AVI workshop on Beyond time and errors: novel evaluation methods for information visualization, May 2006.

Toole, J. & Heift, T. (2002). The Tutor Assistant: An Authoring System for a Web-based Intelligent Language Tutor. Computer Assisted Language Learning, 15(4), 373-86.

Annotating ESL Errors: Challenges and Rewards

Alla Rozovskaya and Dan Roth
University of Illinois at Urbana-Champaign
Urbana, IL 61801
{rozovska,danr}@illinois.edu

Abstract

In this paper, we present a corrected and error-tagged corpus of essays written by non-native speakers of English. The corpus contains 63000 words and includes data by learners of English of nine first language backgrounds. The annotation was performed at the sentence level and involved correcting all errors in the sentence. Error classification includes mistakes in preposition and article usage, errors in grammar, word order, and word choice. We show an analysis of errors in the annotated corpus by error categories and first language backgrounds, as well as inter-annotator agreement on the task.

We also describe a computer program that was developed to facilitate and standardize the annotation procedure for the task. The program allows for the annotation of various types of mistakes and was used in the annotation of the corpus.

1 Introduction

Work on automated methods for detecting and correcting context dependent mistakes (e.g., (Golding and Roth, 1996; Golding and Roth, 1999; Carlson et al., 2001)) has taken an interesting turn over the last few years, and has focused on correcting mistakes made by non-native speakers of English. Non-native writers make a variety of errors in grammar and word usage. Recently, there has been a lot of effort on building systems for detecting mistakes in article and preposition usage (DeFelice, 2008; Eeg-Olofsson, 2003; Gamon et al., 2008; Han et al., 2006; Tetreault and Chodorow, 2008b). Izumi et al. (2003) consider several error types, including article and preposition mistakes, made by Japanese learners of English, and Nagata et al. (2006) focus on the errors in mass/count noun distinctions with an application to detecting article mistakes also made by Japanese speakers. Article and preposition mistakes have been shown to be very common mistakes for learners of different first language (L1) backgrounds (Dagneaux et al., 1998; Gamon et al., 2008; Izumi et al., 2004; Tetreault and Chodorow, 2008a), but there is no systematic study of a whole range of errors non-native writers produce, nor is it clear what the distribution of different types of mistakes is in learner language.

In this paper, we describe a corpus of sentences written by English as a Second Language (ESL) speakers, annotated for the purposes of developing an automated system for correcting mistakes in text. Although the focus of the annotation were errors in article and preposition usage, all mistakes in the sentence have been corrected. The data for annotation were taken from two sources: The International Corpus of Learner English (ICLE, (Granger et al., 2002a)) and Chinese Learners of English Corpus (CLEC, (Gui and Yang, 2003)). The annotated corpus includes data from speakers of nine first language backgrounds. To our knowledge, this is the first corpus of non-native English text (learner corpus) of fully-corrected sentences from such a diverse group of learners[1]. The size of the annotated corpus is 63000 words, or 2645 sentences. While a corpus

[1]Possibly, except for the Cambridge Learner Corpus http://www.cambridge.org/elt

Proceedings of the NAACL HLT 2010 Fifth Workshop on Innovative Use of NLP for Building Educational Applications, pages 28–36,
Los Angeles, California, June 2010.

of this size may not seem significant in many natural language applications, this is in fact a large corpus for this field, especially considering the effort to correct all mistakes, as opposed to focusing on one language phenomenon. This corpus was used in the experiments described in the companion paper (Rozovskaya and Roth, 2010).

The annotation schema that we developed was motivated by our special interest in errors in article and preposition usage, but also includes errors in verbs, morphology, and noun number. The corpus contains 907 article corrections and 1309 preposition corrections, in addition to annotated mistakes of other types.

While the focus of the present paper is on annotating ESL mistakes, we have several goals in mind. First, we present the annotation procedure for the task, including an error classification schema, annotation speed, and inter-annotator agreement. Second, we describe a computer program that we developed to facilitate the annotation of mistakes in text. Third, having such a diverse corpus allows us to analyze the annotated data with respect to the source language of the learner. We show the analysis of the annotated data through an overall breakdown of error types by the writer's first language. We also present a detailed analysis of errors in article and preposition usage. Finally, it should be noted that there are currently very few annotated learner corpora available. Consequently, systems are evaluated on different data sets, which makes performance comparison impossible. The annotation of the data presented here is available[2] and, thus, can be used by researchers who obtain access to these respective corpora[3].

The rest of the paper is organized as follows. First, we describe previous work on the annotation of learner corpora and statistics on ESL mistakes. Section 3 gives a description of the annotation procedure, Section 4 presents the annotation tool that was developed for the purpose of this project and used in the annotation. We then present error statistics based on the annotated corpus across all error types and separately for errors in article and preposition usage. Finally, in Section 6 we describe how we evaluate inter-annotator agreement and show agreement results for the task.

2 Learner Corpora and Error Tagging

In this section, we review research in the annotation and error analysis of learner corpora. For a review of learner corpus research see, for example, (Díaz-Negrillo, 2006; Granger, 2002b; Pravec, 2002). Comparative error analysis is difficult, as there are no standardized error-tagging schemas, but we can get a general idea about the types of errors prevalent with such speakers. Izumi et al. (2004a) describe a speech corpus of Japanese learners of English (NICT JLE). The corpus is corrected and annotated and consists of the transcripts (2 million words) of the audio-recordings of the English oral proficiency interview test. In the NICT corpus, whose error tag set consists of 45 tags, about 26.6% of errors are determiner related, and 10% are preposition related, which makes these two error types the most common in the corpus (Gamon et al., 2008). The Chinese Learners of English corpus (CLEC, (Gui and Yang, 2003)) is a collection of essays written by Chinese learners of beginning, intermediate, and advanced levels. This corpus is also corrected and error-tagged, but the tagging schema does not allow for an easy isolation of article and preposition errors. The International Corpus of Learner English (ICLE, (Granger et al., 2002a)) is a corpus of argumentative essays by advanced English learners. The corpus contains 2 million words of writing by European learners from 14 mother tongue backgrounds. While the entire corpus is not error-tagged, the French subpart of the corpus along with other data by French speakers of a lower level of proficiency has been annotated (Dagneaux et al., 1998). The most common errors for the advanced level of proficiency were found to be lexical errors (words) (15%), register (10%), articles (10%), pronouns (10%), spelling (8%) , verbs (8%).

In a study of 53 post-intermediate ESOL (migrant) learners in New Zealand (Bitchener et al., 2005), the most common errors were found to be prepositions (29%), articles (20%), and verb tense (22%). Dalgish (1985) conducted a study of errors produced by ESL students enrolled at CUNY. It was found that across students of different first

[2]Details about the annotation are accessible from `http://L2R.cs.uiuc.edu/~cogcomp/`

[3]The ICLE and CLEC corpora are commercially available.

languages, the most common error types among 24 different error types were errors in article usage (28%), vocabulary error (20-25%) (word choice and idioms), prepositions (18%), and verb-subject agreement (15%). He also noted that the speakers of languages without article system made considerably more article errors, but the breakdown of other error types across languages was surprisingly similar.

3 Annotation

3.1 Data Selection

Data for annotation were extracted from the ICLE corpus (Granger et al., 2002a) and CLEC (Gui and Yang, 2003). As stated in Section 2, the ICLE contains data by European speakers of advanced level of proficiency, and the CLEC corpus contains essays by Chinese learners of different levels of proficiency. The annotated corpus includes sentences written by speakers of nine languages: Bulgarian, Chinese, Czech, French, German, Italian, Polish, Russian, and Spanish. About half of the sentences for annotation were selected based on their scores with respect to a 4-gram language model built using the English Gigaword corpus (LDC2005T12). This was done in order to exclude sentences that would require heavy editing and sentences with near-native fluency, sentences with scores too high or too low. Such sentences would be less likely to benefit from a system on preposition/article correction. The sentences for annotation were a random sample out of the remaining 80% of the data.

To collect more data for errors in preposition usage, we also manually selected sentences that contained such errors. This might explain why the proportion of preposition errors is so high in our data.

3.2 Annotation Procedure

The annotation was performed by three native speakers of North American English, one undergraduate and two graduate students, specializing in foreign languages and Linguistics, with previous experience in natural language annotation. A sentence was presented to the annotator in the context of the essay from which it was extracted. Essay context can become necessary, especially for the correction of article errors, when an article is acceptable in the context of a sentence, but is incorrect in the context of the essay. The annotators were also encouraged to propose more than one correction, as long as all of their suggestions were consistent with the essay context.

3.3 Annotation Schema

While we were primarily interested in article and preposition errors, the goal of the annotation was to correct all mistakes in the sentence. Thus, our error classification schema[4], though motivated by our interest in errors in article and preposition usage, was also intended to give us a general idea about the types of mistakes ESL students make. A better understanding of the nature of learners' mistakes is important for the development of a robust automated system that detects errors and proposes corrections. Even when the focus of a correction system is on one language phenomenon, we would like to have information about all mistakes in the context: Error information around the target article or preposition could help us understand how noisy data affect the performance.

But more importantly, a learner corpus with error information could demonstrate how mistakes interact in a sentence. A common approach to detecting and correcting context-sensitive mistakes is to deal with each phenomenon independently, but sometimes errors cannot be corrected in isolation. Consider, for example, the following sentences that are a part of the corpus that we annotated.

1. "I should know all important aspects of English." → "I should know all *of the* important aspects of English."
2. "But *some of the* people *thought* about him as a parodist of a rhythm-n-blues singer." → "But *some people considered* him to be a parodist of a rhythm-n-blues singer."
3. "...to be *a* competent avionics *engineer*..." → ..."to become competent avionics *engineers*..."
4. "...which reflect a traditional female role and a traditional attitude to *a woman*..." → "...which reflect a traditional female role and a traditional attitude towards *women*..."
5. "Marx lived in the epoch when there *were* no *entertainments*." → "Marx lived in an era when there *was* no *entertainment*."

In the examples above, errors interact with one another. In example 1, the context requires a definite article, and the definite article, in turn, calls for the

[4]Our error classification was inspired by the classification developed for the annotation of preposition errors (Tetreault and Chodorow, 2008a).

preposition "of". In example 2, the definite article after "some of" is used extraneously, and deleting it also requires deleting preposition "of". Another case of interaction is caused by a word choice error: The writer used the verb "thought" instead of "considered"; replacing the verb requires also changing the syntactic construction of the verb complement. In examples 3 and 4, the article choice before the words "engineer" and "woman" depends on the number value of those nouns. To correctly determine which article should be used, one needs to determine first whether the context requires a singular noun "engineer" or plural "engineers". Finally, in example 5, the form of the predicate in the relative clause depends on the number value of the noun "entertainment".

For the reasons mentioned above, the annotation involved correcting all mistakes in a sentence. The errors that we distinguish are *noun number*, *spelling*, *verb form*, and *word form*, in addition to article and preposition errors . All other corrections, the majority of which are lexical errors, were marked as *word replacement*, *word deletion*, and *word insertion*. Table 1 gives a description of each error type.

4 Annotation Tool

In this section, we describe a computer program that was developed to facilitate the annotation process. The main purpose of the program is to allow an annotator to easily mark the type of mistake, when correcting it. In addition, the tool allows us to provide the annotator with sufficient essay context. As described in Section 3, sentences for annotation came from different essays, so each new sentence was usually extracted from a new context. To ensure that the annotators preserved the meaning of the sentence being corrected, we needed to provide them with the essay context. A wider context could affect the annotator's decision, especially when determining the correct article choice. The tool allowed us to efficiently present to the annotator the essay context for each target sentence.

Fig. 1 shows the program interface. The sentence for annotation appears in the white text box and the annotator can type corrections in the box, as if working in a word processor environment. Above and below the text box we can see the context boxes, where the rest of the essay is shown. Below the lower context box, there is a list of buttons. The pink buttons and the dark green buttons correspond to different error types, the pink buttons are for correcting article and preposition errors, and the dark green buttons – for correcting other errors. The annotator can indicate the type of mistake being corrected by placing the cursor after the word that contains an error and pressing the button that corresponds to this error type. Pressing on an error button inserts a pair of delimiters after the word. The correction can then be entered between the delimiters. The yellow buttons and the three buttons next to the pink ones are the shortcuts that can be used instead of typing in articles and common preposition corrections. The button *None* located next to the article buttons is used for correcting cases of articles and prepositions used superfluously. To correct other errors, the annotator needs to determine the type of error, insert the corresponding delimiters after the word by pressing one of the error buttons and enter the correction between the delimiters.

The annotation rate for the three annotators varied between 30 and 40 sentences per hour.

Table 2 shows sample sentences annotated with the tool. The proposed corrections are located inside the delimiters and follow the word to which the correction refers. When replacing a sequence of words, the sequence was surrounded with curly braces. This is useful if a sequence is a multi-word expression, such as *at last*.

5 Annotation Statistics

In this section, we present the results of the annotation by error type and the source language of the writer.

Table 3 shows statistics for the annotated sentences by language group and error type. Because the sub-corpora differ in size, we show the number of errors per hundred words. In total, the annotated corpus contains 63000 words or 2645 sentences of learner writing. Category *punctuation* was not specified in the annotation, but can be easily identified and includes insertion, deletion, and replacement of punctuation marks. The largest error category is *word replacement*, which combines deleted, inserted words and word substitutions. This is followed by

Error type	**Description**	**Examples**
Article error	Any error involving an article	"Women were indignant at [None/the] inequality from men."
Preposition error	Any error involving a preposition	"...to change their views [to/for] the better."
Noun number	Errors involving plural/singular confusion of a noun	"Science is surviving by overcoming the mistakes not by uttering the [truths/truth] ."
Verb form	Errors in verb tense and verb inflections	"He [write/writes] poetry."
Word form	Correct lexeme, but wrong suffix	"It is not [simply/simple] to make professional army ."
Spelling	Error in spelling	"...if a person [commited/committed] a crime..."
Word insertion, deletion, or replacement	Other corrections that do not fall into any of the above categories	"There is a [probability/possibility] that today's fantasies will not be fantasies tomorrow."

Table 1: Error classification used in annotation

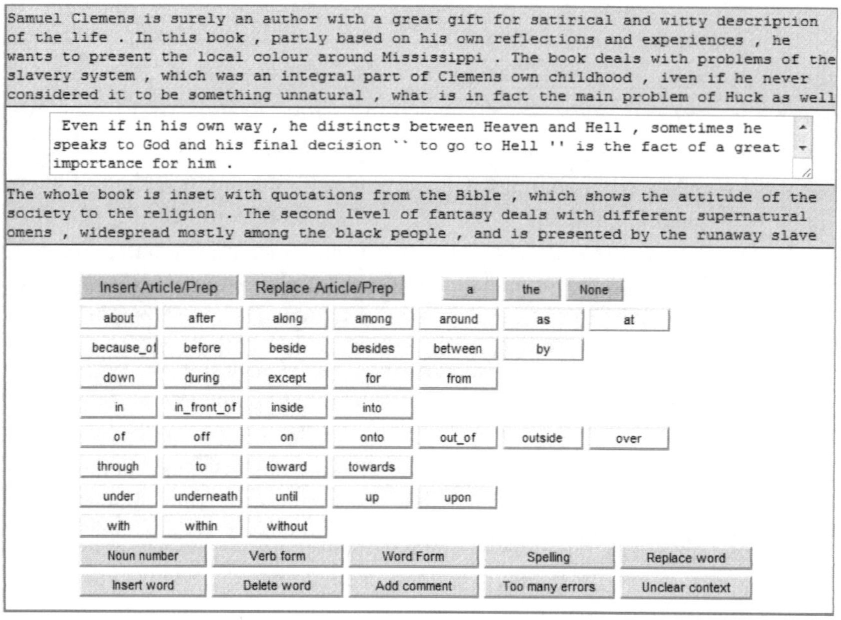

Figure 1: Example of a sentence for annotation as it appears in the annotation tool window. The target sentence is shown in the white box. The surrounding essay context is shown in the brown boxes. The buttons appear below the boxes with text: pink buttons (for marking article and preposition errors), dark green (for marking other errors), light green (article buttons) and yellow (preposition buttons).

Annotated sentence	**Corrected errors**
1. Television becomes their life , and in many cases it replaces their real life /lives/	noun number (*life* → *lives*)
2. Here I ca n't $help$ but mention that all these people were either bankers or the Heads of companies or something of that kind @nature, kind@.	word insertion (*help*); word replacement (*kind* → *kind, nature*)
3. We exterminated *have exterminated* different kinds of animals	verb form (*exterminated* → *have exterminated*)
4. ... nearly 30000 species of plants are under the <a> serious threat of disappearance |disappearing|	article replacement (*the* → *a*); word form (*disappearance* → *disappearing*)
5. There is &a& saying that laziness is the engine of the <None> progress	article insertion (*a*); article deletion (*the*)
6. ...experience teaches people to strive to <for> the <None> possible things	preposition replacement (*to* → *for*); article deletion (*the*)

Table 2: Examples of sentences annotated using the annotation tool. Each type of mistake is marked using a different set of delimiters. The corrected words are enclosed in the delimiters and follow the word to which the correction refers. In example 2, the annotator preserved the author's choice *kind* and added a better choice *nature*.

Source language	Total sent.	Total words	Errors per 100 words	Corrections by Error Type								
				Articles	Prepositions	Verb form	Word form	Noun number	Word order	Spell.	Word repl.	Punc.
Bulgarian	244	6197	11.9	10.3%	12.1%	3.5%	3.1%	3.0%	2.0%	5.0%	46.7%	14.2%
Chinese	468	9327	15.1	12.7%	27.2%	7.9%	3.1%	4.6%	1.4%	5.4%	26.2%	11.3%
Czech	296	6570	12.9	16.3%	10.8%	5.2%	3.4%	2.7%	3.2%	8.3%	32.5%	17.5%
French	238	5656	5.8	6.7%	17.4%	2.1%	4.0%	4.6%	3.1%	9.8%	12.5%	39.8%
German	198	5086	11.4	4.0%	13.0%	4.3%	2.8%	1.9%	2.9%	4.7%	15.4%	51.0%
Italian	243	6843	10.6	5.9%	16.6%	6.4%	1.4%	3.0%	2.4%	4.6%	20.5%	39.3%
Polish	198	4642	10.1	15.1%	16.3%	4.0%	1.3%	1.3%	2.3%	2.1%	12.3%	45.2%
Russian	464	10844	13.0	19.2%	17.8%	3.7%	2.5%	2.5%	2.1%	5.0%	28.3%	18.8%
Spanish	296	7760	15.0	11.5%	14.2%	6.0%	3.8%	2.6%	1.6%	11.9%	37.7%	10.7%
All	**2645**	**62925**	**12.2**	**12.5%**	**17.1%**	**5.2%**	**2.9%**	**3.0%**	**2.2%**	**6.5%**	**28.2%**	**22.5%**

Table 3: Error statistics on the annotated data by source language and error type

the *punctuation* category, which comprises 22% of all corrections. About 12% of all errors involve articles, and prepositions comprise 17% of all errors. We would expect the preposition category to be less significant if we did not specifically look for such errors, when selecting sentences for annotation. Two other common categories are *spelling* and *verb form*. *Verb form* combines errors in verb conjugation and errors in verb tense. It can be observed from the table that there is a significantly smaller proportion of article errors for the speakers of languages that have articles, such as French or German. Lexical errors (word replacement) are more common in language groups that have a higher rate of errors per 100 words. In contrast, the proportion of punctuation mistakes is higher for those learners that make fewer errors overall (cf. French, German, Italian, and Polish). This suggests that punctuation errors are difficult to master, maybe because rules of punctuation are not generally taught in foreign language classes. Besides, there is a high degree of variation in the use of punctuation even among native speakers.

5.1 Statistics on Article Corrections

As stated in Section 2, article errors are one of the most common mistakes made by non-native speakers of English. This is especially true for the speakers of languages that do not have articles, but for advanced French speakers this is also a very common mistake (Dagneaux et al., 1998), suggesting that article usage in English is a very difficult language feature to master.

Han et al. (2006) show that about 13% of noun phrases in TOEFL essays by Chinese, Japanese, and Russian speakers have article mistakes. They also show that learners do not confuse articles randomly and the most common article mistakes are omissions and superfluous article usage. Our findings are summarized in Table 4 and are very similar. We also distinguish between the superfluous use of *a* and *the*, we allows us to observe that most of the cases of extraneously used articles involve article *the* for all language groups. In fact, extraneous *the* is the most common article mistake for the majority of our speakers. Superfluous *the* is usually followed by the omission of *the* and the omission of *a*. Another statistic that our table demonstrates and that was shown previously (e.g. (Dalgish, 1985)) is that learners whose first language does not have articles make more article mistakes: We can see from column 3 of the table that the speakers of German, French and Italian are three to four times less likely to make an article mistake than the speakers of Chinese and all of the Slavic languages. The only exception are Spanish speakers. It is not clear whether the higher error rate is only due to a difference in overall language proficiency (as is apparent from the average number of mistakes by these speakers in Table 3) or to other factors. Finally, the last column in the table indicates that confusing articles with pronouns is a relatively common error and on average accounts for 10% of all article mistakes[5]. Current article correction systems do not address this error type.

[5] An example of such confusion is " To pay for *the* crimes, criminals are put in prison", where *the* is used instead of *their*.

Source language	Errors total	Errors per 100 words	Article mistakes by error type						
			Miss. *the*	Miss. *a*	Extr. *the*	Extr. *a*	Confu-sion	Mult. labels	Other
Bulgarian	76	1.2	9%	25%	41%	3%	8%	1%	13%
Chinese	179	1.9	20%	12%	48%	4%	7%	2%	7%
Czech	138	2.1	29%	13%	29%	9%	7%	4%	9%
French	22	0.4	9%	14%	36%	14%	0%	23%	5%
German	23	0.5	22%	9%	22%	4%	8%	9%	26%
Italian	43	0.6	16%	40%	26%	2%	9%	0%	7%
Polish	71	1.5	37%	18%	17%	8%	11%	4%	4%
Russian	271	2.5	24%	18%	31%	6%	11%	1%	9%
Spanish	134	1.7	16%	10%	51%	7%	3%	1%	10%
All	**957**	**1.5**	**22%**	**16%**	**36%**	**6%**	**8%**	**3%**	**9%**

Table 4: Distribution of article mistakes by error type and source language of the writer. *Confusion* error type refers to confusing articles *a* and *the*. *Multiple labels* denotes cases where the annotator specified more than one article choice, one of which was used by the learner. *Other* refers to confusing articles with possessive and demonstrative pronouns.

5.2 Statistics on Preposition Corrections

Table 5 shows statistics on errors in preposition usage. Preposition mistakes are classified into three categories: *replacements*, *insertions*, and *deletions*. Unlike with article errors, the most common type of preposition errors is confusing two prepositions. This category accounts for more than half of all errors, and the breakdown is very similar for all language groups. The fourth category in the table, *with original*, refers to the preposition usages that were found acceptable by the annotators, but with a better suggestion provided. We distinguish this case as a separate category because preposition usage is highly variable, unlike, for example, article usage. Tetreault and Chodorow (Tetreault and Chodorow, 2008a) show that agreement between two native speakers on a cloze test targeting prepositions is about 76%, which demonstrates that there are many contexts that license multiple prepositions.

Source language	Errors total	Errors per 100 words	Mistakes by error type			
			Repl.	Ins.	Del.	With orig.
Bulgarian	89	1.4	58%	22%	11%	8%
Chinese	384	4.1	52%	24%	22%	2%
Czech	91	1.4	51%	21%	24%	4%
French	57	1.0	61%	9%	12%	18%
German	75	1.5	61%	8%	16%	15%
Italian	120	1.8	57%	22%	12%	8%
Polish	77	1.7	49%	18%	16%	17%
Russian	251	2.3	53%	21%	17%	9%
Spanish	165	2.1	55%	20%	19%	6%
All	**1309**	**2.1**	**54%**	**21%**	**18%**	**7%**

Table 5: Distribution of preposition mistakes by error type and source language of the writer. *With orig* refers to prepositions judged as acceptable by the annotators, but with a better suggestion provided.

6 Inter-annotator Agreement

Correcting non-native text for a variety of mistakes is challenging and requires a number of decisions on the part of the annotator. Human language allows for many ways to express the same idea. Furthermore, it is possible that the corrected sentence, even when it does not contain clear mistakes, does not sound like a sentence produced by a native speaker. The latter is complicated by the fact that native speakers differ widely with respect to what constitutes acceptable usage (Tetreault and Chodorow, 2008a).

To date, a common approach to annotating non-native text has been to use one rater (Gamon et al., 2008; Han et al., 2006; Izumi et al., 2004; Nagata et al., 2006). The output of human annotation is viewed as the gold standard when evaluating an error detection system. The question of reliability of using one rater has been raised in (Tetreault and Chodorow, 2008a), where an extensive reliability study of human judgments in rating preposition usage is described. In particular, it is shown that inter-annotator agreement on preposition correction is low (kappa value of 0.63) and that native speakers do not always agree on whether a specific preposition constitutes acceptable usage.

We measure agreement by asking an annotator whether a sentence corrected by another person is correct. After all, our goal was to make the sentence sound native-like, without enforcing that errors are corrected in the same way. One hundred sentences annotated by each person were selected and the cor-

Agreement set	Rater	Judged correct	Judged incorrect
Agreement set 1	Rater #2	37	63
	Rater #3	59	41
Agreement set 2	Rater #1	79	21
	Rater #3	73	27
Agreement set 3	Rater #1	83	17
	Rater #2	47	53

Table 6: Annotator agreement at the sentence level. The number next to the agreement set denotes the annotator who corrected the sentences on the first pass. *Judged correct* denotes the proportion of sentences in the agreement set that the second rater did not change. *Judged incorrect* denotes the proportion of sentences, in which the second rater made corrections.

rections were applied. This corrected set was mixed with new sentences and given to the other two annotators. In this manner, each annotator received two hundred sentences corrected by the other two annotators. For each pair of the annotators, we compute agreement based on the 100 sentences on which they did a second pass after the initial corrections by the third rater. To compute agreement at the sentence level, we assign the annotated sentences to one of the two categories: "correct" and "incorrect": A sentence is considered "correct" if a rater did not make any corrections in it on the second pass [6]. Table 6 shows for each agreement set the number of sentences that were corrected on the second pass. On average, 40.8% of the agreement set sentences belong to the "incorrect" category, but the proportion of "incorrect" sentences varies across annotators.

We also compute agreement on the two categories, "correct" and "incorrect". The agreement and the kappa values are shown in Table 7. Agreement on the sentences corrected on the second pass varies between 56% to 78% with kappa values ranging from 0.16 to 0.40. The low numbers reflect the difficulty of the task and the variability of the native speakers' judgments about acceptable usage. In fact, since the annotation requires looking at several phenomena, we can expect a lower agreement, when compared to agreement rate on one language phenomenon. Suppose rater A disagrees with rater B on a given phenomenon with probability 1/4, then, when there are two phenomena, the probability that he will disagree with at least on of them is

[6] We ignore punctuation corrections.

Agreement set	Agreement	kappa
Agreement set 1	56%	0.16
Agreement set 2	78%	0.40
Agreement set 3	60%	0.23

Table 7: Agreement at the sentence level. *Agreement* shows how many sentences in each agreement set were assigned to the same category ("correct", "incorrect") for each of the two raters.

$1 - 9/16 = 7/16$. And the probability goes down with the number of phenomena.

7 Conclusion

In this paper, we presented a corpus of essays by students of English of nine first language backgrounds, corrected and annotated for errors. To our knowledge, this is the first fully-corrected corpus that contains such diverse data. We have described an annotation schema, have shown statistics on the error distribution for writers of different first language backgrounds and inter-annotator agreement on the task. We have also described a program that was developed to facilitate the annotation process.

While natural language annotation, especially in the context of error correction, is a challenging and time-consuming task, research in learner corpora and annotation is important for the development of robust systems for correcting and detecting errors.

Acknowledgments

We thank the anonymous reviewers for their helpful comments. This research is partly supported by a grant from the U.S. Department of Education.

References

J. Bitchener, S. Young and D. Cameron. 2005. The Effect of Different Types of Corrective Feedback on ESL Student Writing. *Journal of Second Language Writing*.

A. J. Carlson and J. Rosen and D. Roth. 2001. Scaling Up Context Sensitive Text Correction. *IAAI*, 45–50.

M. Chodorow, J. Tetreault and N-R. Han. 2007. Detection of Grammatical Errors Involving Prepositions. *Proceedings of the Fourth ACL-SIGSEM Workshop on Prepositions*.

E. Dagneaux, S. Denness and S. Granger. 1998. Computer-aided Error Analysis. *System*, 26:163–174.

G. Dalgish. 1985. Computer-assisted ESL Research. *CALICO Journal*, 2(2).

G. Dalgish. 1991. Computer-Assisted Error Analysis and Courseware Design: Applications for ESL in the Swedish Context. *CALICO Journal*, 9.

R. De Felice and S. Pulman. 2008. A Classifier-Based Approach to Preposition and Determiner Error Correction in L2 English. In *Proceedings of COLING-08.*

A. Díaz-Negrillo and J. Fernández-Domínguez. 2006. Error Tagging Systems for Learner Corpora. *RESLA*, 19:83-102.

J. Eeg-Olofsson and O. Knuttson. 2003. Automatic Grammar Checking for Second Language Learners - the Use of Prepositions. In *Nodalida.*

M. Gamon, J. Gao, C. Brockett, A. Klementiev, W. Dolan, D. Belenko and L. Vanderwende. 2008. Using Contextual Speller Techniques and Language Modeling for ESL Error Correction. *Proceedings of IJCNLP.*

A. R. Golding and D. Roth. 1996. Applying Winnow to Context-Sensitive Spelling Correction. *ICML*, 182–190.

A. R. Golding and D. Roth. 1999. A Winnow based approach to Context-Sensitive Spelling Correction. *Machine Learning*, 34(1-3):107–130.

S. Granger, E. Dagneaux and F. Meunier. 2002. *International Corpus of Learner English*

S. Granger. 2002. A Bird's-eye View of Learner Corpus Research. *Computer Learner Corpora, Second Language Acquisition and Foreign Language Teaching*, Eds. S. Granger, J. Hung and S. Petch-Tyson, Amsterdam: John Benjamins. 3–33.

S. Gui and H. Yang. 2003. *Zhongguo Xuexizhe Yingyu Yuliaohu. (Chinese Learner English Corpus).* Shanghai Waiyu Jiaoyu Chubanshe. (In Chinese).

N. Han, M. Chodorow and C. Leacock. 2006. Detecting Errors in English Article Usage by Non-native Speakers. *Journal of Natural Language Engineering*, 12(2):115–129.

E. Izumi, K. Uchimoto, T. Saiga and H. Isahara. 2003. Automatic Error Detection in the Japanese Leaners English Spoken Data. *ACL.*

E. Izumi, K. Uchimoto and H. Isahara. 2004. The Overview of the SST Speech Corpus of Japanese Learner English and Evaluation through the Experiment on Automatic Detection of Learners' Errors. *LREC.*

E. Izumi, K. Uchimoto and H. Isahara. 2004. The NICT JLE Corpus: Exploiting the Language Learner's Speech Database for Research and Education. *International Journal of the Computer, the Internet and Management*, 12(2):119–125.

R. Nagata, A. Kawai, K. Morihiro, and N. Isu. 2006. A Feedback-Augmented Method for Detecting Errors in the Writing of Learners of English. *ACL/COLING.*

N. Pravec. 2002. Survey of learner corpora. *ICAME Journal*, 26:81–114.

A. Rozovskaya and D. Roth 2010. Training Paradigms for Correcting Errors in Grammar and Usage. In *Proceedings of the NAACL-HLT*, Los-Angeles, CA.

J. Tetreault and M. Chodorow. 2008. Native Judgments of Non-Native Usage: Experiments in Preposition Error Detection. *COLING Workshop on Human Judgments in Computational Linguistics*, Manchester, UK.

J. Tetreault and M. Chodorow. 2008. The Ups and Downs of Preposition Error Detection in ESL Writing. *COLING*, Manchester, UK.

Search right and thou shalt find ...
Using Web Queries for Learner Error Detection

Michael Gamon
Microsoft Research
One Microsoft Way
Redmond, WA 981052, USA
mgamon@microsoft.com

Claudia Leacock
Butler Hill Group
P.O. Box 935
Ridgefield, CT 06877, USA
Claudia.leacock@gmail.com

Abstract

We investigate the use of web search queries for detecting errors in non-native writing. Distinguishing a correct sequence of words from a sequence with a learner error is a baseline task that any error detection and correction system needs to address. Using a large corpus of error-annotated learner data, we investigate whether web search result counts can be used to distinguish correct from incorrect usage. In this investigation, we compare a variety of query formulation strategies and a number of web resources, including two major search engine APIs and a large web-based n-gram corpus.

1 Introduction

Data-driven approaches to the detection and correction of non-native errors in English have been researched actively in the past several years. Such errors are particularly amenable to data-driven methods because many prominent learner writing errors involve a relatively small class of phenomena that can be targeted with specific models, in particular article and preposition errors. Preposition and determiner errors (most of which are article errors) are the second and third most frequent errors in the *Cambridge Learner Corpus* (after the more intractable problem of content word choice). By targeting the ten most frequent prepositions involved in learner errors, more than 80% of preposition errors in the corpus are covered.

Typically, data-driven approaches to learner errors use a classifier trained on contextual information such as tokens and part-of-speech tags within a window of the preposition/article (Gamon et al. 2008, 2010, DeFelice and Pulman 2007, 2008, Han et al. 2006, Chodorow et al. 2007, Tetreault and Chodorow 2008).

Language models are another source of evidence that can be used in error detection. Using language models for this purpose is not a new approach, it goes back to at least Atwell (1987). Gamon et al. (2008) and Gamon (2010) use a combination of classification and language modeling. Once language modeling comes into play, the *quantity* of the training data comes to the forefront. It has been well-established that statistical models improve as the size of the training data increases (Banko and Brill 2001a, 2001b). This is particularly true for language models: other statistical models such as a classifier, for example, can be targeted towards a specific decision/classification, reducing the appetite for data somewhat, while language models provide probabilities for any sequence of words - a task that requires immense training data resources if the language model is to consider increasingly sparse longer n-grams.

Language models trained on data sources like the Gigaword corpus have become commonplace, but of course there is one corpus that dwarfs any other resource in size: the World Wide Web. This has drawn the interest of many researchers in natural language processing over the past decade. To mention just a few examples, Zhu and Rosenfeld (2001) combine trigram counts from the web with an existing language model where the estimates of the existing model are unreliable because of data sparseness. Keller and Lapata (2003) advocate the use of the web as a corpus to retrieve backoff probabilities for unseen bigrams. Lapata and Keller (2005) extend this method to a range of additional natural language processing tasks, but also caution that web counts have limitations and add noise. Kilgariff (2007) points out the shortcomings of

Proceedings of the NAACL HLT 2010 Fifth Workshop on Innovative Use of NLP for Building Educational Applications, pages 37–44,
Los Angeles, California, June 2010.

accessing the web as a corpus through search queries: (a) there is no lemmatization or part-of-speech tagging in search indices, so a linguistically meaningful query can only be approximated, (b) search syntax, as implemented by search engine providers, is limited, (c) there is often a limit on the number of automatic queries that are allowed by search engines, (c) hit count estimates are estimates of retrieved *pages*, not of retrieved words. We would like to add to that list that hit count estimates on the web are just that -- estimates. They are computed on the fly by proprietary algorithms, and apparently the algorithms also access different slices of the web index, which causes a fluctuation over time, as Tetrault and Chodorow (2009) point out.

In 2006, Google made its web-based 5gram language model available through the Linguistic Data Consortium, which opens the possibility of using real n-gram statistics derived from the web directly, instead of using web search as a proxy.

In this paper we explore the use of the web as a corpus for a very specific task: distinguishing between a learner error and its correction. This is obviously not the same as the more ambitious question of whether a system can be built to detect and correct errors on the basis of web counts alone, and this is a distinction worth clarifying. Any system that successfully detects and corrects an error will need to accomplish three tasks[1]: (1) find a part of the user input that contains an error (*error detection*). (2) find one or multiple alternative string(s) for the alleged error (*candidate generation*) and (3) score the alternatives and the original to determine which alternative (if any) is a likely correction (*error correction*). Here, we are only concerned with the third task, specifically the comparison between the incorrect and the correct choice. This is an easily measured task, and is also a minimum requirement for any language model or language model approximation: if the model cannot distinguish an error from a well-formed string, it will not be useful.

[1] Note that these tasks need not be addressed by separate components. A contextual classifier for preposition choice, for example, can generate a probability distribution over a set of prepositions (candidate generation). If the original preposition choice has lower probability than one or more other prepositions, it is a potential error (error detection), and the prepositions with higher probability will be potential corrections (error correction).

We focus on two prominent learner errors in this study: preposition inclusion and choice and article inclusion and choice. These errors are among the most frequent learner errors (they comprise nearly one third of all errors in the learner corpus used in this study).

In this study, we compare three web data sources: The public Bing API, Google API, and the Google 5-gram language model. We also pay close attention to strategies of query formulation. The questions we address are summarized as follows:

> Can web data be used to distinguish learner errors from correct phrases?
>
> What is the better resource for web-data: the Bing API, the Google API, or the Google 5-gram data?
>
> What is the best query formulation strategy when using web search results for this task? How much context should be included in the query?

2 Related Work

Hermet et al. (2008) use web search hit counts for preposition error detection and correction in French. They use a set of confusable prepositions to create a candidate set of alternative prepositional choices and generate queries for each of the candidates and the original. The queries are produced using linguistic analysis to identify both a governing and a governed element as a minimum meaningful context. On a small test set of 133 sentences, they report accuracy of 69.9% using the Yahoo! search engine.

Yi et al. (2008) target article use and collocation errors with a similar approach. Their system first analyzes the input sentence using part-of-speech tagging and a chunk parser. Based on this analysis, potential error locations for determiners and verb-noun collocation errors are identified. Query generation is performed at three levels of granularity: the sentence (or clause) level, chunk level and word level. Queries, in this approach, are not exact string searches but rather a set of strings combined with the chunk containing the potential error through a boolean operator. An example for a chunk level query for the sentence "I am learning economics at university" would be "[economics] AND [at university] AND [learning]". For article errors the hit count estimates (normalized for query length) are used directly. If the ratio of the normalized hit count estimate for the alternative article choice to the normalized hit count estimate of the original choice exceeds a manually determined threshold, the alternative is suggested as a correction. For verb-noun collocations, the situation is more complex since the system does not automatically generate possible alternative choices for noun/verb collocations. Instead, the snippets (document summaries) that are returned by the initial web search are analyzed and potential alternative collocation candidates are identified. They then submit a second round of queries to determine whether the suggestions are more frequent than the original collocation. Results on a 400+ sentence corpus of learner writing show 62% precision and 41% recall for determiners, and 30.7% recall and 37.3% precision for verb-noun collocation errors.

Tetreault and Chodorow (2009) make use of the web in a different way. Instead of using global web count estimates, they issue queries with a region-specific restriction and compare statistics across regions. The idea behind this approach is that regions that have a higher density of non-native speakers will show significantly higher frequency of erroneous productions than regions with a higher proportion of native speakers. For example, the verb-preposition combinations *married to* versus *married with* show very different counts in the UK versus France regions. The ratio of counts for *married to*/*married with* in the UK is 3.28, whereas it is 1.18 in France. This indicates that there is significant over-use of *married with* among native French speakers, which serves as evidence that this verb-preposition combination is likely to be an error predominant for French learners of English. They test their approach on a list of known verb-preposition errors. They also argue that, in a state-of-the-art preposition error detection system, recall on the verb-preposition errors under investigation is still so low that systems can only benefit from increased sensitivity to the error patterns that are discoverable through the region web estimates.

Bergsma et al (2009) are the closest to our work. They use the Google N-gram corpus to disambiguate usage of 34 prepositions in the *New York Times* portion of the Gigaword corpus. They use a sliding window of n-grams (n ranging from 2 to 5) across the preposition and collect counts for all resulting n-grams. They use two different methods to combine these counts. Their *SuperLM* model combines the counts as features in a linear SVM classifier, trained on a subset of the data. Their *SumLM* model is simpler, it sums all log counts across the n-grams. The preposition with the highest score is then predicted for the given context. Accuracy on the *New York Times* data in these experiments reaches 75.4% for SuperLM and 73.7% for SumLM.

Our approach differs from Bergsma et al. in three crucial respects. First, we evaluate insertion, deletion, and substitution operations, not just substitution, and we extend our evaluation to article errors. Second, we focus on finding the best query mechanism for each of these operations, which requires only a single query to the Web source. Finally, the focus of our work is on learner error detection, so we evaluate on real learner data as opposed to well-formed news text. This distinction is important: in our context, evaluation on edited text artificially inflates both precision and recall because the context surrounding the potential error site is error-free whereas learner writing can be, and often is, surrounded by errors. In addition, *New York Times* writing is highly idiomatic while learner productions often include unidiomatic word choices, even though the choice may not be considered an error.

3 Experimental Setup

3.1 Test Data

Our test data is extracted from the *Cambridge University Press Learners' Corpus* (CLC). Our version of CLC currently contains 20 million words from non-native English essays written as part of one of Cambridge's English language proficiency tests (ESOL) – at all proficiency levels. The essays are annotated for error type, erroneous span and suggested correction. We perform a number of preprocessing steps on the data. First, we correct all errors that were flagged as being spelling errors. Spelling errors that were flagged as morphology errors were left alone. We also changed confusable words that are covered by MS Word. In addition, we changed British English spelling to American English. We then eliminate all annotations for non-pertinent errors (i.e. non-preposition/article errors, or errors that do not involve any of the targeted prepositions), but we retain the original (erroneous) text for these. This makes our task harder since we will have to make predictions in text containing multiple errors, but it is more realistic given real learner writing. Finally, we eliminate sentences containing nested errors (where the annotation of one error contains an annotation for another error) and multiple article/preposition errors. Sentences that were flagged for a replacement error but contained no replacement were also eliminated from the data. The final set we use consists of a random selection of 9,006 sentences from the CLC with article errors and 9,235 sentences with preposition errors.

3.2 Search APIs and Corpora

We examine three different sources of data to distinguish learner errors from corrected errors. First, we use two web search engine APIs, Bing and Google. Both APIs allow the retrieval of a *page-count estimate* for an exact match query. Since these estimates are provided based on proprietary algorithms, we have to treat them as a "black box". The third source of data is the Google 5-gram corpus (Linguistic Data Consortium 2006) which contains n-grams with n ranging from 1 to 5. The count cutoff for unigrams is 200, for higher order n-grams it is 40.

3.3 Query Formulation

There are many possible ways to formulate an exact match (i.e. quoted) query for an error and its correction, depending on the amount of context that is included on the right and left side of the error. Including too little context runs the risk of missing the linguistically relevant information for determining the proper choice of preposition or determiner. Consider, for example, the sentence *we rely most of/on friends*. If we only include one word to the left and one word to the right of the preposition, we end up with the queries "most on friends" and "most of friends" - and the web hit count estimate may tell us that the latter is more frequent than the former. However, in this example, the verb *rely* determines the choice of preposition and when it is included in the query as in "rely most on friends" versus "rely most of friends", the estimated hit counts might correctly reflect the incorrect versus correct choice of preposition. Extending the query to cover too much of the context, on the other hand, can lead to low or zero web hit estimates because of data sparseness - if we include the pronoun *we* in the query as in "we rely most on friends" versus "we rely most of friends", we get zero web count estimates for both queries.

Another issue in query formulation is what strategy to use for corrections that involve deletions and insertions, where the number of tokens changes. If, for example, we use queries of length 3, the question for deletion queries is whether we use two words to the left and one to the right of the deleted word, or one word to the left and two to the right. In other words, in the sentence *we traveled to/0 abroad last year*, should the query for the correction (deletion) be "we traveled abroad" or "traveled abroad last"?

Finally, we can employ some linguistic information to design our query. By using part-of-speech tag information, we can develop heuristics to include a governing content word to the left and the head of the noun phrase to the right.

The complete list of query strategies that we tested is given below.

SmartQuery: using part-of-speech information to include the first content word to the left and the head noun to the right. If the content word on the left cannot be established within a window of 2 tokens and the noun phrase edge within 5 tokens, select a fixed window of 2 tokens to the left and 2 tokens to the right.

FixedWindow Queries: include *n* tokens to the left and *m* tokens to the right. We experimented with the following settings for *n* and *m*: 1_1, 2_1, 1_2, 2_2, 3_2, 2_3. The latter two 6-grams were only used for the API's, because the Google corpus does not contain 6-grams.

FixedLength Queries: queries where the length in tokens is identical for the error and the correction. For substitution errors, these are the same as the corresponding *FixedWindow* queries, but for substitutions and deletions we either favor the left or right context to include one additional token to make up for the deleted/inserted token. We experimented with trigrams, 4-grams, 5-grams and 6-grams, with left and right preference for each, they are referred to as *Left4g* (4-gram with left preference), etc.

3.4 Evaluation Metrics

For each query pair <q_{error}, $q_{correction}$>, we produce one of three different outcomes:

correct (the query results favor the correction of the learner error over the error itself):

$count(q_{correction}) > count(q_{error})$

incorrect (the query results favor the learner error over its correction):

$count(q_{error}) >= count(q_{correction})$
where($count(q_{error}) \neq 0$ OR $count(q_{correction}) \neq 0$)

noresult:

$count(q_{correction}) = count(q_{error}) = 0$

For each query type, each error (preposition or article), each correction operation (deletion, insertion, substitution) and each web resource (Bing API, Google API, Google N-grams) we collect these counts and use them to calculate three different metrics. *Raw accuracy* is the ratio of correct predictions to all query pairs:

$$Raw\ accuracy = \frac{corr}{corr + incorr + noresult}$$

We also calculate accuracy for the subset of query pairs where at least one of the queries resulted in a successful hit, i.e. a non-zero result. We call this metric *Non-Zero-Result-Accurracy (NZRA)*, it is the ratio of correct predictions to incorrect predictions, ignoring noresults:

$$NonZeroResultAccuracy = \frac{corr}{corr + incorr}$$

Finally, *retrieval ratio* is the ratio of queries that returned non-zero results:

4 Results

We show results from our experiments in Table 1 - Table 6. Since space does not permit a full tabulation of all the individual results, we restrict ourselves to listing only those query types that achieve best results (highlighted) in at least one metric.

Google 5-grams show significantly better results than both the Google and Bing APIs. This is good news in terms of implementation, because it frees the system from the vagaries involved in relying on search engine page estimates: (1) the latency, (2) query quotas, and (3) fluctuations of page estimates over time. The bad news is that the 5-gram corpus has much lower retrieval ratio because, presumably, of its frequency cutoff. Its use also limits the maximum length of a query to a 5-gram (although neither of the APIs outperformed Google 5-grams when retrieving 6-gram queries).

The results for substitutions are best, for fixed window queries. For prepositions, the SmartQueries perform with about 86% NZRA while a fixed length 2_2 query (targeted word with a ±2-token window) achieves the best results for articles, at about 85% (when there was at least one non-zero match). Retrieval ratio for the prepositions was about 6% lower than retrieval ratio for articles – 41% compared to 35%.

The best query type for insertions was fixed-length LeftFourgrams with about 95% NZRA and 71% retrieval ratio for articles and 89% and 78% retrieval ratio for prepositions. However, LeftFourgrams favor the suggested rewrites because, by keeping the query length at four tokens, the original has more syntactic/semantic context. If the original sentence contains *is referred as the* and the annotator inserted *to* before *as*, the original query will be *is referred as the* and the correction query *is referred to as*.

Conversely, with deletion, having a fixed window favors the shorter rewrite string. The best query types for deletions were: 2_2 queries for articles (94% NZRA and 46% retrieval ratio) and SmartQueries for prepositions (97% NZRA and 52% retrieval ratio). For prepositions the fixed length 1_1 query performs about the same as the SmartQueries, but that query is a trigram (or smaller at the edges of a sentence) whereas the average length of SmartQueries is 4.7 words for prepositions and 4.3 words for articles. So while the coverage for SmartQueries is much lower, the longer query string cuts the risk of matching on false positives.

The Google 5-gram Corpus differs from search engines in that it is sensitive to upper and lower case distinctions and to punctuation. While intuitively it seemed that punctuation would hurt n-gram performance, it actually helps because the punctuation is an indicator of a clause boundary. A recent Google search for *have a lunch* and *have lunch* produced estimates of about 14 million web pages for the former and only 2 million for the latter. Upon inspecting the snippets for *have a lunch*, the next word was almost always a noun such as *menu, break, date, hour, meeting, partner,* etc. The relative frequencies for *have a lunch* would be much different if a clause boundary marker were required. The 5-gram corpus also has sentence boundary markers which is especially helpful to identify changes at the beginning of a sentence.

	non-zero-result accuracy			retrieval ratio			raw accuracy		
Query type	B-API	G-API	G-Ngr	B-API	G-API	G-Ngr	B-API	G-API	G-Ngr
SmartQuery	0.8637	0.9548	**0.9742**	0.8787	0.8562	0.5206	0.7589	0.8176	0.5071
1_1	0.4099	0.9655	0.9721	**0.9986**	0.9978	0.9756	0.4093	**0.9634**	0.9484

Table 1: Preposition deletions (1395 query pairs).

	non-zero-result accuracy			retrieval ratio			raw accuracy		
Query type	B-API	G-API	G-Ngr	B-API	G-API	G-Ngr	B-API	G-API	G-Ngr
Left4g	0.7459	0.8454	**0.8853**	0.9624	0.9520	0.7817	0.7178	0.8048	0.6920
1_1	0.5679	0.2983	0.3550	**0.9973**	0.9964	0.9733	0.5661	0.2971	0.3456
Right3g	0.6431	0.8197	0.8586	0.9950	0.9946	0.9452	0.6399	**0.8152**	0.8116

Table 2: Preposition insertions (2208 query pairs).

	non-zero-result accuracy			retrieval ratio			raw accuracy		
Query type	B-API	G-API	G-Ngr	B-API	G-API	G-Ngr	B-API	G-API	G-Ngr
SmartQuery	0.7396	0.8183	**0.8633**	0.7987	0.7878	0.4108	0.5906	0.6446	0.5071
1_1=L3g=R3g	0.4889	0.6557	0.6638	**0.9870**	0.9856	0.9041	0.4826	0.6463	0.6001
1_2=R4g	0.6558	0.7651	0.8042	0.9178	0.9047	0.6383	0.6019	**0.6921**	0.5133

Table 3: Preposition substitutions (5632 query pairs).

	non-zero-result accuracy			retrieval ratio			raw accuracy		
Query type	B-API	G-API	G-Ngr	B-API	G-API	G-Ngr	B-API	G-API	G-Ngr
2_2	0.7678	0.9056	**0.9386**	0.8353	0.8108	0.4644	0.6414	0.7342	0.4359
1_1	0.3850	0.8348	0.8620	**0.9942**	0.9924	0.9606	0.3828	0.8285	0.8281
1_2	0.5737	0.8965	0.9097	0.9556	0.9494	0.7920	0.5482	**0.8512**	0.7205

Table 4: Article deletions (2769 query pairs).

	non-zero-result accuracy			retrieval ratio			raw accuracy		
Query type	B-API	G-API	G-Ngr	B-API	G-API	G-Ngr	B-API	G-API	G-Ngr
Left4g	0.8292	0.9083	**0.9460**	0.9505	0.9428	0.7072	0.7880	0.8562	0.6690
1_1	0.5791	0.3938	0.3908	**0.9978**	0.9975	0.9609	0.5777	0.3928	0.3755
Left3g	0.6642	0.8983	0.8924	0.9953	0.9955	0.9413	0.6611	**0.8942**	0.8400

Table 5: Article insertions (5520 query pairs).

	non-zero-result accuracy			retrieval ratio			raw accuracy		
Query type	B-API	G-API	G-Ngr	B-API	G-API	G-Ngr	B-API	G-API	G-Ngr
2_2=Left5g= Right5g	0.6970	0.7842	**0.8486**	0.8285	0.8145	0.4421	0.5774	0.6388	0.3752
1_1=L3g=R3g	0.4385	0.7063	0.7297	**0.9986**	0.9972	0.9596	0.4379	0.7043	0.7001
1_2=R4g	0.5268	0.7493	0.7917	0.9637	0.9568	0.8033	0.5077	**0.7169**	0.6360

Table 6: Article substitutions (717 query pairs).

5 Error Analysis

We manually inspected examples where the matches on the original string were greater than matches on the corrected string. The results of this error analysis are shown in table 7. Most of the time, (1) the context that determined article or preposition use and choice was not contained within the query. This includes, for articles, cases where article usage depends either on a previous mention or on the intended sense of a polysemous head noun. Some other patterns also emerged. Sometimes (2) both and the original and the correction seemed equally good in the context of the entire sentence, for example *it's very important to us* and *it's very important for us*. In other cases, (3) there was another error in the query string (recall that we retained all of the errors in the original sentences that were not the targeted error). Then there is a very subjective category (4) where the relative n-gram frequencies are unexpected, for example where the corpus has 171 trigrams *guilty for you* but only 137 for *guilty about you*. These often occur when both of the frequencies are either low and/or close. This category includes cases where it is very likely that one of the queries is retrieving an n-gram whose right edge is the beginning of a compound noun (as in with the trigram *have a lunch*). Finally, (5) some of the "corrections" either introduced an error into the sentence or the original and "correction" were equally bad. In this category, we also include British English article usage like *go to hospital*. For prepositions, (6) some of the corrections changed the meaning of the sentence – where the disambiguation context is often not in the sentence itself and either choice is syntactically correct, as in *I will buy it from you* changed to *I will buy it for you*.

	Articles		Preps	
	freq	ratio	freq	ratio
1.N-gram does not contain necessary context	187	.58	183	.52
2.Original and correction both good	39	.12	51	.11
3.Other error in n-gram	30	.9	35	.10
4.Unexpected ratio	36	.11	27	.09
5.Correction is wrong	30	.9	30	.08
6.Meaning changing	na	na	24	.07

Table 7: Error analysis

If we count categories 2 and 5 in Table 7 as not being errors, then the error rate for articles drops 20% and the error rate for prepositions drops 19%.

A disproportionately high subcategory of query strings that did not contain the disambiguating context (category 1) was at the edges of the sentence – especially for the LeftFourgrams at the beginning of a sentence where the query will always be a bigram.

6 Conclusion and Future Work

We have demonstrated that web source counts can be an accurate predictor for distinguishing between a learner error and its correction - as long as the query strategy is tuned towards the error type. Longer queries, i.e. 4-grams and 5-grams achieve the best non-zero-result accuracy for articles, while SmartQueries perform best for preposition errors. Google N-grams across the board achieve the best non-zero-result accuracy, but not surprisingly they have the lowest retrieval ratio due to count cutoffs. Between the two search APIs, Bing tends to have better retrieval ratio, while Google achieves higher accuracy.

In terms of practical use in an error detection system, a general "recipe" for a high precision component can be summarized as follows. First, use the Google Web 5-gram Corpus as a web source. It achieves the highest NZRA, and it avoids multiple problems with search APIs: results do not fluctuate over time, results are real n-gram counts as opposed to document count estimates, and a local implementation can avoid the high latency associated with search APIs. Secondly, carefully select the query strategy depending on the correction operation and error type.

We hope that this empirical investigation can contribute to a more solid foundation for future work in error detection and correction involving the web as a source for data. While it is certainly not sufficient to use only web data for this purpose, we believe that the accuracy numbers reported here indicate that web data can provide a strong additional signal in a system that combines different detection and correction mechanisms. One can imagine, for example, multiple ways to combine the n-gram data with an existing language model. Alternatively, one could follow Bergsma et al. (2009) and issue not just a single pair of queries but a whole series of queries and sum over the results. This would increase recall since at least some of the shorter queries are likely to return non-zero results. In a real-time system, however, issuing several dozen queries per potential error location and potential correction could cause performance issues. Finally, the n-gram counts can be incorporated as one of the features into a system such as the one described in Gamon (2010) that combines evidence from various sources in a principled way to optimize accuracy on learner errors.

Acknowledgments

We would like to thank Yizheng Cai for making the Google web ngram counts available through a web service and to the anonymous reviewers for their feedback.

References

Eric Steven Atwell. 1987. How to detect grammatical errors in a text without parsing it. *Proceedings of the 3rd EACL, Copenhagen, Denmark*, pp 38 - 45.

Michele Banko and Eric Brill. 2001a. Mitigating the paucity-of-data problem: Exploring the effect of training corpus size on classifier performance for natural language processing. In James Allan, editor, *Proceedings of the First International Conference on Human Language Technology Research*. Morgan Kaufmann, San Francisco.

Michele Banko and Eric Brill. 2001b. Scaling to very very large corpora for natural language disambiguation. In *Proceedings of the 39th Annual Meeting of the Association for Computational Linguistics and the 10th Conference of the European Chapter of the Association for Computational Linguistics*, pp. 26–33, Toulouse, France.

Shane Bergsma, Dekang Lin, and Randy Goebel. 2009. Web-scale n-gram models for lexical disambiguation. In Proceedings for the 21st International Joint *Conference on Artificial Intelligence*, pp. 1507 – 1512.

Martin Chodorow, Joel Tetreault, and Na-Rae Han. 2007. Detection of grammatical errors involving prepositions. In *Proceedings of the Fourth ACL-SIGSEM Workshop on Prepositions,* pp. 25-30.

Rachele De Felice and Stephen G. Pulman. 2007. Automatically acquiring models of preposition use. In *Proceedings of the Fourth ACL-SIGSEM Workshop on Prepositions*, pp. 45-50. Prague.

Rachele De Felice and Stephen Pulman. 2008. A classifier-based approach to preposition and determiner error correction in L2 English. *COLING*. Manchester, UK.

Michael Gamon, Jianfeng Gao, Chris Brockett, Alexander Klementiev, William Dolan, Dmitriy Belenko, and Lucy Vanderwende. 2008. Using contextual speller techniques and language modeling for ESL error correction. In P*roceedings of IJCNLP*, Hyderabad, India.

Michael Gamon. 2010. Using mostly native data to correct errors in learners' writing. In *Proceedings of NAACL.*

Na-Rae Han, Martin Chodorow, and Claudia Leacock. 2006. Detecting errors in English article usage by non-native speakers. *Natural Language Engineering*, 12(2), 115-129.

Matthieu Hermet, Alain Désilets, Stan Szpakowicz. 2008. Using the web as a linguistic resource to automatically correct lexico-syntactic errors. In *Proceedings of the 6th Conference on Language Resources and Evaluation* (LREC), pp. 874-878.

Frank Keller and Mirella Lapata. 2003. Using the web to obtain frequencies for unseen bigrams. *Computational Linguistics,* 29(3): 459-484.

Adam Kilgariff. 2007. Googleology is bad science. *Computational Linguistics* 33(1): 147-151.

Mirella Lapata and Frank Keller. 2005. Web-Based Models for Natural Language Processing. *ACM Transactions on Speech and Language Processing (TSLP)*, 2(1):1-31.

Linguistic Data Consortium. 2006. Web 1T 5-gram version 1. http://www.ldc.upenn.edu/Catalog/CatalogEntry.jsp?catalogId=LDC2006T13 .

Joel Tetreault and Martin Chodorow. 2008. The ups and downs of preposition error detection in ESL. *COLING*. Manchester, UK.

Joel Tetreault and Martin Chodorow. 2009. Examining the use of region web counts for ESL error detection. *Web as Corpus Workshop* (WAC-5), San Sebastian, Spain.

Xing Yi, Jianfeng Gao and Bill Dolan. 2008. A web-based English proofing system for English as a second language users. In *Proceedings of the Third International Joint Conference on Natural Language Processing* (IJCNLP). Hyderabad, India.

Zhu, X. and Rosenfeld, R. 2001. Improving trigram language modeling with the world wide web. In *Proceedings of International Conference on Acoustics Speech and Signal Processing*. Salt Lake City.

Rethinking Grammatical Error Annotation and Evaluation with the Amazon Mechanical Turk

Joel R. Tetreault
Educational Testing Service
Princeton, NJ, 08540, USA
JTetreault@ets.org

Elena Filatova
Fordham University
Bronx, NY, 10458, USA
filatova@fordham.edu

Martin Chodorow
Hunter College of CUNY
New York, NY, USA
martin.chodorow@hunter.cuny.edu

Abstract

In this paper we present results from two pilot studies which show that using the Amazon Mechanical Turk for preposition error annotation is as effective as using trained raters, but at a fraction of the time and cost. Based on these results, we propose a new evaluation method which makes it feasible to compare two error detection systems tested on different learner data sets.

1 Introduction

The last few years have seen an explosion in the development of NLP tools to detect and correct errors made by learners of English as a Second Language (ESL). While there has been considerable emphasis placed on the system development aspect of the field, with researchers tackling some of the toughest ESL errors such as those involving articles (Han et al., 2006) and prepositions (Gamon et al., 2008), (Felice and Pullman, 2009), there has been a woeful lack of attention paid to developing best practices for annotation and evaluation.

Annotation in the field of ESL error detection has typically relied on just one trained rater, and that rater's judgments then become the gold standard for evaluating a system. So it is very rare that inter-rater reliability is reported, although, in other NLP subfields, reporting reliability is the norm. Time and cost are probably the two most important reasons why past work has relied on only one rater because using multiple annotators on the same ESL texts would obviously increase both considerably. This is especially problematic for this field of research since some ESL errors, such as preposition usage, occur at error rates as low as 10%. This means that to collect a corpus of 1,000 preposition errors, an annotator would have to check over 10,000 prepositions.[1]

(Tetreault and Chodorow, 2008b) challenged the view that using one rater is adequate by showing that preposition usage errors actually do not have high inter-annotator reliability. For example, trained raters typically annotate preposition errors with a kappa around 0.60. This low rater reliability has repercussions for system evaluation: Their experiments showed that system precision could vary as much as 10% depending on which rater's judgments they used as the gold standard. For some grammatical errors such as subject-verb agreement, where rules are clearly defined, it may be acceptable to use just one rater. But for usage errors, the rules are less clearly defined and two native speakers can have very different judgments of what is acceptable. One way to address this is by aggregating a multitude of judgments for each preposition and treating this as the gold standard, however such a tactic has been impractical due to time and cost limitations.

While annotation is a problem in this field, comparing one system to another has also been a major issue. To date, *none* of the preposition and article error detection systems in the literature have been evaluated on the same corpus. This is mostly due to the fact that learner corpora are difficult to acquire (and then annotate), but also to the fact that they are

[1](Tetreault and Chodorow, 2008b) report that it would take 80hrs for one of their trained raters to find and mark 1,000 preposition errors.

Proceedings of the NAACL HLT 2010 Fifth Workshop on Innovative Use of NLP for Building Educational Applications, pages 45–48,

usually proprietary and cannot be shared. Examples include the Cambridge Learners Corpus[2] used in (Felice and Pullman, 2009), and TOEFL data, used in (Tetreault and Chodorow, 2008a). This makes it difficult to compare systems since learner corpora can be quite different. For example, the "difficulty" of a corpus can be affected by the L1 of the writers, the number of years they have been learning English, their age, and also where they learn English (in a native-speaking country or a non-native speaking country). In essence, learner corpora are not equal, so a system that performs at 50% precision in one corpus may actually perform at 80% precision on a different one. Such an inability to compare systems makes it difficult for this NLP research area to progress as quickly as it otherwise might.

In this paper we show that the Amazon Mechanical Turk (AMT), a fast and cheap source of untrained raters, can be used to alleviate several of the evaluation and annotation issues described above. Specifically we show:

- In terms of cost and time, AMT is an effective alternative to trained raters on the tasks of preposition selection in well-formed text and preposition error annotation in ESL text.
- With AMT, it is possible to efficiently collect multiple judgments for a target construction. Given this, we propose a new method for evaluation that finally allows two systems to be compared to one another even if they are tested on different corpora.

2 Amazon Mechnical Turk

Amazon provides a service called the Mechanical Turk which allows requesters (companies, researchers, etc.) to post simple tasks (known as Human Intelligence Tasks, or HITs) to the AMT website for untrained raters to perform for payments as low as $0.01 in many cases (Sheng et al., 2008). Recently, AMT has been shown to be an effective tool for annotation and evalatuation in NLP tasks ranging from word similarity detection and emotion detection (Snow et al., 2008) to Machine Translation quality evaluation (Callison-Burch, 2009). In these cases, a handful of untrained AMT workers (or Turkers) were found to be as effective as trained raters, but with the advantage of being considerably faster and less expensive. Given the success of using AMT in other areas of NLP, we test whether we can leverage it for our work in grammatical error detection, which is the focus of the pilot studies in the next two sections.

The presence of a *gold standard* in the above papers is crucial. In fact, the usability of AMT for text annotation has been demostrated in those studies by showing that non-experts' annotation converges to the gold standard developed by expert annotators. However, in our work we concentrate on tasks where there is no single gold standard, either because there are multiple prepositions that are acceptable in a given context or because the conventions of preposition usage simply do not conform to strict rules.

3 Selection Task

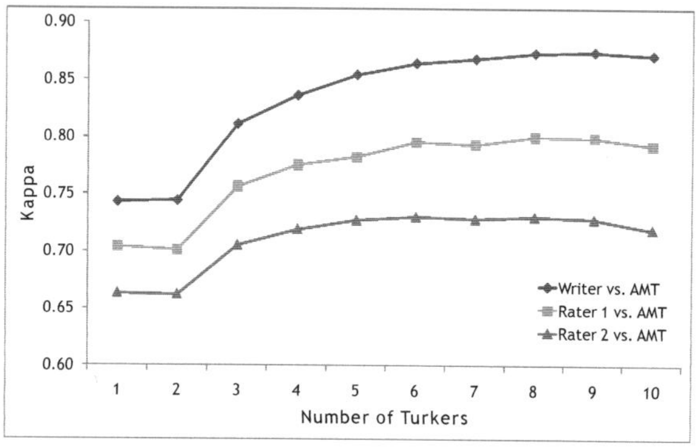

Figure 1: Error Detection Task: Reliability of AMT as a function of number of judgments

Typically, an early step in developing a preposition or article error detection system is to test the system on well-formed text written by native speakers to see how well the system can predict, or select, the writer's preposition given the context around the preposition. (Tetreault and Chodorow, 2008b) showed that trained human raters can achieve very high agreement (78%) on this task. In their work, a rater was shown a sentence with a target preposition replaced with a blank, and the rater was asked to select the preposition that the writer may have used. We replicate this experiment not with trained raters but with the AMT to answer two research questions: 1. Can untrained raters be as effective as trained

[2] http://www.cambridge.org/elt

raters? 2. If so, how many raters does it take to match trained raters?

In the experiment, a Turker was presented with a sentence from Microsoft's Encarta encyclopedia, with one preposition in that sentence replaced with a blank. There were 194 HITs (sentences) in all, and we requested 10 Turker judgments per HIT. Some Turkers did only one HIT, while others completed more than 100, though none did all 194. The Turkers' performance was analyzed by comparing their responses to those of two trained annotators and to the Encarta writer's preposition, which was considered the gold standard in this task. Comparing each trained annotator to the writer yielded a kappa of 0.822 and 0.778, and the two raters had a kappa of 0.742. To determine how many Turker responses would be required to match or exceed these levels of reliability, we randomly selected samples of various sizes from the sets of Turker responses for each sentence. For example, when samples were of size $N = 4$, four responses were randomly drawn from the set of ten responses that had been collected. The preposition that occurred most frequently in the sample was used as the Turker response for that sentence. In the case of a tie, a preposition was randomly drawn from those tied for most frequent. For each sample size, 100 samples were drawn and the mean values of agreement and kappa were calculated. The reliability results presented in Table 1 show that, with just three Turker responses, kappa with the writer (top line) is comparable to the values obtained from the trained annotators (around 0.8). Most notable is that with ten judgments, the reliability measures are much higher than those of the trained annotators. [3]

4 Error Detection Task

While the previous results look quite encouraging, the task they are based on, preposition selection in well-formed text, is quite different from, and less challenging than, the task that a system must perform in detecting errors in learner writing. To examine the reliability of Turker preposition error judgments, we ran another experiment in which Turkers were presented with a preposition highlighted in a sentence taken from an ESL corpus, and were instructed to judge its usage as either *correct*, *incorrect*, or *the context is too ungrammatical to make a judgment*. The set consisted of 152 prepositions in total, and we requested 20 judgments per preposition. Previous work has shown this task to be a difficult one for trainer raters to attain high reliability. For example, (Tetreault and Chodorow, 2008b) found kappa between two raters averaged 0.630.

Because there is no gold standard for the error detection task, kappa was used to compare Turker responses to those of three trained annotators. Among the trained annotators, inter-kappa agreement ranged from 0.574 to 0.650, for a mean kappa of 0.606. In Figure 2, kappa is shown for the comparisons of Turker responses to each annotator for samples of various sizes ranging from $N = 1$ to $N = 18$. At sample size $N = 13$, the average kappa is 0.608, virtually identical to the mean found among the trained annotators.

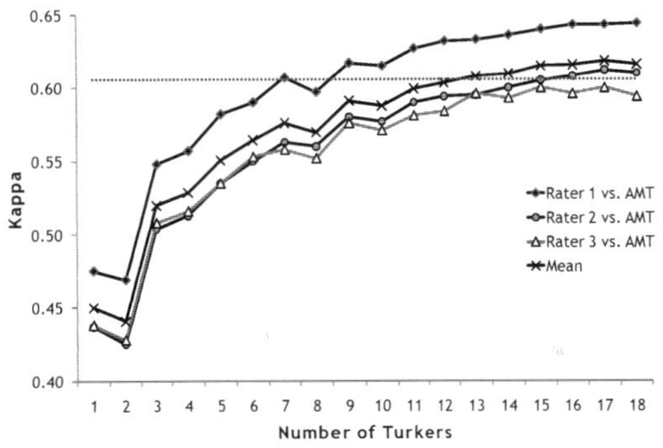

Figure 2: Error Detection Task: Reliability of AMT as a function of number of judgments

5 Rethinking Evaluation

We contend that the Amazon Mechanical Turk can not only be used as an effective alternative annotation source, but can also be used to revamp evaluation since multiple judgments are now easily acquired. Instead of treating the task of error detection as a "black or white" distinction, where a preposition is either correct or incorrect, cases of preposition use can now be grouped into bins based on the level of agreement of the Turkers. For example, if 90% or more judge a preposition to be an error,

[3]We also experimented with 50 judgments per sentence, but agreement and kappa improved only negligibly.

Task	# of HITs	Judgments/HIT	Total Judgments	Cost	Total Cost	# of Turkers	Total Time
Selection	194	10	1,940	$0.02	$48.50	49	0.5 hours
Error Detection	152	20	3,040	$0.02	$76.00	74	6 hours

Table 1: AMT Experiment Statistics

the high agreement is strong evidence that this is a clear case of an error. Conversely, agreement levels around 50% would indicate that the use of a particular preposition is highly contentious, and, most likely, it should not be flagged by an automated error detection system.

The current standard method treats all cases of preposition usage equally, however, some are clearly harder to annotate than others. By breaking an evaluation set into agreement bins, it should be possible to separate the "easy" cases from the "hard" cases and report precision and recall results for the different levels of human agreement represented by different bins. This method not only gives a clearer picture of how a system is faring, but it also ameliorates the problem of cross-system evaluation when two systems are evaluated on different corpora. If each evaluation corpus is annotated by the same number of Turkers and with the same annotation scheme, it will now be possible to compare systems by simply comparing their performance on each respective bin. The assumption here is that prepositions which show X% agreement in corpus A are of equivalent difficulty to those that show X% agreement in corpus B.

6 Discussion

In this paper, we showed that the AMT is an effective tool for annotating grammatical errors. At a fraction of the time and cost, it is possible to acquire high quality judgments from *multiple* untrained raters without sacrificing reliability. A summary of the cost and time of the two experiments described here can be seen in Table 1. In the task of preposition selection, only three Turkers are needed to match the reliability of two trained raters; in the more complicated task of error detection, up to 13 Turkers are needed. However, it should be noted that these numbers can be viewed as upper bounds. The error annotation scheme that was used is a very simple one. We intend to experiment with different guidelines and instructions, and to screen (Callison-Burch, 2009) and weight Turkers' responses (Snow et al., 2008), in order to lower the number of Turkers required for this task. Finally, we will look at other errors, such as articles, to determine how many Turkers are necessary for optimal annotation.

Acknowledgments

We thank Sarah Ohls and Waverely VanWinkle for their annotation work, and Jennifer Foster and the two reviewers for their comments and feedback.

References

Chris Callison-Burch. 2009. Fast, cheap, and creative: Evaluating translation quality using Amazon's Mechanical Turk. In *EMNLP*.

Rachele De Felice and Stephen G. Pullman. 2009. Automatic detection of preposition errors in learner writing. *CALICO Journal*, 26(3).

Michael Gamon, Jianfeng Gao, Chris Brockett, Alex Klementiev, William B. Dolan, Dmitriy Belenko, and Lucy Vanderwende. 2008. Using contextual speller techniques and language modeling for esl error correction. In *Proceedings of IJCNLP*, Hyderabad, India, January.

Na-Rae Han, Martin Chodorow, and Claudia Leacock. 2006. Detecting errors in English article usage by non-native speakers. *Natural Language Engineering*, 12:115–129.

Victor Sheng, Foster Provost, and Panagiotis Ipeirotis. 2008. Get another label? Improving data quality and data mining using multiple, noisy labelers. In *Proceeding of ACM SIGKDD*, Las Vegas, Nevada, USA.

Rion Snow, Brendan O'Connor, Daniel Jurafsky, and Andrew Ng. 2008. Cheap and fast – but is it good? evaluating non-expert annotations for natural language tasks. In *EMNLP*.

Joel R. Tetreault and Martin Chodorow. 2008a. The ups and downs of preposition error detection in ESL writing. In *COLING*.

Joel Tetreault and Martin Chodorow. 2008b. Native Judgments of non-native usage: Experiments in preposition error detection. In *COLING Workshop on Human Judgments in Computational Linguistics*.

Predicting Cloze Task Quality for Vocabulary Training

Adam Skory **Maxine Eskenazi**
Language Technologies Institute
Carnegie Mellon University
Pittsburgh PA 15213, USA
{askory,max}@cs.cmu.edu

Abstract

Computer generation of cloze tasks still falls short of full automation; most current systems are used by teachers as authoring aids. Improved methods to estimate cloze quality are needed for full automation. We investigated lexical reading difficulty as a novel automatic estimator of cloze quality, to which co-occurrence frequency of words was compared as an alternate estimator. Rather than relying on expert evaluation of cloze quality, we submitted open cloze tasks to workers on Amazon Mechanical Turk (AMT) and discuss ways to measure of the results of these tasks. Results show one statistically significant correlation between the above measures and estimators, which was lexical co-occurrence and Cloze Easiness. Reading difficulty was not found to correlate significantly. We gave subsets of cloze sentences to an English teacher as a gold standard. Sentences selected by co-occurrence and Cloze Easiness were ranked most highly, corroborating the evidence from AMT.

1 Cloze Tasks

Cloze tasks, described in Taylor (1953), are activities in which one or several words are removed from a sentence and a student is asked to fill in the missing content. That sentence can be referred to as the 'stem', and the removed term itself as the 'key'. (Higgins, 2006) The portion of the sentence from which the key has been removed is the 'blank'. 'Open cloze' tasks are those in which the student can propose any answer. 'Closed cloze' describes multiple choice tasks in which the key is presented along with a set of several 'distractors'.

1.1 Cloze Tasks in Assessment

Assessment is the best known application of cloze tasks. As described in (Alderson, 1979), the “cloze procedure” is that in which multiple words are removed at intervals from a text. This is mostly used in first language (L1) education. Alderson describes three deletion strategies: random deletion, deletion of every n^{th} word, and targeted deletion, in which certain words are manually chosen and deleted by an instructor. Theories of lexical quality (Perfetti & Hart, 2001) and word knowledge levels (Dale, 1965) illustrate why cloze tasks can effectively assess multiple dimensions of vocabulary knowledge.

Perfetti & Hart explain that lexical knowledge can be decomposed into orthographic, phonetic, syntactic, and semantic constituents. The lexical quality of a given word can then be defined as a measure based on both the depth of knowledge of each constituent and the degree to which those constituents are bonded together. Cloze tasks allow a test author to select for specific combinations of constituents to assess (Bachman, 1982).

1.2 Instructional Cloze Tasks

Cloze tasks can be employed for instruction as well as assessment. Jongsma (1980) showed that targeted deletion is an effective use of instructional passage-based cloze tasks. Repeated exposure to frequent words leads first to familiarity with those words, and increasingly to suppositions about their semantic and syntactic constituents. Producing cloze tasks through targeted deletion takes implicit, receptive word knowledge, and forces the student

Proceedings of the NAACL HLT 2010 Fifth Workshop on Innovative Use of NLP for Building Educational Applications, pages 49–56,
Los Angeles, California, June 2010.

to consider explicitly how to match features of the stem with what is known about features of any keys she may consider.

2 Automatic Generation of Cloze Tasks

Most cloze task "generation" systems are really cloze task *identification* systems. That is, given a set of requirements, such as a specific key and syntactic structure (Higgins 2006) for the stem, a system looks into a database of pre-processed text and attempts to identify sentences matching those criteria. Thus, the content generated for a closed cloze is the stem (by deletion of the key), and a set of distractors. In the case of some systems, a human content author may manually tailor the resulting stems to meet further needs.

Identifying suitable sentences from natural language corpora is desirable because the sentences that are found will be authentic. Depending on the choice of corpora, sentences should also be well-formed and suitable in terms of reading level and content. Newspaper text is one popular source (Hoshino & Nakagawa, 2005; Liu et al., 2005; Lee & Seneff, 2007). Pino et al. (2008) use documents from a corpus of texts retrieved from the internet and subsequently filtered according to readability level, category, and appropriateness of content. Using a broader corpus increases the number and variability of potential matching sentences, but also lowers the confidence that sentences will be well-formed and contain appropriate language (Brown & Eskenazi, 2004).

2.1 Tag-based Sentence Search

Several cloze item authoring tools (Liu et al. 2005; Higgins, 2006) implement specialized tag-based sentence search. This goes back to the original distribution of the Penn Treebank and the corresponding *tgrep* program. Developed by Pito in 1992 (Pito, 1994) this program allows researchers to search for corpus text according to sequences of part of speech (POS) tags and tree structure.

The linguists' Search Engine (Resnik & Elkiss, 2005) takes the capabilities of *tgrep* yet further, providing a simplified interface for linguists to search within tagged corpora along both syntactic and lexical features.

Both *tgrep* and the Linguists' Search Engine were not designed as cloze sentence search tools, but they paved the way for similar tools specialized for this task. For example, Higgins' (2006) system uses a regular expression engine that can work either on the tag level, the text level or both. This allows test content creators to quickly find sentences within very narrow criteria. They can then alter these sentences as necessary.

Liu et al. (2005) use sentences from a corpus of newspaper text tagged for POS and lemma. Candidate sentences are found by searching on the key and its POS as well as the POS sequence of surrounding terms. In their system results are filtered for proper word sense by comparing other words in the stem with data from WordNet and HowNet, databases of inter-word semantic relations.

2.2 Statistical Sentence Search

Pino et al (2009) use co-occurrence frequencies to identify candidate sentences. They used the Stanford Parser (Klein & Manning, 2003) to detect sentences within a desired range of complexity and likely well-formedness. Co-occurrence frequencies of words in the corpus were calculated and keys were compared to other words in the stem to determine cloze quality, producing suitable cloze questions 66.53% of the time. This method operates on the theory that the quality of the context of a stem is based on the co-occurrence scores of other words in the sentence. Along with this result, Pino et al. incorporated syntactic complexity in terms of the number of parses found.

Hoshino & Nakagawa (2005) use machine learning techniques to train a cloze task search system. Their system, rather than finding sentences suitable for cloze tasks, attempts to automate deletion for passage-based cloze. The features used include sentence length and POS of keys and surrounding words. Both a Naïve Bayes and a K-Nearest Neighbor classifier were trained to find the most likely words for deletion within news articles. To train the system they labeled cloze sentences from a TOEIC training test as *true*, then shifted the position of the blanks from those sentences and labeled the resulting sentences as *false*. Manual evaluation of the results showed that, for both classifiers, experts saw over 90% of the deletions as either easy to solve or merely possible to solve.

3 Reading Level and Information Theory

An information-theoretical basis for an entirely novel approach to automated cloze sentence search is found in Finn (1978). Finn defines *Cloze Easiness* as "the percent of subjects filling in the correct word in a cloze task." Another metric of the quality of a cloze task is context restriction; the number of solutions perceived as acceptable keys for a given stem. Finn's theory of lexical feature transfer provides one mechanism to explain context restriction. The theory involves the *information* content of a blank.

According to Shannon's (1948) seminal work on information theory, the *information* contained in a given term is inverse to its predictability. In other words, if a term appears despite following a history after which is it considered very unlikely to occur, that word has high *information* content. For example, consider the partial sentence *"She drives a nice..."*. A reader forms hypotheses about the next word before seeing it, and thus expects an overall meaning of the sentence. A word that conforms to this hypothesis, such as the word 'car', does little to change a reader's knowledge and thus has little *information*. If instead the next word is 'taxi', 'tank', or 'ambulance', unforeseen knowledge is gained and relative *information* is higher.

According to Finn (1978) the applicability of this theory to Cloze Easiness can be explained though lexical transfer features. These features can be both syntactic and semantic, and they serve to interrelate words within a sentence. If a large number of lexical transfer features are within a given proximity of a blank, then the set of words matching those features will be highly restricted. Given that each choice of answer will be from a smaller pool of options, the probability of that answer will be much higher. Thus, a highly probable key has correspondingly low *information* content.

Predicting context restriction is of benefit to automatic generation of cloze tasks. Cloze Easiness improves if a student chooses from a smaller set of possibilities. The instructional value of a highly context-restricted cloze task is also higher by providing a richer set of lexical transfer features with which to associate vocabulary.

Finn's application of information theory to Cloze Easiness and context restriction provides one possible new avenue to improve the quality of generated cloze tasks. We hypothesize that words of higher reading levels contain higher numbers of transfer features and thus their presence in a sentence can be correlated with its degree of context restriction. To the authors' knowledge reading level has not been previously applied to this problem.

We can use a unigram reading level model to investigate this hypothesis. Returning to the example words for the partial sentence *"She drives a nice..."*, we can see that our current model classifies the highly expected word, 'car', at reading level *1*, while 'taxi','tank', and 'ambulance', are at reading levels *5*, *6*, and *11* respectively.

3.1 Reading Level Estimators

The estimation of reading level is a complex topic unto itself. Early work used heuristics based on average sentence length and the percentage of words deemed unknown to a baseline reader. (Dale & Chall, 1948; Dale, 1965) Another early measure, the Flesch-Kincaid measure, (Kincaid et al., 1975) uses a function of the syllable length of words in a document and the average sentence length.

More recent work on the topic also focuses on readability classification at the document level. Collins-Thompson & Callan (2005) use unigram language models without syntactic features. Heilman et al. (2008) use a probabilistic parser and unigram language models to combine grammatical and lexical features. (Petersen & Ostendorf, 2006) add higher-order n-gram features to the above to train support vector machine classifiers for each grade level.

These recent methods perform well to characterize the level of an entire document, but they are untested for single sentences. We wish to investigate if a robust unigram model of reading level can be employed to improve the estimation of cloze quality at the sentence level. By extension of Finn's (1978) hypothesis, it is in fact not the overall level of the sentence that has a predicted effect on cloze context restriction, but rather the reading level of the words in proximity to the blank. Thus we propose that it should be possible to find a correlation between cloze quality and the reading levels of words in near context to the blank of a cloze task.

4 The Approach

We investigate a multi-staged filtering approach to cloze sentence generation. Several variations of the final filtering step of this approach were employed and correlations sought between the resulting sets of each filter variation. The subset predicted to contain the best sentences by each filter was finally submitted to expert review as a gold standard test of cloze quality.

This study compares two features of sentences, finding the levels of context restriction experimentally. The first feature in question is the maximum reading level found in near-context to the blank. The second feature is the mean skip bigram co-occurrence score of words within that context.

Amazon Mechanical Turk (AMT) is used as a novel cloze quality evaluation method. This method is validated by both positive correlation with the known-valid (Pino et al., 2008) co-occurrence score predictor, and an expert gold standard. Experimental results from AMT are then used to evaluate the hypothesis that reading level can be used as a new, alternative predictor of cloze quality.

4.1 Cloze Sentence Filtering

The first step in preparing material for this study was to obtain a set of keys. We expect that in most applications of sentence-based cloze tasks the set of keys is pre-determined by instructional goals. Due to this constraint, we choose a set of keys distributed across several reading levels and hold it as fixed. Four words were picked from the set of words common in texts labeled as grades four, six, eight, ten, and twelve respectively.

4th: 'little', 'thought', 'voice', 'animals'
6th: ‘president', 'sportsmanship', 'national', experience'
8th: 'college', 'wildlife', 'beautiful', 'competition'
10th: 'medical', 'elevations','qualities', 'independent'
12th: 'scientists', 'citizens', 'discovered', 'university'

Figure 1: common words per grade level.

201,025 sentences containing these keys were automatically extracted from a corpus of web documents as the initial filtering step. This collection of sentences was then limited to sentences of length 25 words or less. Filtering by sentence length reduced the set to 136,837 sentences.

A probabilistic parser was used to score each sentence. This parser gives log-probability values corresponding to confidence of the best parse. A threshold for this confidence score was chosen manually and sentences with scores below the threshold were removed, reducing the number of sentences to 29,439.

4.2 Grade Level

Grade level in this study is determined by a smoothed unigram model based on normalized concentrations within labeled documents. A sentence is assigned the grade level of the highest level word in context of the key.

4.3 Co-occurrence Scores

Skip bigram co-occurrence counts were calculated from the Brown (Francis & Kucera, 1979) and OANC (OANC, 2009) corpora. A given sentence's score is calculated as the mean of the probabilities of finding that sentence's context for the key.

These probabilities are defined on the triplet (*key*, *word*, *window size*), in which *key* is the target word to be removed, *word* any term in the corpus, and *window size* is a positive integer less than or equal to the length of the sentence.

This probability is estimated as the number of times *word* is found within the same sentence as *key* and within an absolute *window size* of *2* positions from *key*, divided by the total number of times all terms are found in that window. These scores are thus maximum likelihood estimators of the probability of *word* given *key* and *window size:*

(1) For some key k , word w, and window-size m :

$C_j(w, k)$:= count of times w found j words from the position of k, within the same sentence.

(2) For a vocabulary V and for some positive integer window-size m, let $n = (m-1) / 2$, then:

$$P(w|k,m) = \frac{\sum_{j \in [-n,n], j \neq 0} C_j(w,k)}{\sum_{t_i \in V} \sum_{j \in [-n,n], j \neq 0} C_j(t_i,k)}$$

i.e. if our corpus consisted of the single sentence *"This is a good example sentence."*:

$C{-1}$ (w = good, k = example) = 1
$C1$ (w = sentence, k = example) = 1
P (w = good | k = example, m = 3) = $1 / (1+1)$= .5

Finally, the overall score of the sentence is taken to be the mean of the skip bigram probabilities of all words in context of the key.

4.4 Variable Filtering by Grade and Score

Skip bigram scores were calculated for all words co-occurrent in a sentence with each of our 20 keys. To maximize the observable effect of the two dimensions of grade level and co-occurrence score, the goal was to find sentences representing combinations of ranges within those dimensions. To achieve this it was necessary to pick the window size that best balances variance of these dimensions with a reasonably flat distribution of sentences.

In terms of grade level, smaller window sizes resulted in very few sentences with at least one high-level word, while larger window sizes resulted in few sentences with no high-level words. Variance in co-occurrence score, on the other hand, was maximal at a window size of 3 words, and dropped off until nearly flattening out at a window size of 20 words. A window size of 15 words was found to offer a reasonable distribution of grade level while preserving sufficient variance of co-occurrence score.

Using the above window-size, we created filters according to maximum grade level: one each for the grade ranges 5-6, 7-8, 9-10, and 11-12. Four more filters were created according to co-occurrence score: one selecting the highest-scoring quartile of sentences, one the second highest-scoring quartile, and so on. Each grade level filter was combined with each co-occurrence score filter creating 4x4=16 composite filters. By combining these filters we can create a final set of sentences for analysis with high confidence of having a significant number of sentences representing all possible values of grade level and co-occurrence score. At most two sentences were chosen for each of the 20 keys using these composite filters. The final number of sentences was 540.

4.5 Experimental Cloze Quality

Previous evaluation of automatically generated cloze tasks has relied on expert judgments. (Pino et al., 2008; Liu et al., 2005) We present the use of crowdsourcing techniques as a new approach for this evaluation. We believe the approach can be validated by statistically significant correlations with predicted cloze quality and comparison with expert judgments.

The set of 540 sentences were presented to workers from Amazon Mechanical Turk (AMT), an online marketplace for "human intelligence tasks." Each worker was shown up to twenty of the stems of these sentences as open cloze tasks. No worker was allowed to see more than one stem for the same key. Workers were instructed to enter only those words that "absolutely make sense in this context", but were not encouraged to submit any particular number of answers. Workers were paid US$.04 per sentence, and the task was limited to workers with approval ratings on past tasks at or above 90%.

For each sentence under review each worker contributes one subset of answers. Cloze Easiness, as defined by Finn (1978) is calculated as the percentage of these subsets containing the original key. We define *context restriction* on n as the percentage of answer subsets containing n or fewer words.

Using the example sentence: "Take this cloze sentence, for <u>(example)</u>." We can find the set of answer subsets A:

A = { A_1={example, free, fun, me}
A_2={example,instance}
A_3={instance} }

Then, Cloze Easiness is $|\{A_1,A_2\}| / |A| \approx .67$ and Context restriction (on one or two words) is $|\{A_2,A_3\}| / |A| \approx .67$

5 Results

Each sentence in the final set was seen, on average, by 27 Mechanical Turk workers. We wish to correlate measures of Cloze Easiness and context restriction with cloze quality predictors of maximum grade level and score. We use the Pearson correlation coefficient (PCC) to test the linear relationship between each measure of cloze quality and each predictor.

Table (1) shows these PCC values. All of the values are positive, meaning there is a correlation showing that one value will tend to increase as the other increases. The strongest correlation is that of co-occurrence and Cloze Easiness. This is also the only statistically significant correlation. The value of $P(H_0)$ represents the likelihood of the null hypothesis: that two random distributions generated the same correlation. Values of $P(H_0)$ under 0.05 can be considered statistically significant.

Cloze Easiness	PCC = 0.2043 $P(H_0)$=1.6965e-06	PCC = 0.0671 $P(H_0)$=0.1193
Context Restriction (2)	PCC = 0.0649 $P(H_0)$=0.1317	PCC = 0.07 $P(H_0)$=0.1038
	Co-occurrence	Maximum Grade

Table (1): Pearson Correlation Coefficient and probability of null hypothesis for estimators and measures of cloze quality.

Figure (3) shows scatter plots of these four correlations in which each dot represents one sentence.

The top-leftmost plot shows the correlation of co-occurrence score (on the x-axis), and Cloze Easiness (on the y-axis). Co-occurrence scores are shown on a log-scale. The line through these points represents a linear regression, which is in this case statistically significant.

The bottom-left plot shows correlation of co-occurrence score (x-axis) with context restriction. In this case context restriction was calculated on *n=2*, i.e. the percent of answers containing only

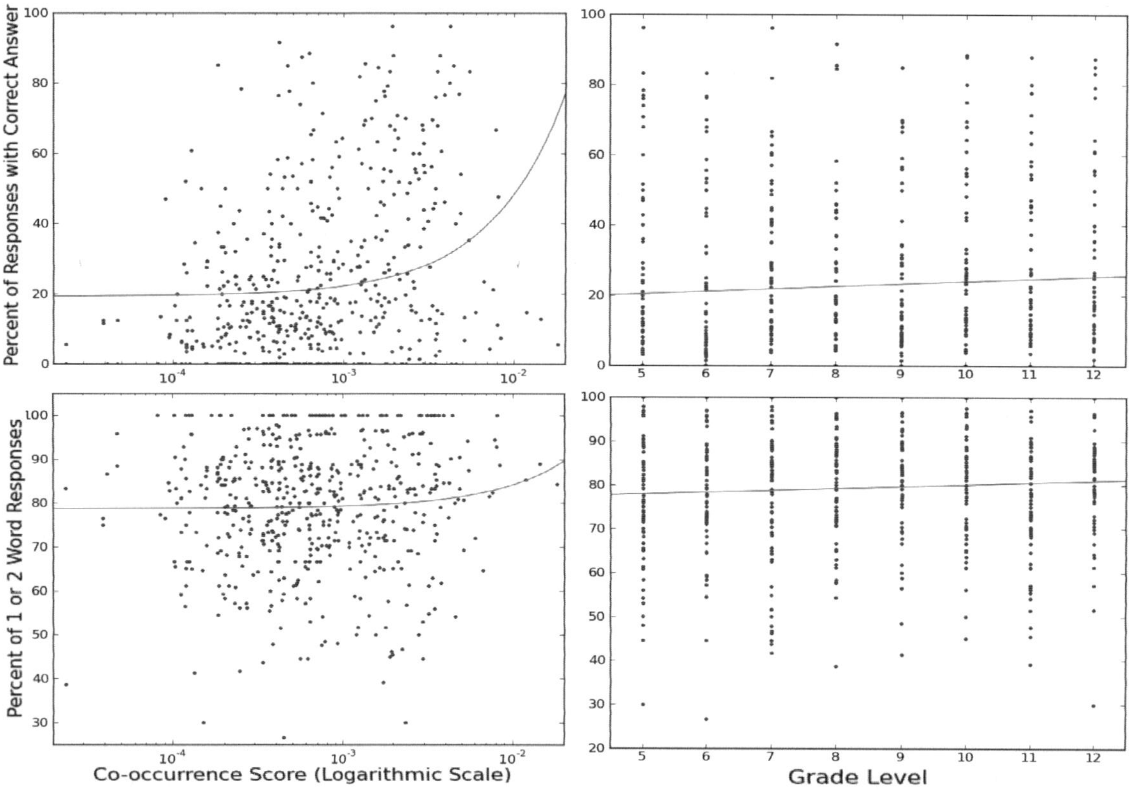

Figure (3): Scatter plots of all sentences with cloze quality measure as y-axis, and cloze quality estimator as x-axis. The linear regression of each distribution is shown.

one or two words. The linear regression shows there is a small (statistically insignificant) correlation.

The top-right plot shows Cloze Easiness (y-axis) per grade level (x-axis). The bottom left shows context restriction (y-axis) as a function of grade level. In both cases linear regressions here also show small, statistically insignificant positive correlations.

The lack of significant correlations for three out of four combinations of measures and estimators is not grounds to dismiss these measures. Across all sentences, the measure of context restriction is highly variant, at 47.9%. This is possibly the result of the methodology; in an attempt to avoid biasing the AMT workers, we did not specify the desirable number of answers. This led to many workers interpreting the task differently.

In terms of maximum grade level, the lack of a significant correlation with context restriction does not absolutely refute Finn (1978)'s hypothesis. Finn specifies that semantic transfer features should be in "lexical scope" of a blank. A clear definition of "lexical scope" was not presented. We generalized scope to mean proximity within a fixed contextual window size. It is possible that a more precise definition of "lexical scope" will provide a stronger correlation of reading level and context restriction.

5.1 Expert Validation

Finally, while we have shown a statistically significant positive correlation between co-occurrence scores and Cloze Easiness, we still need to demonstrate that Cloze Easiness is a valid measure of cloze quality. To do so, we selected the set of 20 sentences that ranked highest by co-occurrence score and by Cloze Easiness to submit to expert evaluation. Due to overlap between these two sets, choosing distinct sentences for both would require choosing some sentences ranked below the top 20 for each category. Accordingly, we chose to submit just one set based on both criteria in combination.

Along with these 20 sentences, as controls, we also selected two more distinct sets of 20 sentences: one set of sentences measuring most highly in context restriction, and one set most highly estimated by maximum grade level.

We asked a former English teacher to read each open cloze, without the key, and rate, on a five point Likert scale, her agreement with the statement "*This is a very good fill-in-the-blank sentence.*" where 1 means strong agreement, and 5 means strong disagreement.

		Expert evaluation on 5-point Scale	
		Mean	Standard Deviation
20 best sentences as determined by:	Cloze Easiness and co-occurrence score	2.25	1.37
	Context restriction	3.05	1.36
	Maximum grade level	3.15	1.2

Table (2): Mean ratings for each sentence category.

The results in Table (2) show that, on average, the correlated results of selecting sentences based on Cloze Easiness and co-occurrence score are in fact rated more highly by our expert as compared to sentences selected based on context restriction, which is, in turn, rated more highly than sentences selected by maximum grade level. Using a one-sample t-test and a population mean of 2.5, we find a p-value of .0815 for our expert's ratings.

6 Conclusion

We present a multi-step filter-based paradigm under which diverse estimators of cloze quality can be applied towards the goal of full automation of cloze task generation. In our implementation of this approach sentences were found for a set of keys, and then filtered by maximum length and likelihood of well-formedness. We then tested combinations of two estimators and two experimental measures of cloze quality for the next filtering step.

We presented an information-theoretical basis for the use of reading level as a novel estimator for cloze quality. The hypothesis that maximum grade level should be correlated with context restriction was not, however, shown with statistical significance. A stronger correlation might be shown with a different experimental methodology and a more refined definition of lexical scope.

As an alternative to expert evaluation of cloze quality, we investigated the use of non-expert workers on AMT. A statistically significant correlation was found between the co-occurrence score of a sentence and its experimental measure of Cloze Easiness. This is evidence that crowdsourcing techniques agree with expert evaluation of co-occurrence scores in past studies.

To gain further evidence of the validity of these experimental results, sentences selected by a composite filter of co-occurrence score and Cloze Easiness were compared to sentences selected by context restriction and reading level. An expert evaluation showed a preference for sentences selected by the composite filter.

We believe that this method of cloze task selection is promising. It will now be tested in a real learning situation. This work contributes insight into methods for improving technologies such as intelligent tutoring systems and language games.

References

Alderson, J. C. (1979). The Cloze Procedure and Proficiency in English as a Foreign Language. *TESOL Quarterly*, *13*(2), 219-227. doi: 10.2307/3586211.

Bachman, L. F. (1982). The Trait Structure of Cloze Test Scores. *TESOL Quarterly*, *16*(1), 61.

Brown, J., & Eskenazi, M. (2004). Retrieval of Authentic Documents for Reader-Specific Lexical Practice. In *InSTIL/ICALL Symposium* (Vol. 2). Venice, Italy.

Collins-Thompson, K., & Callan, J. (2005). Predicting reading difficulty with statistical language models. *Journal of the American Society for Information Science and Technology*, *56*(13), 1448-1462.

Dale, E. (1965). Vocabulary measurement: Techniques and major findings. *Elementary English*, *42*, 395-401.

Dale, E., & Chall, J. S. (1948). A Formula for Predicting Readability: Instructions. *Educational Research Bulletin*, *Vol. 27*(2), 37-54.

Finn, P. J. (1978). Word frequency, information theory, and cloze performance: A transfer feature theory of processing in reading. *Reading Research Quarterly*, *13*(4), 508-537.

Francis, W. N. & Kucera, H. (1979). Brown Corpus Manual, *Brown University Department of Linguistics*. Providence, RI

Heilman, M., Collins-Thompson, K., & Eskenazi, M. (2008). An Analysis of Statistical Models and Features for Reading Difficulty Prediction. *3rd Workshop on Innovative Use of NLP for Building Educational Applications*. Assoc. for Computational Linguistics.

Higgins, D. (2006). Item Distiller: Text retrieval for computer-assisted test item creation. ETS, Princeton, NJ.

Hoshino, A., & Nakagawa, H. (2005). A real-time multiple-choice question generation for language testing – a preliminary study–. In *2nd Workshop on Building Educational Applications Using NLP* (pp. 17-20). Ann Arbor, MI: Association for Computational Linguistics.

Jongsma, E. (1980). Cloze instructional research: A second look. Newark, DE: International Reading Association. Urbana, IL.

Kincaid, J., Fishburne, R., Rodgers, R., & Chissom, B. (1975). Derivation of new readability formulas for navy enlisted personnel. *Research Branch Report*. Millington, TN.

Klein, D. & Manning, C. (2003). Accurate Unlexicalized Parsing. (pp. 423-430) In *Proceedings of the 41st Meeting of the Assoc. for Computational Linguistics.*

Lee, J., & Seneff, S. (2007). Automatic Generation of Cloze Items for Prepositions. *Proceedings of In*.

Liu, C., Wang, C., Gao, Z., & Huang, S. (2005). Applications of Lexical Information for Algorithmically Composing Multiple-Choice Cloze Items. In *Proceedings of the 2nd Workshop on Building Educational Applications Using NLP* (p. 1–8). Ann Arbor, MI: Association for Computational Linguistics.

Open American National Corpus (2009) *americannationalcorpus.org/OANC/*

Perfetti, C., & Hart, L. (2001). *Lexical bases of comprehension skill*. (D. Gorfein) (pp. 67-86). Washington D.C.: American Psychological Association.

Petersen, S. E., & Ostendorf, M. (2006). Assessing the reading level of web pages. In *ICSLP* (Vol. pages, pp. 833-836).

Pino, J., Heilman, M., & Eskenazi, M. (2008). A Selection Strategy to Improve Cloze Question Quality. In *Proceedings of the Workshop on Intelligent Tutoring Systems for Ill-Defined Domains*.

Pito, R. (1994). tgrep README *www.ldc.upenn.edu/ldc/online/treebank/README.long*

Resnik, P., & Elkiss, A. (2005). The Linguist's Search Engine: An Overview. *Association for Computational Linguistics*, (June), 33-36.

Shannon, C. (1948). A Mathematical Theory of Communication. *Bell System Technical Journal*, *27*, 379–423, 623–656.

Taylor, W. L. (1953). Cloze procedure: a new tool for measuring readability. *Journalism Quarterly*, *30*, 415-453.

Generating Quantifiers and Negation to Explain Homework Testing

Jason Perry and **Chung-chieh Shan**
Rutgers University
Department of Computer Science

Abstract

We describe Prograder, a software package for automatic checking of requirements for programming homework assignments. Prograder lets instructors specify requirements in natural language as well as explains grading results to students in natural language. It does so using a grammar that generates as well as parses to translate between a small fragment of English and a first-order logical specification language that can be executed directly in Python. This execution embodies multiple semantics—both to check the requirement and to search for evidence that proves or disproves the requirement. Such a checker needs to interpret and generate sentences containing quantifiers and negation. To handle quantifier and negation scope, we systematically simulate continuation grammars using record structures in the Grammatical Framework.

1 Introduction

The typical programming assignment in a computer-science course comes with not only a problem description but also correctness and stylistic requirements such as

(1) Every source file compiles and has comments, and a text file mentions every source file and every header file.

Although the requirements do not usually specify exactly how the students' work will be judged, they make it much easier to grade and respond to the submitted work. Many requirements can be checked automatically by computer, and often they are—perhaps even right after each student uploads their work so that the student can revise their work using the immediate feedback.

This common workflow is wanting in two aspects. First, the requirements are both specified to the students in English and coded into a testing harness by the course staff. Keeping the two versions is a hassle that involves much boilerplate text as well as boilerplate code. Second, students rightfully demand comprehensible explanations when their work is rejected by the requirement tester. It is tricky to code up a tester that produces error messages neither too terse nor too verbose, when one student might forget to comment just one file and another might not know the lexical syntax of comments at all.

A natural approach to improve this workflow, then, is to specify the requirements in a formal language and to implement an interpreter for the language that produces explanations. Because many instructors, like students, are averse to learning new languages, we pursue the use of a controlled subset of English as that formal language. In short, we aim to produce a programming-assignment tester that allows instructors to specify requirements for programming assignments in natural language, checks those requirements automatically by executing commands on the submitted assignment files, and generates for the student a natural-language explanation of the results. For example, in an introductory programming class, a professor may write the specification sentence (1). The system would then grade all students' programming assignments according to these criteria, and return individualized explanations

Proceedings of the NAACL HLT 2010 Fifth Workshop on Innovative Use of NLP for Building Educational Applications, pages 57–65,
Los Angeles, California, June 2010.

to students like

(2) Credit was lost because `bar.c` did not compile and no text file mentioned the files `foo.h` and `baz.h`.

As this example illustrates, the tester needs to interpret and generate sentences with quantifiers and negation. Although the interpretation of quantifiers and negation is a traditional research area in computational linguistics (VanLehn, 1978; Hobbs and Shieber, 1987; Moran, 1988), their generation is much less studied (Gailly, 1988). Even if our system were to compose explanations entirely from the input specification sentences and their negation, it cannot negate a specification sentence merely by adding or removing verbal auxiliaries: the negation of "a source file defines `main()`" is not "a source file does not define `main()`".

1.1 Contributions

We have built Prograder, a rudimentary programming-assignment tester that correctly interprets and generates a small fragment of English that includes quantifiers and negation. This paper describes the architecture of Prograder. Our implementation uses a declarative grammar that simultaneously supports interpretation and generation by relating English phrase structure to type-logical semantics. This paper details the new techniques we use in this grammar to represent quantifier scope and De Morgan duality in a tractable way.

Prograder also lets us investigate how to make a computer program explain its own execution. The concerns for a tester that must justify its output to students are not merely grammatical, but involve the semantics and pragmatics of summarization and justification. For example, when is it semantically correct to combine entities within an NP, as in "`foo.h` and `baz.h`" above? When is an explanation pragmatically enough for a student who has a right to know why she lost credit on a programming assignment? Which pieces of evidence must be stated and which are better left out? We plan to study these questions within type-logical semantics as well.

1.2 Organization of This Paper

In Section 1, we have introduced the problem and outlined the contributions of the research carried out in building Prograder. In Section 2, we give a high-level overview of the architecture of the system, including the representation of natural-language syntax and type-logical semantics, as well as the procedure of operation. Section 3 describes Prograder's checking procedure and how it generates explanations in tandem with the checking. In Section 4, we begin to describe the details of the grammatical framework that allows us to handle bidirectional translation between English and the logical form. Continuing in Section 5, we discuss the handling of negation and quantifier scoping by means of a record-based implementation of continuation grammars. Section 6 reviews the architecture of the system with additional implementation details, and Section 7 concludes with future work.

2 System Overview

We explain the architecture of our Prograder system using a simplified example. Suppose that the instructor specifies the requirement that

(3) Every source file compiles.

Prograder begins by parsing this sentence into an abstract syntax tree:

(4)
```
               ApplyS
              /      \
EverySourceFile      Compiles
```

Interpreting this tree compositionally gives the meaning of the sentence:

(5)
```
everysourcefile(lambda x:
                compiles(x))
```

On one hand, this expression is a formula in predicate logic. In general, each requirement specification is a sentence, whose truth value is determined by checking a single student's programming assignment. We use the types of Montague grammar (1974), which are the base type of entities e, the base type of propositions t, and function types notated by $\to$. Our logical language is defined by a domain-specific vocabulary of typed predicates and entities (Hudak, 1996). Naturally, the files submitted by the student are entities.

For example, the unary predicates `compiles` and `hascomments` have the type $e \to t$, and the binary predicate `mentions` has the type $e \to e \to t$. These predicates in our vocabulary represent various properties of submitted files that instructors may want to check. Logical connectives are also part of the vocabulary; for instance, `and` and `or` have the type $t \to t \to t$, `not_b` has the type $t \to t$, and `everysourcefile` has the type $(e \to t) \to t$. Therefore, the expression (5) has the type t, as do the expressions

(6) `compiles("foo.c")`

(7)
```
and(compiles("foo.c"),
    hascomments("bar.c"))
```

On the other hand, the expressions (5–7) are executable Python code. Prograder includes a library of Python functions such as `everysourcefile`, which iterates over the source files submitted, and `compiles`, which invokes `gcc`. As each student submits their homework, we evaluate the expression (5) to check the requirement (3). We use Python's own lambda abstraction and first-class functions to express quantified statements. For example, evaluating (5) invokes `gcc` on each source file submitted.

Evaluation not only computes a Boolean value but also yields a tree of evidence statements to justify the result. At the root of the tree is either the requirement (5) or its negation:

(8)
```
asourcefile(lambda x:
            not_b(compiles(x)))
```

Each node's children are the premises that together justify the conclusion at that node. For example, if every source file submitted by the student compiles successfully except one, then (8) would be justified by a sole child:

(9) `not_b(compiles("bar.c"))`

Prograder then parses each evidence statement into abstract syntax:

(10)

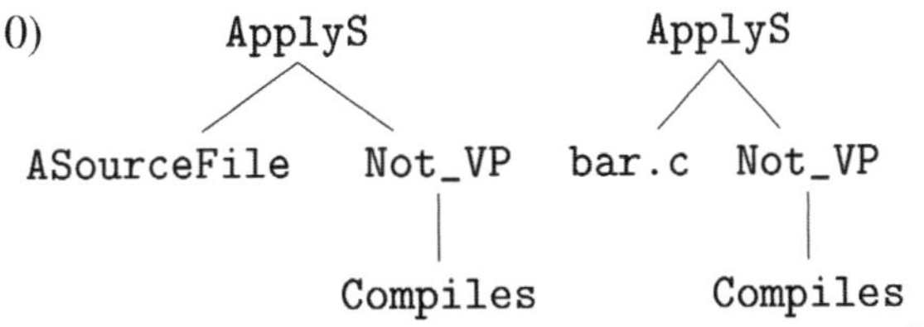

From these trees, Prograder finally renders each evidence statement as an English clause:

(11) A source file does not compile because `bar.c` does not compile.

To summarize, Prograder's steps of operation are as follows:

1. Parse the natural-language requirement statement into a phrase-structure syntax tree.
2. Produce a logical semantic representation from the syntax tree.
3. Execute the semantic representation to check the requirement and produce a semantic representation of each evidence statement.
4. Parse the evidence statements into phrase-structure syntax trees.
5. Produce natural-language explanation from the syntax trees.

From end to end, these steps operate on just three levels of representation: the abstract syntax trees in (4) and (10) can be spelled out either in natural language (English) as in (3) and (11) or in predicate logic (Python) as in (5–9). Thus, Prograder interprets natural-language requirements and generates natural-language explanations using the same executable semantic representations. In fact, it uses the same grammar, as described in Section 4.

3 Gathering Evidence while Testing Truth

As sketched above, evaluating a proposition gives a Boolean result along with a tree of evidence propositions that justify that result. That is, we represent the type t in Python as an ordered pair, not just a Boolean value. This is straightforward for primitive first-order predicates. For example, the `compiles` function, when invoked with the argument `"foo.c"`, tries to compile `foo.c`, then either returns `True` along with a trivial evidence tree containing just the proposition `compiles("foo.c")`, or returns `False` along with a trivial evidence tree containing just the proposition `not_b(compiles("foo.c"))`. In short, we hold whether a file compiles to be self-evident.

The picture is more complex for logical connectives, especially higher-order functions such as the quantifier `everysourcefile`. Ideally, the falsity of (3) should be justified by an explanation like

(12) Not every source file compiles because `foo.c` and `bar.c` do not compile.

Also, the explanation should be generated by composing the implementations of `everysourcefile` and of `compiles`, so that new quantifiers ("most source files") and predicates ("has comments") can be added as separate modules. For example, evaluating the proposition `not_b(compiles("foo.c"))` first evaluates `compiles("foo.c")` then negates the Boolean while keeping the evidence the same.

Prograder currently justifies quantified propositions in the following compositional way. When the higher-order function `everysourcefile` is invoked with the predicate argument `p`, it invokes `p` on each source file submitted and collects the resulting Boolean-evidence pairs. If any of the Boolean results is `False`, then the overall Boolean result is of course also `False`. This result is justified by an evidence tree whose root proposition is

(13) `not_b(everysourcefile(p))`

and whose subtrees are the evidence trees for all the `False` results. (After all, the primary mode of explanation required in grading a programming assignment is to say why credit has been subtracted.) Prograder then produces the serviceable explanation

(14) Not every source file compiles because `foo.c` does not compile and `bar.c` does not compile.

(We are working on simplifying this explanation to (12).) This process generalizes immediately to propositions with multiple quantifiers, such as

(15) Every text file mentions a source file.

```
everytextfile(lambda x:
  asourcefile(lambda y:
    mentions(y)(x)))
```

For example, Prograder might explain that

(16) Not every text file mentions a source file because `README` mentions no source file.

In sum, Prograder generates explanations in the same process—the same sequence of function calls and returns—as it computes Boolean values. In this way, the checking process gains an additional interpretation as a process of gathering evidence for the explanation. The explanation itself is a tree structure corresponding to the pattern of function calls in the computation; in fact, it is a proof tree for the requirements specification statement (or its negation). Once all the evidence has been gathered, a textual version of the explanation can be generated by traversing the tree and concatenating evidence statements, possibly using summarization techniques to make the explanation more concise.

We have so far glossed over how English sentences, especially those with quantification and negation such as (14) and (16), are parsed into and generated from logical representations. The rest of this paper describes our principled approach to this problem, based on a consistent mapping between syntactic categories and semantic types.

4 Using the Grammatical Framework

We relate natural language (English) to logical semantics (Python) using the Grammatical Framework (GF) of Ranta (2004). GF is a mature system that allows linguists and logicians to define grammars for both natural and formal languages using a Haskell-like syntax. Once defined, the grammars can be used for parsing as well as generation (*linearization*) with no further programming.

In GF, grammars are specified in two parts: an abstract grammar and a concrete grammar. An abstract grammar specifies the set of well-formed abstract syntax trees, whereas a concrete grammar specifies how to spell out abstract syntax as strings. For example, an abstract grammar can admit the abstract syntax tree in (4) by specifying that `EverySourceFile` is an NP, `Compiles` is a VP, and `ApplyS` combines an NP and a VP into an S:

```
fun EverySourceFile: NP;
fun Compiles: VP;
fun ApplyS: NP -> VP -> S;
```

A concrete grammar for English can then specify that the linearization of `EverySourceFile` is a singular (`Sg`) string,

```
lin EverySourceFile = {
  s = "every source file"; n = Sg };
```

the linearization of `Compiles` is a pair of strings,

```
lin Compiles = {
  s = { Sg => "compiles";
        Pl => "compile" } };
```

and the linearization of ApplyS is a function that combines these two linearizations into the string (3).

```
lin ApplyS NP VP = {
  s = NP.s ++ (VP.s ! NP.n) };
```

Here ++ denotes string concatenation and ! denotes table lookup.

Multiple concrete grammars can share the same abstract grammar in GF, as in synchronous grammars (Aho and Ullman, 1969) and abstract categorial grammars (de Groote, 2002). This sharing is meant to enable multilingual applications, in which the same meaning representation defined by a single abstract grammar can be rendered into various natural languages by different concrete grammars.

This separation into abstract and concrete grammars lets us use one concrete grammar to model English and another to model the Python syntax of Prograder's logical forms. For example, the linearization of `Compiles` into Python is simply `compiles`, which can be combined with `"foo.c"` by the linearization of `ApplyS` to form `compiles("foo.c")`. The system can thus parse a natural-language specification into an abstract syntax tree using the first concrete grammar, then produce the corresponding semantic representation using the second concrete grammar. Since each concrete grammar can be used for both parsing and generation, the system can also be run in the other direction, to parse the semantic representations of an explanation, then generate that explanation in natural language.

Since the linearization `compiles("foo.c")` in Python is virtually isomorphic to its abstract syntax tree, one may wonder why we bother with the second concrete grammar at all. Why not just express the type-theoretical semantic structure in the abstract syntax and relate it to English in a single concrete grammar? The answer is that using two concrete grammars lets us represent quantifier meanings and scope preferences. Without the distinction between abstract syntax and logical semantics, we would have to specify how to linearize `everysourcefile` and `asourcefile` so that the Python in (15) linearizes to the English. Moreover, Prograder should disprefer the inverse-scope reading

(17)
```
asourcefile(lambda y:
  everytextfile(lambda x:
    mentions(y)(x)))
```

for the same English sentence. We do not see a way to achieve these goals given GF's limited support for higher-order abstract syntax. Instead, we keep our grammars first-order and let our abstract grammar express only the surface structure of English, where quantifiers stay "in situ" just like proper names.

Below we describe how even a first-order concrete grammar for semantic representations can represent quantifier meanings and scope preferences.

5 Quantifier Scope, Negation and Continuation Grammars

Quantifier scoping has long been a key source of difficulty in mapping natural language sentences to logical forms. Scope ambiguities arise even in relatively simple sentences such as (15), which any instructor might be expected to generate in specifying programming assignment requirements. The scope of negation is also problematic. An algorithm for generating all possible quantifier scopings was detailed by Hobbs and Shieber (1987). However, we need a solution that prefers one highly likely default scoping, that supports both interpretation and generation, and that is integrated with the type structure of our semantic representation.

Compositional semantics based on *continuations* (Barker, 2002) can represent preferred scoping of quantifiers and negation without the semantic type-shifting or syntactic underspecification (Hendriks, 1993; Steedman, 1996; Bos, 1995; Koller et al., 2003) that typically complicates interpreting and generating quantification. The rough idea is to generalize Montague's PTQ (1974), so that every constituent's semantic type has the form $(\cdots \to t) \to t$: not only does every NP denote the type $(e \to t) \to t$ instead of e, but every VP also denotes the type $((e \to t) \to t) \to t$ instead of $e \to t$. For example (as in PTQ),

(18) "foo.c" denotes `lambda c: c("foo.c")`

(19) "every text file" denotes
```
lambda c:
  everytextfile(lambda x: c(x))
```

Analogously (but unlike in PTQ),

(20) "compiles" denotes `lambda c: c(compiles)`

(21) "mentions a source file" denotes

```
lambda c:
  asourcefile(lambda x:
    c(mentions(x)))
```

Recall from Section 4 that we model denotations as the linearizations of abstract syntax trees. Therefore, in GF, we want to specify linearizations like

```
lin EverySourceFile =
  lambda c:
    everysourcefile(lambda x: c(x));
lin Compiles = lambda c: c(compiles);
```

to be combined by the linearization of `ApplyS`

```
lin ApplyS NP VP =
  NP(lambda n: VP(lambda v: v(n)));
```

into the expression (5).

In this last linearization, the innermost application `v(n)` means to apply the VP's predicate meaning to the subject NP's entity meaning. The surrounding `NP(lambda n: VP(lambda v: ...))` lets a quantificational subject take wide scope over the VP. This general composition rule thus yields surface scope to the exclusion of inverse scope. In particular, it equally well combines the denotations in (19) and (21) into the expression (15), rather than (17). In the present implementation of Prograder, the rules all encode surface scope for the quantifiers. A similar linearization forms the VP denotation in (21) by composing a transitive verb and its object NP:

```
lin ApplyVP VT NP =
  lambda c: NP(lambda n: c(VT(n)))
```

The same machinery generalizes to handle possessives, ditransitive verbs, relative clauses, and so on.

5.1 Simulating higher-order functions

As shown above, denotations using continuations are higher-order functions. However, linearization in GF does not allow higher-order functions—in fact, the only "functions" allowed in GF are record or table structures indexed by a finite set of parameters. To keep parsing tractable, GF only lets strings be concatenated, not beta-reduced as lambda-terms; the one extension that GF makes to the context-free model is allowing argument suppression and repetition. In other words, GF cannot equate logical forms by beta-equivalence. Therefore, we cannot just feed the pseudocode above into GF to generate explanations. This is an instance of the problem of logical-form equivalence (Shieber, 1993).

Fortunately, because denotations using continuations are always of a certain form (Danvy and Filinski, 1992), we can simulate these higher-order functions using first-order records. Specifically, we simulate a higher-order function of the form

(22) `lambda c:` s_l `c(`s_m`)` s_r

by the *triple of strings*

(23) `{ s_l =` s_l`; s_m =` s_m`; s_r =` s_r `}`

in GF. The middle string s_m corresponds to the "core" of the phrase, and the left and right strings s_l, s_r are those parts which may take scope over other phrases. For example, following the pseudocode above, we write

```
lin EverySourceFile = {
  s_l = "everysourcefile ( lambda x :";
  s_m = "x";
  s_r = ")" };
lin Compiles = {
  s_l = "";
  s_m = "compiles";
  s_r = "" };
```

in our GF concrete grammar. Continuing to follow the pseudocode above, we can also implement the linearizations of `ApplyS` and `ApplyVP` to operate on triples rather than the functions they simulate:

```
lin ApplyS NP VP = {
  s = NP.s_l ++ VP.s_l ++
      VP.s_m ++ "(" ++ NP.s_m ++ ")" ++
      VP.s_r ++ NP.s_r };
lin ApplyVP VT NP = {
  s_l = NP.s_l;
  s_m = VT.s ++ NP.s_m;
  s_r = NP.s_r };
```

Here the linearization of the transitive verb `VT` consists of a single string `s`.

This simulation is reminiscent of Barker and Shan's "tower notation" (2008). In general, we can simulate a n-level semantic tower by a tuple of

$2n - 1$ strings. Overall, this simulation makes us hopeful that linearization in GF can be extended to a broad, useful class of higher-order expressions while keeping parsing tractable.

5.2 Maintaining De Morgan duals

Both to interpret requirements and to generate explanations, our system needs to deal with negation correctly. Whether in the form of a negative quantifier such as "no source file" or a VP modifier such as "don't", negation takes scope. (In the case of the determiner "no", the scope of negation is linked to the containing NP.) We use continuations to account for the scope of negation, as for all scope-taking.

When scope ambiguities arise, negation exhibits the same preference for surface scope as other quantifiers. For example, all of the sentences below prefer the reading where the subject takes wide scope.

(24) A source file doesn't compile.

(25) A text file mentions no source file.

(26) No text file mentions a source file.

The linearization of `ApplyS` shown above already captures this preference; we just need to specify new linearizations with `not_b` in them. The pseudocode

```
lin NoSourceFile =
  lambda c:
    not_b(asourcefile(lambda x: c(x)));
lin Not_VP VP =
  lambda c:
    not_b(VP(lambda v: c(v)));
```

captures the fact that the negation of "A source file compiles" is not (24) but "No source file compiles".

To generate natural-sounding negations of sentences containing quantification, some simple logical equivalences are necessary. To take an extreme example, suppose that Prograder needs to negate the requirement specification

(27) Every text file mentions no source file.

Strictly speaking, it would be correct to generate

(28) Not every text file mentions no source file.

However, it would be much more comprehensible for Prograder to report instead

(29) A text file mentions a source file.

One heuristic for preferring (29) over (28) is to use as few negations as possible. But to apply this heuristic, Prograder must first realize that (29) is a correct negation of (27). In general, our concrete grammar ought to equate formulas that are equivalent by De Morgan's laws. Unfortunately, GF can no more equate formulas by De Morgan equivalence than by beta-equivalence.

In lieu of equating formulas, we normalize them: we use De Morgan's laws to move negations logically as far "inside" as possible. In other words, we impose an invariant on our semantic representation, that `not_b` applies only to atomic formulas (as in (8–9)). This invariant is easy to enforce in our Python code for gathering evidence, because we can rewrite each evidence statement after generating it. It is trickier to enforce the invariant in our GF concrete grammar for semantic representations, because (to keep parsing tractable) linearizations can only be concatenated, never inspected and rewritten. Therefore, our linearizations must maintain formulas alongside their De Morgan duals.

Specifically, we revise the simulation described in the previous section as follows. The record

(30) `{ spl =` s_l^+`; spm =` s_m^+`; spr =` s_r^+`;`
`snl =` s_l^-`; snm =` s_m^-`; snr =` s_r^-`;`
`switched = False }`

represents a higher-order function of the form

(31) `lambda c:` s_l^+ `c(`s_m^+`)` s_r^+

assuming that it is equivalent to

(32) `lambda c: not_b(`s_l^- `not_b(c(`s_m^-`))` s_r^-`)`

Dually, the record

(33) `{ spl =` s_l^+`; spm =` s_m^+`; spr =` s_r^+`;`
`snl =` s_l^-`; snm =` s_m^-`; snr =` s_r^-`;`
`switched = True }`

represents a higher-order function of the form

(34) `lambda c:` s_l^+ `not_b(c(`s_m^+`))` s_r^+

assuming that it is equivalent to

(35) `lambda c: not_b(`s_l^- `c(`s_m^-`)` s_r^-`)`

For example, given the linearizations

```
lin NoSourceFile = {
  spl = "everysourcefile ( lambda x :";
  spm = "x"; spr = ")";
  snl = "asourcefile ( lambda x :";
  snm = "x"; snr = ")";
  switched = True };
lin EverySourceFile = {
  spl = "everysourcefile ( lambda y :";
  spm = "y"; spr = ")";
  snl = "asourcefile ( lambda y :";
  snm = "y"; snr = ")";
  switched = False };
lin ASourceFile = {
  spl = "asourcefile ( lambda x :";
  spm = "x"; spr = ")";
  snl = "everysourcefile ( lambda x :";
  snm = "x"; snr = ")";
  switched = False };
```

(and an alphabetic variant of `ASourcefile`), Prograder uses the `switched` flags to deduce that one way to negate "Every source file mentions no source file" is "A source file mentions a source file".

Our solution demonstrates that an existing grammatical software package can express continuation grammars. While the record-based implementation is somewhat unwieldy when encoded in the grammar by hand, restricting ourselves to GF's context-free rewrite grammars also ensures efficient parsing.

6 Putting It All Together

Currently, our English grammar supports declarative sentences with a small vocabulary of transitive and intransitive verbs ("exists", "compiles", "has comments", "mentions"), proper noun phrases referring to specific source files, noun phrases representing quantified nouns, and negations.

Given that the grammars correctly specify logical scoping and natural language syntax for parsing and generation, the Python code that implements requirement checking and evidence gathering is relatively straightforward. As described above, the logical form of the requirements specification is executable Python, and their execution emits an evidence statement in the same logical language for each check performed, in a tree structure. Thus the execution of the checking code is an evidence-gathering or proof-search process. The evidence statements are then translated to natural language by means of the two GF grammars.

A Python "glue script" ties the Python and GF components together and manages the dataflow of the end-to-end system. This script provides a simple scanner and symbol table to replace file names with standardized placeholders from the grammar. The variables used in lambda expressions also need to be renamed in order to prevent conflicts.

Here is a sample output of the system as it currently runs:

```
./runPrograder.py 'every source file
    compiles and every source file has
    comments'
******************************
RESULT: False, because:
some source files don't compile and
some source files don't have
comments:
"nowork2.c" doesn't compile
"nowork.c" doesn't compile
"nowork2.c" doesn't have comments
"nowork.c" doesn't have comments
```

7 Conclusions and Future Work

To our knowledge, Prograder incorporates the first implementation of continuation-based semantics within a grammatical framework that supports efficient parsing and generation. Consequently, our declarative grammar uniformly expresses quantifier meanings and scope preferences.

We want to see how far we can stretch a record-based grammar system such as GF to handle quantifiers and negation using continuations. In the end, the boilerplate ingredients of our solution ought to be automated, so as to combine the expressivity of continuation-based semantics with the usability and efficiency of GF. This will also make it easier to expand the range of natural-language constructs that the system handles. Of course, this development should be driven by feedback from actual instructors using the system, which we also intend to obtain.

Our second area of future work is the summarization of explanations. We plan to use Prograder to investigate the semantics and pragmatics of summarization, and to search for underlying principles based on proofs and types.

References

Alfred V. Aho and Jeffrey D. Ullman. 1969. Syntax directed translations and the pushdown assembler. *Journal of Computer and System Sciences*, 3(1):37–56, February.

Chris Barker and Chung-chieh Shan. 2008. Donkey anaphora is in-scope binding. *Semantics and Pragmatics*, 1(1):1–46.

Chris Barker. 2002. Continuations and the nature of quantification. *Natural Language Semantics*, 10(3):211–242.

Johan Bos. 1995. Predicate logic unplugged. In Paul Dekker and Martin Stokhof, editors, *Proceedings of the 10th Amsterdam Colloquium*, pages 133–142. Institute for Logic, Language and Computation, Universiteit van Amsterdam.

Olivier Danvy and Andrzej Filinski. 1992. Representing control: A study of the CPS transformation. *Mathematical Structures in Computer Science*, 2(4):361–391, December.

Philippe de Groote. 2002. Towards abstract categorial grammars. In *Proceedings of the 40th Annual Meeting of the Association for Computational Linguistics*, pages 148–155, San Francisco, CA, July. Morgan Kaufmann.

Pierre-Joseph Gailly. 1988. Expressing quantifier scope in French generation. In *COLING '88: Proceedings of the 12th International Conference on Computational Linguistics*, volume 1, pages 182–184.

Herman Hendriks. 1993. *Studied Flexibility: Categories and Types in Syntax and Semantics*. Ph.D. thesis, Institute for Logic, Language and Computation, Universiteit van Amsterdam.

Jerry R. Hobbs and Stuart M. Shieber. 1987. An algorithm for generating quantifier scopings. *Computational Linguistics*, 13(1–2):47–63.

Paul Hudak. 1996. Building domain-specific embedded languages. *ACM Computing Surveys*, 28.

Alexander Koller, Joachim Niehren, and Stefan Thater. 2003. Bridging the gap between underspecification formalisms: Hole semantics as dominance constraints. In *Proceedings of the 10th Conference of the European Chapter of the Association for Computational Linguistics*, pages 195–202, Somerset, NJ. Association for Computational Linguistics.

Richard Montague. 1974. The proper treatment of quantification in ordinary English. In Richmond H. Thomason, editor, *Formal Philosophy: Selected Papers of Richard Montague*, pages 247–270. Yale University Press, New Haven.

Douglas B. Moran. 1988. Quantifier scoping in the SRI core language engine. In *Proceedings of the 26th Annual Meeting of the Association for Computational Linguistics*, pages 33–40, Somerset, NJ. Association for Computational Linguistics.

Aarne Ranta. 2004. Grammatical Framework: A type-theoretical grammar formalism. *Journal of Functional Programming*, 14(2):145–189.

Stuart M. Shieber. 1993. The problem of logical-form equivalence. *Computational Linguistics*, 19(1):179–190.

Mark J. Steedman. 1996. *Surface Structure and Interpretation*. MIT Press, Cambridge.

Kurt A. VanLehn. 1978. Determining the scope of English quantifiers. Master's thesis, Department of Electrical Engineering and Computer Science, Massachusetts Institute of Technology.

Leveraging Hidden Dialogue State to Select Tutorial Moves

Kristy Elizabeth Boyer[a] | Robert Phillips[ab] | Eun Young Ha[a] | Michael D. Wallis[ab] | Mladen A. Vouk[a] | James C. Lester[a]

[a]Department of Computer Science, North Carolina State University
[b]Applied Research Associates
Raleigh, NC, USA

{keboyer, rphilli, eha, mdwallis, vouk, lester}@ncsu.edu

Abstract

A central challenge for tutorial dialogue systems is selecting an appropriate move given the dialogue context. Corpus-based approaches to creating tutorial dialogue management models may facilitate more flexible and rapid development of tutorial dialogue systems and may increase the effectiveness of these systems by allowing data-driven adaptation to learning contexts and to individual learners. This paper presents a family of models, including first-order Markov, hidden Markov, and hierarchical hidden Markov models, for predicting tutor dialogue acts within a corpus. This work takes a step toward fully data-driven tutorial dialogue management models, and the results highlight important directions for future work in unsupervised dialogue modeling.

1 Introduction

A central challenge for dialogue systems is selecting appropriate system dialogue moves (Bangalore, Di Fabbrizio, & Stent, 2008; Frampton & Lemon, 2009; Young et al., 2009). For tutorial dialogue systems, which aim to support learners during conceptual or applied learning tasks, selecting an appropriate dialogue move is particularly important because the tutorial approach could significantly influence cognitive and affective outcomes for the learner (Chi, Jordan, VanLehn, & Litman, 2009). The strategies implemented in tutorial dialogue systems have historically been based on handcrafted rules derived from observing human tutors (e.g., Aleven, McLaren, Roll, & Koedinger, 2004; Evens & Michael, 2006; Graesser, Chipman, Haynes, & Olney, 2005; Jordan, Makatchev, Pappuswamy, VanLehn, & Albacete, 2006). While these systems can achieve results on par with unskilled human tutors, tutorial dialogue systems have not yet matched the effectiveness of expert human tutors (VanLehn et al., 2007).

A more flexible model of strategy selection may enable tutorial dialogue systems to increase their effectiveness by responding adaptively to a broader range of contexts. A promising method for deriving such a model is to learn it directly from corpora of effective human tutoring. Data-driven approaches have shown promise in task-oriented domains outside of tutoring (Bangalore et al., 2008; Hardy et al., 2006; Young et al., 2009), and automatic dialogue policy creation for tutoring has been explored recently (Chi, Jordan, VanLehn, & Hall, 2008; Tetreault & Litman, 2008). Ultimately, devising data-driven approaches for developing tutorial dialogue systems may constitute a key step towards achieving the high learning gains that have been observed with expert human tutors.

The work presented in this paper focuses on learning a model of tutorial moves within a corpus of human-human dialogue in the task-oriented domain of introductory computer science. Unlike the majority of task-oriented domains that have been studied to date, our domain involves the separate creation of a persistent artifact by the user (the student). The modification of this artifact, in our case a computer program, is the focus of the dialogues. Our corpus consists of textual dialogue utterances and a separate synchronous stream of

Proceedings of the NAACL HLT 2010 Fifth Workshop on Innovative Use of NLP for Building Educational Applications, pages 66–73,
Los Angeles, California, June 2010.

task actions. Our goal is to extract a data-driven dialogue management model from the corpus, as evidenced by predicting system (tutor) dialogue acts.

In this paper, we present an annotation approach that addresses dialogue utterances and task actions, and we propose a unified sequential representation for these separate synchronous streams of events. We explore the predictive power of three stochastic models — first-order Markov models, hidden Markov models, and hierarchical hidden Markov models — for predicting tutor dialogue acts in the unified sequences. By leveraging these models to capture effective tutorial dialogue strategies, this work takes a step toward creating data-driven tutorial dialogue management models.

2 Related Work

Much of the research on selecting system dialogue acts relies on a Markov assumption (Levin, Pieraccini, & Eckert, 2000). This formulation is often used in conjunction with reinforcement learning (RL) to derive optimal dialogue policies (Frampton & Lemon, 2009). Sparse data and large state spaces can pose serious obstacles to RL, and recent work aims to address these issues (Ai, Tetreault, & Litman, 2007; Henderson, Lemon, & Georgila, 2008; Heeman, 2007; Young et al., 2009). For tutorial dialogue, RL has been applied to selecting a state space representation that best facilitates learning an optimal dialogue policy (Tetreault & Litman, 2008). RL has also been used to compare specific tutorial dialogue tactic choices (Chi et al., 2008).

While RL learns a dialogue policy through exploration, our work assumes that a flexible, good (though possibly not *optimal*) dialogue policy is realized in successful human-human dialogues. We extract this dialogue policy by predicting tutor (system) actions within a corpus. Using human dialogues directly in this way has been the focus of work in other task-oriented domains such as finance (Hardy et al., 2006) and catalogue ordering (Bangalore et al., 2008). Like the parse-based models of Bangalore et al., our hierarchical hidden Markov models (HHMM) explicitly capture the hierarchical nesting of tasks and subtasks in our domain. In other work, this level of structure has been studied from a slightly different perspective as conversational game (Poesio & Mikheev, 1998).

For tutorial dialogue, there is compelling evidence that human tutoring is a valuable model for extracting dialogue system behaviors. The CIRCSIM-TUTOR (Evens & Michael, 2006), ITSPOKE (Forbes-Riley, Rotaru, Litman, & Tetreault, 2007; Forbes-Riley & Litman, 2009), and KSC-PAL (Kersey, Di Eugenio, Jordan, & Katz, 2009) projects have made extensive use of data-driven techniques based on human corpora. Perhaps most directly comparable to the current work are the bigram models of Forbes-Riley et al.; we explore first-order Markov models, which are equivalent to bigram models, for predicting tutor dialogue acts. In addition, we present HMMs and HHMMs trained on our corpus. We found that both of these models outperformed the bigram model for predicting tutor moves.

3 Corpus and Annotation

The corpus was collected during a human-human tutoring study in which tutors and students worked to solve an introductory computer programming problem (Boyer et al., in press). The dialogues were effective: on average, students exhibited a 7% absolute gain from pretest to posttest (N=48, paired t-test $p<0.0001$).

The corpus contains 48 textual dialogues with a separate, synchronous task event stream. Tutors and students collaborated to solve an introductory computer programming problem using an online tutorial environment with shared workspace viewing and textual dialogue. Each student participated in exactly one tutoring session. The corpus contains 1,468 student utterances, 3,338 tutor utterances, and 3,793 student task actions. In order to build the dialogue model, we annotated the corpus with dialogue act tags and task annotation labels.

3.1 Dialogue Act Annotation

We have developed a dialogue act tagset inspired by schemes for conversational speech (Stolcke et al., 2000), task-oriented dialogue (Core & Allen, 1997), and tutoring (Litman & Forbes-Riley, 2006). The dialogue act tags are displayed in Table 1. Overall reliability on 10% of the corpus for two annotators was κ=0.80.

Table 1. Dialogue act tags

DA	Description	Stu. Rel. Freq.	Tut. Rel. Freq.	κ
ASSESSING QUESTION (AQ)	Request for feedback on task or conceptual utterance.	.20	.11	.91
EXTRA-DOMAIN (EX)	Asides not relevant to the tutoring task.	.08	.04	.79
GROUNDING (G)	Acknowledgement/thanks	.26	.06	.92
LUKEWARM CONTENT FEEDBACK (LCF)	Negative assessment with explanation.	.01	.03	.53
LUKEWARM FEEDBACK (LF)	Lukewarm assessment of task action or conceptual utterance.	.02	.03	.49
NEGATIVE CONTENT FEEDBACK (NCF)	Negative assessment with explanation.	.01	.10	.61
NEGATIVE FEEDBACK (NF)	Negative assessment of task action or conceptual utterance.	.05	.02	.76
POSITIVE CONTENT FEEDBACK (PCF)	Positive assessment with explanation.	.02	.03	.43
POSITIVE FEEDBACK (PF)	Positive assessment of task action or conceptual utterance.	.09	.16	.81
QUESTION (Q)	Task or conceptual question.	.09	.03	.85
STATEMENT (S)	Task or conceptual assertion.	.16	.41	.82

3.2 Task Annotation

The dialogues focused on the task of solving an introductory computer programming problem. The task actions were recorded as a separate but synchronous event stream. This stream included 97,509 keystroke-level user task events. These events were manually aggregated and annotated for subtask structure and then for correctness. The task annotation scheme was hierarchical, reflecting the nested nature of the subtasks. An excerpt from the task annotation scheme is depicted in Figure 1; the full scheme contains 66 leaves. The task annotation scheme was designed to reflect the different depth of possible subtasks nested within the overall task. Each labeled task action was also judged for correctness according to the requirements of the task, with categories CORRECT, BUGGY, INCOMPLETE, and DISPREFERRED (technically correct but not accomplishing the pedagogical goals of the task).

Each group of task keystrokes that occurred between dialogue utterances was tagged, possibly with many subtask labels, by a human judge. A second judge tagged 20% of the corpus in a reliability study for which one-to-one subtask identification was not enforced (giving judges maximum flexibility to apply the tags). To ensure a conservative reliability statistic, all unmatched subtask tags were treated as disagreements. The resulting unweighted kappa statistic was κ_{simple}= 0.58, but the weighted Kappa $\kappa_{weighted}$=0.86 is more meaningful because it takes into account the ordinal nature of the labels that result from sequential subtasks. On task actions for which the two judges agreed on subtask tag, the agreement statistic for correctness was κ_{simple}=0.80.

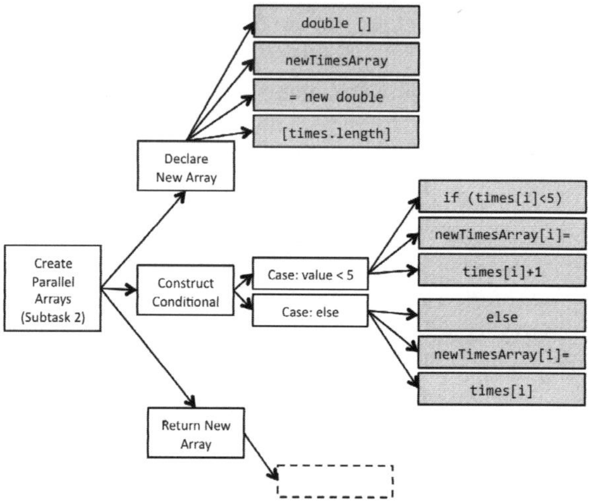

Figure 1. Portion of task annotation scheme

3.3 Adjacency Pair Joining

Some dialogue acts establish an expectation for another dialogue act to occur next (Schegloff & Sacks, 1973). Our previous work has found that identifying the statistically significant *adjacency pairs* in a corpus and joining them as atomic observations prior to model building produces more interpretable descriptive models. The models reported here were trained on hybrid sequences of dialogue acts and adjacency pairs. A full description of the adjacency pair identification methodology and joining algorithm is reported in (Boyer et al., 2009). A partial list of the most highly statistically significant adjacency pairs, which for this work include task actions, is displayed in Table 2.

Table 2. Subset of significant adjacency pairs

CorrectTaskAction-CorrectTaskAction;
ExtraDomain$_S$-ExtraDomain$_T$; Grounding$_S$-Grounding$_T$;
AssessingQuestion$_T$-PositiveFeedback$_S$;
AssessingQuestion$_S$-PositiveFeedback$_T$; Question$_T$-Statement$_S$;
AssessingQuestion$_T$-Statement$_S$; ExtraDomain$_T$-ExtraDomain$_S$;
Question$_S$-Statement$_T$; NegativeFeedback$_S$-Grounding$_T$;
IncompleteTaskAction-IncompleteTaskAction;
PositiveFeedback$_S$-Grounding$_T$;
BuggyTaskAction-BuggyTaskAction

4 Models

We learned three types of models using cross-validation with systematic sampling of training and testing sets.

4.1 First-Order Markov Model

The simplest model we discuss is the first-order Markov model (MM), or bigram model (Figure 2). A MM that generates observation (state) sequence $o_1o_2...o_t$ is defined in the following way. The observation symbols are drawn from the alphabet $\sum=\{\sigma_1, \sigma_2, ..., \sigma_M\}$, and the initial probability distribution is $\Pi=[\pi_i]$ where π_i is the probability of a sequence beginning with observation symbol σ_i. The transition probability distribution is $A=[a_{ij}]$, where a_{ij} is the probability of observation j occurring immediately after observation i.

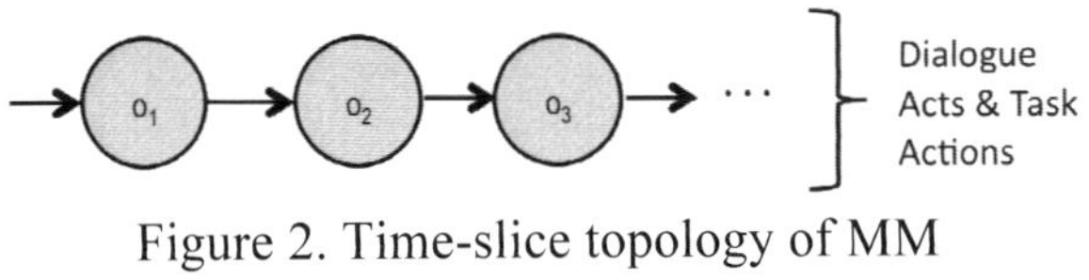

Figure 2. Time-slice topology of MM

We trained MMs on our corpus of dialogue acts and task events using ten-fold cross-validation to produce a model that could be queried for the next predicted tutorial dialogue act given the history.

4.2 Hidden Markov Model

A hidden Markov model (HMM) augments the MM framework, resulting in a doubly stochastic structure (Rabiner, 1989). For a first-order HMM, the observation symbol alphabet is defined as above, along with a set of hidden states $S=\{s_1,s_2,...,s_N\}$. The transition and initial probability distributions are defined analogously to MMs, except that they operate on hidden states rather than on observation symbols (Figure 3). That is, $\Pi=[\pi_i]$ where π_i is the probability of a sequence beginning in hidden state s_i. The transition matrix is $A=[a_{ij}]$, where a_{ij} is the probability of the model transitioning from hidden state i to hidden state j. This framework constitutes the first stochastic layer of the model, which can be thought of as modeling hidden, or unobservable, structure. The second stochastic layer of the model governs the production of observation symbols: the emission probability distribution is $B=[b_{ik}]$ where b_{ik} is the probability of state i emitting observation symbol k.

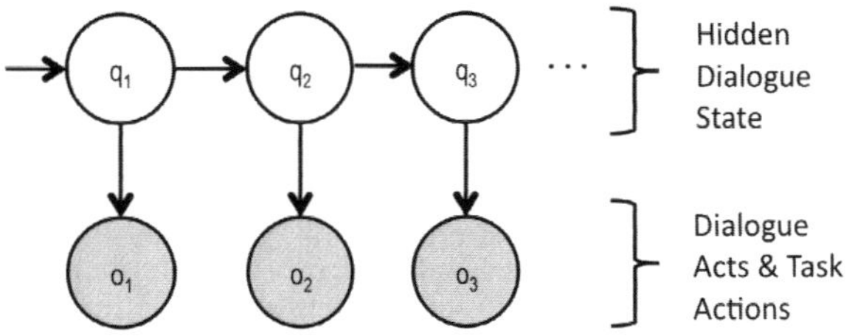

Figure 3. Time-slice topology of HMM

The notion that dialogue has an overarching unobservable structure that influences the observations is widely accepted. In tutoring, this overarching structure may correspond to tutorial strategies. We have explored HMMs' descriptive power for extracting these strategies (Boyer et al., 2009), and this paper explores the hypothesis that HMMs provide better predictive power than MMs on our dialogue sequences. We trained HMMs on the corpus using the standard Baum-Welch expectation maximization algorithm and applied state labels that reflect post-hoc interpretation (Figure 4).

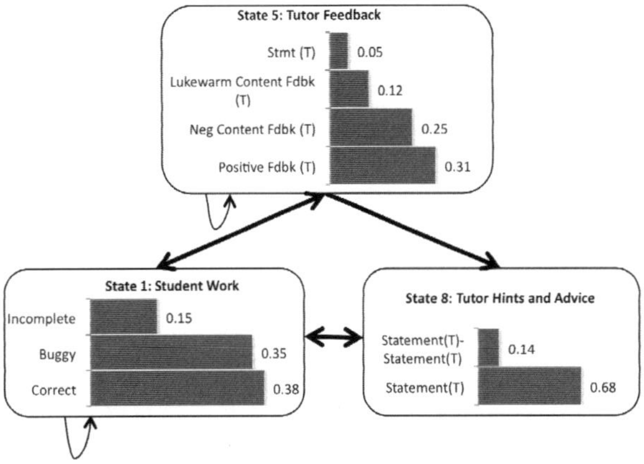

Figure 4. Portion of learned HMM

4.3 Hierarchical Hidden Markov Model

Hierarchical hidden Markov models (HHMMs) allow for explicit representation of multilevel stochastic structure. A complete formal definition of HHMMs can be found in (Fine, Singer, & Tishby, 1998), but here we present an informal description. HHMMs include two types of hidden states: internal nodes, which do not produce observation symbols, and production nodes, which do produce observations. An internal node includes a set of substates that correspond to its potential children, $S=\{s_1, s_2, ..., s_N\}$, each of which is itself the root of an HHMM. The initial probability distribution $\Pi=[\pi_i]$ for each internal node governs the probability that the model will make a vertical transition to substate s_i from this internal node; that is, that this internal node will produce substate s_i as its leftmost child. Horizontal transitions are governed by a transition probability distribution similar to that described above for flat HMMs. Production nodes are defined by their observation symbol alphabet and an emission probability distribution over the symbols; HHMMs do not require a global observation symbol alphabet. The generative topology of our HHMMs is illustrated in Figure 5.

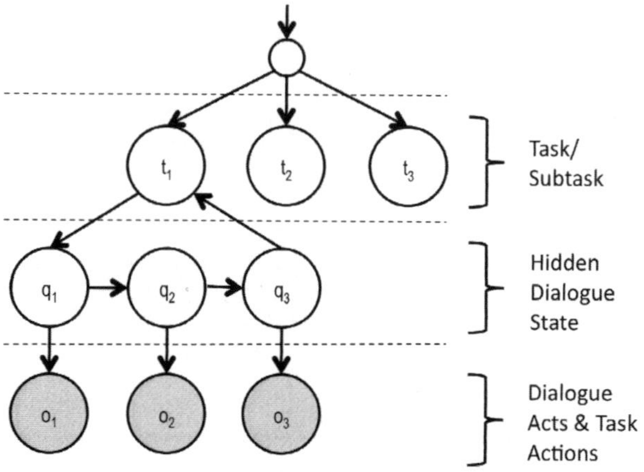

Figure 5. Generative topology of HHMM

HHMMs of arbitrary topology can be trained using a generalized version of the Baum-Welch algorithm (Fine et al., 1998). Our HHMMs featured a pre-specified model topology based on known task/subtask structure. A Bayesian view of a portion of the best-fit HHMM is depicted in Figure 6. This model was trained using five-fold cross-validation to address the absence of symbols from the training set that were present in the testing set, a sparsity problem that arose from splitting the data hierarchically.

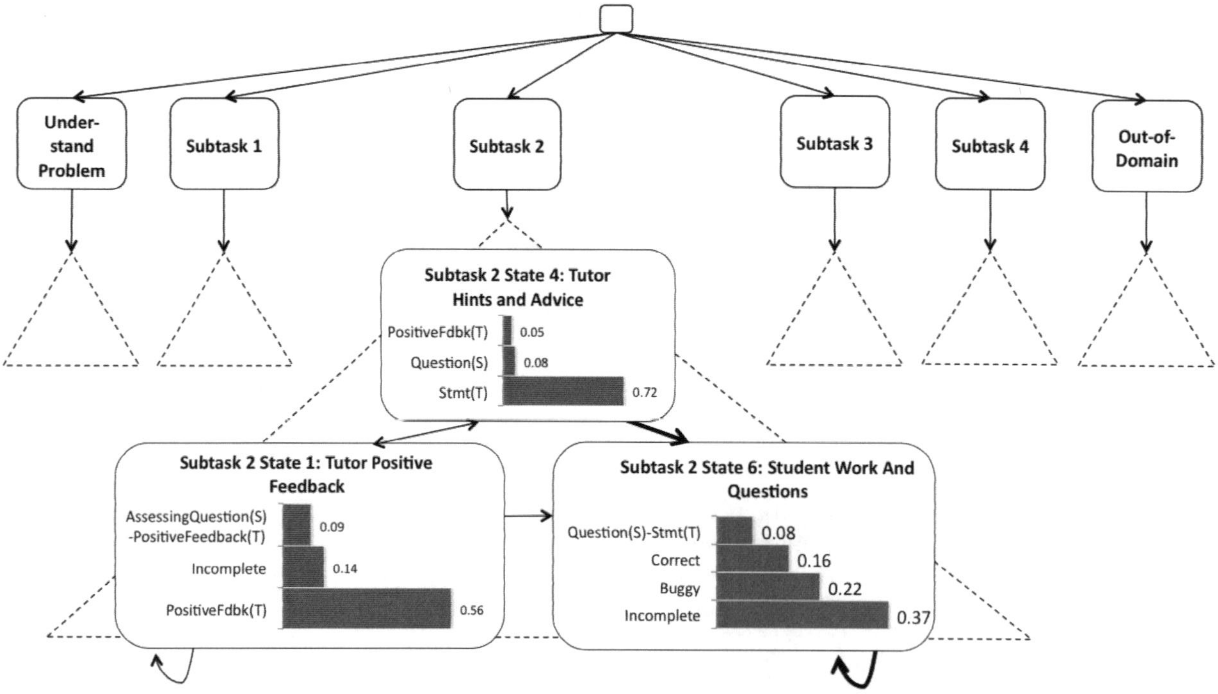

Figure 6. Portion of learned HHMM

5 Results

We trained and tested MMs, HMMs, and HHMMs on the corpus and compared prediction accuracy for tutorial dialogue acts by providing the model with partial sequences from the test set and querying for the next tutorial move. The baseline prediction accuracy for this task is 41.1%, corresponding to the most frequent tutorial dialogue act (STATEMENT). As depicted in Figure 7, a first-order MM performed worse than baseline ($p<0.001$)[1] at 27% average prediction accuracy ($\hat{\sigma}_{MM}$=6%). HMMs performed better than baseline ($p<0.0001$), with an average accuracy of 48% ($\hat{\sigma}_{HMM}$=3%). HHMMs averaged 57% accuracy, significantly higher than baseline ($p=0.002$) but weakly significantly higher than HMMs ($p=0.04$), and with high variation ($\hat{\sigma}_{HHMM}$=23%).

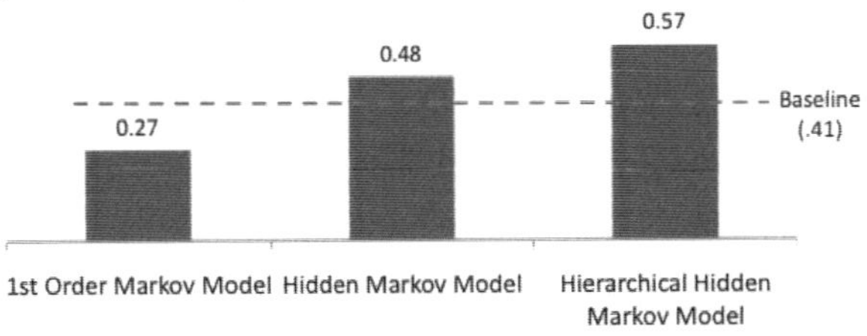

Figure 7. Average prediction accuracies of three model types on tutor dialogue acts

To further explore the performance of the HHMMs, Figure 8 displays their prediction accuracy on each of six labeled subtasks. These subtasks correspond to the top level of the hierarchical task/subtask annotation scheme. The UNDERSTAND THE PROBLEM subtask corresponds to the initial phase of most tutoring sessions, in which the student and tutor agree to some extent on a problem-solving plan. Subtasks 1, 2, and 3 account for the implementation and debugging of three distinct modules within the learning task, and Subtask 4 involves testing and assessing the student's finalized program. The EXTRA-DOMAIN subtask involves side conversations whose topics are outside of the domain.

The HHMM performed as well as or better ($p<0.01$) than baseline on the first three in-domain subtasks. The performance on SUBTASK 4 was not distinguishable from baseline ($p=0.06$); relatively few students reached this subtask. The model did not outperform baseline ($p=0.40$) for the UNDERSTAND THE PROBLEM subtask, and qualitative inspection of the corpus reveals that the dialogue during this phase of tutoring exhibits limited regularities between students.

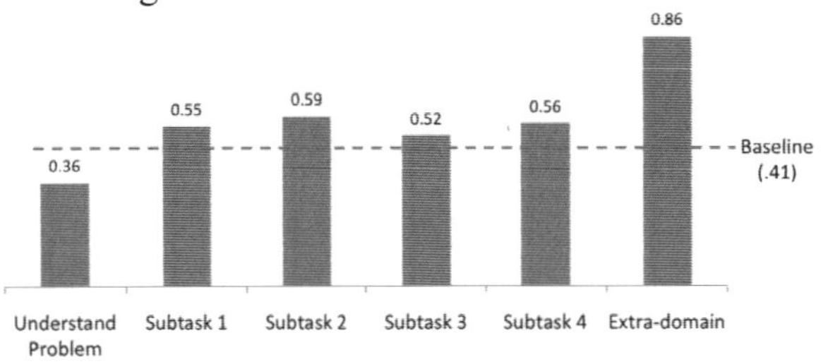

Figure 8. Average prediction accuracies of HHMMs by subtask

6 Discussion

The results support our hypothesis that HMMs, because of their capacity for explicitly representing dialogue structure at an abstract level, perform better than MMs for predicting tutor moves. The results also suggest that explicitly modeling hierarchical task structure can further improve prediction accuracy of the model. The below-baseline performance of the bigram model illustrates that in our complex task-oriented domain, an immediately preceding event is not highly predictive of the next move. While this finding may not hold for conversational dialogue or some task-oriented dialogue with a more balanced distribution of utterances between speakers, the unbalanced nature of our tutoring sessions may not be as easily captured.

In our corpus, tutor utterances outnumber student utterances by more than two to one. This large difference is due to the fact that tutors frequently guided students and provided multi-turn explanations, the impetus for which are not captured in the corpus, but rather, involve external pedagogical goals. The MM, or bigram model, has no mechanism for capturing this layer of stochastic behavior. On the other hand, the HMM can account for unobserved influential variables, and the HHMM can do so to an even greater extent by explicitly modeling task/subtask structure.

Considering the performance of the HHMM on individual subtasks reveals interesting properties of our dialogues. First, the HHMM is unable to outperform baseline on the UNDERSTAND THE PROBLEM subtask. To address this issue, our ongoing work investigates taking into account

[1] All p-values in this section were produced by two-sample one-tailed t-tests with unequal sample variances.

student characteristics such as incoming knowledge level and self-confidence. On all four in-domain subtasks, the HHMM achieved a 30% to 50% increase over baseline. For extra-domain dialogues, which involve side conversations that are not task-related, the HHMM achieved 86% prediction accuracy on tutor moves, which constitutes a 115% improvement over baseline. This high accuracy may be due in part to the fact that out-of-domain asides were almost exclusively initiated by the student, and tutors rarely engaged in such exchanges beyond providing a single response. This regularity likely facilitated prediction of the tutor's dialogue moves during out-of-domain talk.

We are aware of only one recent project that reports extensively on predicting system actions from a corpus of human-human dialogue. Bangalore et al.'s (2008) flat task/dialogue model in a catalogue-ordering domain achieved a prediction accuracy of 55% for system dialogue acts, a 175% improvement over baseline. When explicitly modeling the hierarchical task/subtask dialogue structure, they report a prediction accuracy of 35.6% for system moves, approximately 75% above baseline (Bangalore & Stent, 2009). These findings were obtained by utilizing a variety of lexical and syntactic features along with manually annotated dialogue acts and task/subtask labels. In comparison, our HHMM achieved an average 42% improvement over baseline using only annotated dialogue acts and task/subtask labels. In ongoing work we are exploring the utility of additional features for this prediction task.

Our best model performed better than baseline by a significant margin. The absolute prediction accuracy achieved by the HHMM was 57% across the corpus, which at first blush may appear too low to be of practical use. However, the choice of tutorial move involves some measure of subjectivity, and in many contexts there may be no uniquely appropriate dialogue act. Work in other domains has dealt with this uncertainty by maintaining multiple hypotheses (Wright Hastie, Poesio, & Isard, 2002) and by mapping to clustered sets of moves rather than maintaining policies for each possible system selection (Young et al., 2009). Such approaches may prove useful in our domain as well, and may help to more fully realize the potential of a learned dialogue management model.

7 Conclusion and Future Work

Learning models that predict system moves within a corpus is a first step toward building fully data-driven dialogue management models. We have presented Markov models, hidden Markov models, and hierarchical hidden Markov models trained on sequences of manually annotated dialogue acts and task events. Of the three models, the hierarchical models appear to perform best in our domain, which involves an intrinsically hierarchical task/subtask structure.

The models' performance points to promising future work that includes utilizing additional lexical and syntactic features along with fixed user (student) characteristics within a hierarchical hidden Markov modeling framework. More broadly, the results point to the importance of considering task structure when modeling a complex domain such as those that often accompany task-oriented tutoring. Finally, a key direction for data-driven dialogue management models involves learning unsupervised dialogue act and task classification models.

Acknowledgements. This work is supported in part by the North Carolina State University Department of Computer Science and the National Science Foundation through a Graduate Research Fellowship and Grants CNS-0540523, REC-0632450 and IIS-0812291. Any opinions, findings, conclusions, or recommendations expressed in this report are those of the participants, and do not necessarily represent the official views, opinions, or policy of the National Science Foundation.

References

Ai, H., Tetreault, J. R., & Litman, D. J. (2007). Comparing user simulation models for dialog strategy learning. *Proceedings of NAACL HLT, Companion Volume,* Rochester, New York. 1-4.

Aleven, V., McLaren, B., Roll, I., & Koedinger, K. (2004). Toward tutoring help seeking: Applying cognitive modeling to meta-cognitive skills. *Proceedings of ITS,* 227-239.

Bangalore, S., Di Fabbrizio, G., & Stent, A. (2008). Learning the structure of task-driven human-human dialogs. *IEEE Transactions on Audio, Speech, and Language Processing, 16*(7), 1249-1259.

Bangalore, S., & Stent, A. J. (2009). Incremental parsing models for dialog task structure. *Proceedings of the EACL,* 94-102.

Boyer, K. E., Phillips, R., Ha, E. Y., Wallis, M. D., Vouk, M. A., & Lester, J. C. (2009). Modeling dialogue structure with adjacency pair analysis and hidden Markov models. *Proceedings of NAACL HLT (Short Papers),* 19-26.

Boyer, K. E., Phillips, R., Ingram, A., Ha, E. Y., Wallis, M. D., Vouk, M. A., & Lester, J. C. (In press). Characterizing the effectiveness of tutorial dialogue with hidden Markov models. *Proceedings of ITS,* Pittsburgh, Pennsylvania.

Chi, M., Jordan, P., VanLehn, K., & Hall, M. (2008). Reinforcement learning-based feature selection for developing pedagogically effective tutorial dialogue tactics. *Proceedings of EDM,* Montreal, Canada. 258-265.

Chi, M., Jordan, P., VanLehn, K., & Litman, D. (2009). To elicit or to tell: Does it matter? *Proceedings of AIED,* 197-204.

Core, M., & Allen, J. (1997). Coding dialogs with the DAMSL annotation scheme. *AAAI Fall Symposium on Communicative Action in Humans and Machines,* 28–35.

Evens, M., & Michael, J. (2006). *One-on-one tutoring by humans and computers.* Mahwah, New Jersey: Lawrence Erlbaum Associates.

Fine, S., Singer, Y., & Tishby, N. (1998). The hierarchical hidden Markov model: Analysis and applications. *Machine Learning, 32*(1), 41-62.

Forbes-Riley, K., Rotaru, M., Litman, D. J., & Tetreault, J. (2007). Exploring affect-context dependencies for adaptive system development. *Proceedings of NAACL HLT (Short Papers),* 41-44.

Forbes-Riley, K., & Litman, D. (2009). Adapting to student uncertainty improves tutoring dialogues. *Proceedings of AIED,* 33-40.

Frampton, M., & Lemon, O. (2009). Recent research advances in reinforcement learning in spoken dialogue systems. *The Knowledge Engineering Review, 24*(4), 375-408.

Graesser, A. C., Chipman, P., Haynes, B. C., & Olney, A. (2005). AutoTutor: An intelligent tutoring system with mixed-initiative dialogue. *IEEE Transactions on Education, 48*(4), 612-618.

Hardy, H., Biermann, A., Inouye, R. B., McKenzie, A., Strzalkowski, T., Ursu, C., Webb, N., & Wu, M. (2006). The Amitiés system: Data-driven techniques for automated dialogue. *Speech Communication, 48*(3-4), 354-373.

Heeman, P. A. (2007). Combining reinforcement learning with information-state update rules. *Proceedings of NAACL HLT,* 268-275.

Henderson, J., Lemon, O., & Georgila, K. (2008). Hybrid reinforcement/supervised learning of dialogue policies from fixed data sets. *Computational Linguistics, 34*(4), 487-511.

Jordan, P., Makatchev, M., Pappuswamy, U., VanLehn, K., & Albacete, P. (2006). A natural language tutorial dialogue system for physics. *Proceedings of FLAIRS,* 521-526.

Kersey, C., Di Eugenio, B., Jordan, P., & Katz, S. (2009). KSC-PaL: A peer learning agent that encourages students to take the initiative. *Proceedings of the NAACL HLT Workshop on Innovative use of NLP for Building Educational Applications,* Boulder, Colorado. 55-63.

Levin, E., Pieraccini, R., & Eckert, W. (2000). A stochastic model of human-machine interaction for learning dialog strategies. *IEEE Transactions on Speech and Audio Processing, 8*(1), 11-23.

Litman, D., & Forbes-Riley, K. (2006). Correlations between dialogue acts and learning in spoken tutoring dialogues. *Natural Language Engineering, 12*(2), 161-176.

Poesio, M., & Mikheev, A. (1998). The predictive power of game structure in dialogue act recognition: Experimental results using maximum entropy estimation. *Proceedings of ICSLP,* 90-97.

Rabiner, L. R. (1989). A tutorial on hidden Markov models and selected applications in speech recognition. *Proceedings of the IEEE, 77*(2), 257-286.

Schegloff, E., & Sacks, H. (1973). Opening up closings. *Semiotica, 7*(4), 289-327.

Stolcke, A., Ries, K., Coccaro, N., Shriberg, E., Bates, R., Jurafsky, D., Taylor, P., Martin, R., Van Ess-Dykema, C., & Meteer, M. (2000). Dialogue act modeling for automatic tagging and recognition of conversational speech. *Computational Linguistics, 26*(3), 339-373.

Tetreault, J. R., & Litman, D. J. (2008). A reinforcement learning approach to evaluating state representations in spoken dialogue systems. *Speech Communication, 50*(8-9), 683-696.

VanLehn, K., Graesser, A. C., Jackson, G. T., Jordan, P., Olney, A., & Rose, C. P. (2007). When are tutorial dialogues more effective than reading? *Cognitive Science, 31*(1), 3-62.

Wright Hastie, H., Poesio, M., & Isard, S. (2002). Automatically predicting dialogue structure using prosodic features. *Speech Communication, 36*(1-2), 63-79.

Young, S., Gasic, M., Keizer, S., Mairesse, F., Schatzmann, J., Thomson, B., & Yu, K. (2009). The hidden information state model: A practical framework for POMDP-based spoken dialogue management. *Computer Speech and Language, 24*(2), 150-174.

Towards Using Structural Events To Assess Non-native Speech

Lei Chen, Joel Tetreault, Xiaoming Xi
Educational Testing Service (ETS)
Princeton, NJ 08540, USA
{LChen,JTetreault,XXi}@ets.org

Abstract

We investigated using structural events, e.g., clause and disfluency structure, from transcriptions of spontaneous non-native speech, to compute features for measuring speaking proficiency. Using a set of transcribed audio files collected from the TOEFL Practice Test Online (TPO), we conducted a sophisticated annotation of structural events, including clause boundaries and types, as well as disfluencies. Based on words and the annotated structural events, we extracted features related to syntactic complexity, e.g., the mean length of clause (MLC) and dependent clause frequency (DEPC), and a feature related to disfluencies, the interruption point frequency per clause (IPC). Among these features, the IPC shows the highest correlation with holistic scores ($r = -0.344$). Furthermore, we increased the correlation with human scores by normalizing IPC by (1) MLC ($r = -0.386$), (2) DEPC ($r = -0.429$), and (3) both ($r = -0.462$). In this research, the features derived from structural events of speech transcriptions are found to predict holistic scores measuring speaking proficiency. This suggests that structural events estimated on speech word strings provide a potential way for assessing non-native speech.

1 Introduction

In the last decade, a breakthrough in speech processing is the emergence of a lot of active research work on automatic estimation of structural events, e.g., sentence structure and disfluencies, on spontaneous speech (Shriberg et al., 2000; Liu, 2004; Ostendorf et al., 2008). The detected structural events have been successfully used in many natural language processing (NLP) applications (Ostendorf et al., 2008).

However, the structural events in speech data haven't been largely utilized by the research on using automatic speech recognition (ASR) technology to assess speech proficiency (Neumeyer et al., 2000; Zechner et al., 2007), which mainly used cues derived at the word level, such as timing information of spoken words. The information beyond the word level, e.g., clause/sentence structure of utterances and disfluency structure, has not been or is poorly represented. For example, in Zechner et al. (2007), only special words for filled pauses such as *um* and *uh* were obtained from ASR results to represent disfluencies.

Given the successful usage of structural events on a wide range of NLP applications and the fact that the usage of these events is missing in the automatic speech assessment research, a research question emerges: Can we use structural events of spontaneous speech to assess non-native speech proficiency?

We will address this question in this paper. The paper is organized as follows: Section 2 reviews previous research. Section 3 describes our annotation convention. Section 4 reports on the data collection, annotation, and quality control. Section 5 reports on features based on structural event annotations. Section 6 reports on our experiments. Section 7 discusses our findings and plans for future research work.

Proceedings of the NAACL HLT 2010 Fifth Workshop on Innovative Use of NLP for Building Educational Applications, pages 74–79,
Los Angeles, California, June 2010.

2 Previous Work

In the last decade, a large amount of research (Ostendorf et al., 2008) has been conducted on detection of structural events, e.g., sentence structure and disfluency structure, in spontaneous speech. In these research works, the structural events were detected with a quite high accuracy. Furthermore, the detected sentence and disfluency structures have been found to help many of the following NLP tasks, e.g., speech parsing, information retrieval, machine translation, and extractive speech summary (Ostendorf et al., 2008).

In the second language acquisition (SLA) and child language development research fields, the language development is measured according to fluency, accuracy, and complexity (Iwashita, 2006). The syntactic complexity of learners' writing data has been extensively studied in the SLA community (Ortega, 2003). Recently, this study has been extended to the learner's speaking data (Iwashita, 2006). Typical metrics for examining syntactic complexity include: length of production unit (e.g., T-unit, which is defined as essentially a main clause plus any other clauses which are dependent upon it (Hunt, 1970), clauses, verb phrases, and sentences), amount of embedding, subordination and coordination, range of structural types, and structure sophistication.

Iwashita (2006) investigated several measures for syntactic complexity on the data from learners of Japanese. The author reported that some measurements, e.g., T-unit length, the number of clauses per T-unit, and the number of independent clauses per T-Unit, were good at predicting learners' proficiency levels.

In addition, some previous studies used measurements related to disfluencies to assess speaking proficiency. For example, Lennon (1990) used a dozen features related to speed, pauses, and several disfluency markers, such as filler pauses per T-unit, to measure four German-speaking women's English improvement during a half year study in England. He found a significant change in filled pauses per T-unit during the studying process.

The features related to syntactic complexity and the features related to "smoothness" (disfluency) of speech were jointly used in some previous studies. For example, Mizera (2006) used fluency factors related to speed, voiced smoothness (frequencies of repetitions or self-corrections), pauses, syntactic complexity (mean length of T-units), and accuracy, to measure speaking proficiency on 20 non-native English speakers. In this experiment, disfluency-related factors, such as total voiced disfluencies, had a high correlation with fluency ($r = -0.45$). However, the syntactic complexity factor only showed a moderate correlation ($r = 0.310$). Yoon (2009) implemented an automated disfluency detection method and found that the disfluency-related features lead to the moderate improvement in the automated speech proficiency scoring.

There were limitations on using the features reported in these SLA studies on standard language tests. For example, only a very limited number of subjects (from 20 to 30 speakers) were used in these studies. Second, the speaking content was narrations of picture books or cartoon videos rather than standard test questions. Therefore, we conducted a study using a much larger data set obtained from real speech tests to address these limitations.

3 Structural Event Annotation Convention

To annotate structural events of speech content, we have developed a convention based on previous studies and our observations on the TOEFL Practice Online (TPO) test data. Defining clauses is a relatively simple task; however, defining clause boundaries and specifying which elements fall within a particular clause is a much more challenging task for spoken discourse, due to the presence of grammatical errors, fragments, repetitions, self corrections, and conversation fillers.

Foster et al. (Foster et al., 2000) review various units for analyzing spoken language, including syntactic, semantic and intonational units, and propose a new analysis of speech unit (AS-Unit) that they claim is appropriate for many different purposes. In this study, we focused on clauses given the characteristics of spontaneous speech. Also, we defined clause types based on grammar books such as (Azar, 2003). The following clause types were defined:

- Simple sentence (**SS**) contains a subject and a verb, and expresses a complete thought.

- Independent clause (**I**) is the main clause that can stand along syntactically as a complete sentence. It consists minimally a subject and a finite verb (a verb that shows tense, person, or singular/plural, e.g., *he goes*, *I went*, and *I was*).

- Subordinate clause is a clause in a complex sentence that cannot stand alone as a complete sentence and that functions within the sentence as a noun, a verb complement, an adjective or an adverb. There are three types of subordinate clauses: noun clause (**NC**), relative clause that functions as an adjective (**ADJ**), adverbial clause that functions as an adverb (**ADV**).

- Coordinate clause (**CC**) is a clause in a compound sentence that is grammatically equivalent to the main clause and that performs the same grammatical function.

- Adverbial phrase (**ADVP**) is a separate clause from the main clause that contains a non-finite verb (a verb that does not show tense, person, or singular/plural).

The clause boundaries and clause types were annotated on the word transcriptions. Round brackets were used to indicate the beginning and end of a clause. Then, the abbreviations described above for clause types were added. Also, if a specific boundary serves as the boundaries for both the local and global clause, the abbreviation of the local clause was followed by that of the global. Some examples of clause boundaries and types are reported in Table 1.

In our annotation manual, a speech disfluency contains three parts:

- *Reparandum*: the speech portion that will be repeated, corrected, or even abandoned. The end of the reparandum is called the interruption point (**IP**), which indicates the stop of a normal fluent speech stream.

- *Editing phrase*: optional inserted words, e.g., *um*.

- *Correction*: the speech portion that repeats, corrects, or even starts new content.

In our annotation manual, the reparandum was enclosed by "*", the editing phrase was enclosed by "%", and the correction was enclosed by "$". For example, in the following utterance, "He is a * very mad * % er % $ very bad $ cop", "very mad" was corrected by "very bad" and an editing phrase, *er*, was inserted.

4 Data Collection and Annotation

4.1 Audio data collection and scoring

About 1300 speech responses from the TPO test were collected and transcribed. Each item was scored by two experienced human raters independently using a 4-point holistic score based on the scoring rubrics designed for the test.

In the TPO test, some tasks required test-takers to provide information or opinions on familiar topics based on their personal experience or background knowledge. Others required them to summarize and synthesize information presented in listening and/or reading materials. Each test-taker was required to finish six items in one test session. Each item has a 45 or 60 seconds response time.

4.2 Annotation procedure

Two annotators (who were not the human raters mentioned above) with a linguistics background and past linguistics annotation experience were first presented with a draft of the annotation convention. After reading through it, the annotators, as well as the second and third author completed four iterative loops of rating 4 or 5 responses per meeting. All four discussed differences in annotations and the convention was refined as needed. After the final iteration of comparisons, the raters seemed to have very few disagreement and thus began annotating sets of responses. Each set consisted of roughly 50-75 responses and then a kappa set of 30-50 responses which both annotators completed. Accordingly, between the two annotators, a set comprised roughly 130 to 200 responses. Each response takes roughly 3-8 minutes to annotate. The annotators were instructed to listen to the corresponding audio file if they needed the prosodic information to annotate a particular speech disfluency event.

Clause type	Example
SS	(That's right |SS)
I	(He turned away |I) as soon as he saw me |ADV)
NC	((What he did |NC) shocked me |I)
ADJ	(She is the woman (I told you about |ADJ)|I)
ADV	(As soon as he saw me |ADV) (he turned away |I)
CC	(I will go home |I) (and he will go to work |CC)
ADVP	(While walking to class |ADVP) (I ran into a friend |I)

Table 1: Examples of clause boundary and type annotation

4.3 Evaluation of annotation

To evaluate the quality of structural event annotation, we measured the inter-rater agreement on clause boundary (CB) annotation and interruption point (IP) of disfluencies[1].

We used Cohen's κ to calculate the annotator agreement on each kappa set. κ is calculated on the absence or presence of a boundary marker (either a clause boundary (CB) or an interruption point (IP) between consecutive words). For each consecutive pair of words, we check for the existence of one or more boundaries, and collapse the set into one term "boundary" and then compute the agreement on this reduced annotation.

In Table 2, we list the annotator agreement for both boundary events over 4 kappa sets. The second column refers to the number of speech responses in the kappa set, the next two columns refer to the annotator agreement using the Cohen's κ value on CB and IP annotation results.

Set	N	κ CB	κ IP
Set1	54	0.886	0.626
Set2	71	0.847	0.687
Set3	35	0.855	0.695
Set4	34	0.899	0.833

Table 2: Between-rater agreement of structural event annotation

In general, a κ of 0.8-1.0 represents excellent agreement, 0.6-0.8 represents good agreement, and so forth. Over each kappa set, κ for CB annotations ranges between 0.8 and 0.9, which is an excellent agreement; κ for IP annotation ranges between 0.6 and 0.8, which is a good agreement. Compared to annotating clauses, marking disfluencies is more challenging. As a result, a lower between-rater agreement is expected.

5 Features Derived On Structural Events

Based on the structural event annotations, including clause boundaries and their types, as well as disfluencies, some features measuring syntactic complexity and disfluency profile were derived.

Since simple sentence (SS), independent clause (I), and conjunct clause (CC) represent a complete idea, we treat them as an approximate to a T-unit (T). The clauses that have no complete idea, are dependent clauses (DEP), including noun clauses (N), relative clauses that function as adjective (ADJ), adverbial clauses (ADV), and adverbial phrases (ADVP). The total number of clauses is a summation of the number of T-units (T), dependent clauses (DEP), and fragments[2] (denoted as F). Therefore,

$$\begin{aligned} N_T &= N_{SS} + N_I + N_{CC} \\ N_{DEP} &= N_{NC} + N_{ADJ} + N_{ADV} + N_{ADVP} \\ N_C &= N_T + N_{DEP} + N_F \end{aligned}$$

Assuming N_w is the total number of words in the speech response (without pruning speech repairs), the following features, including mean length of clause (MLC), dependent clauses per clause (DEPC), and interruption points per clause (IPC), are derived:

$$MLC = N_w / N_C$$

[1]Measurement on CBs and IPs can provide a rough quality measurement of annotations. In addition, doing so is more important to us since automatic detection of these two types of events will be investigated in future.

[2]It is either a subordinate clause that does not have a corresponding independent clause or a string of words without a subject or a verb that does not express a complete thought.

$$DEPC = N_{DEP}/N_C$$
$$IPC = N_{IP}/N_C$$

Furthermore, we elaborated the IPC feature. Disfluency is a complex behavior and is influenced by a variety of factors, such as proficiency level, speaking rate, and familiarity with speaking content. The complexity of utterances is also an important factor on the disfluency pattern. For example, Roll et al. (Roll et al., 2007) found that complexity of expression computed based on the language's parsing tree structure influenced the frequency of disfluencies in their experiment on Swedish. Therefore, since disfluency frequency was not only influenced by the test-takers' speaking proficiency but also by the utterance's syntactic structure's difficulty, we reduced the impact from the syntactic structure so that we can focus on speakers' ability. For this purpose, we normalized IPC by dividing by some features related to syntactic-structure's complexity, including MLC, DEPC, and both. Therefore, the following elaborated disfluency-related features were derived:

$$IPCn1 = IPC/MLC$$
$$IPCn2 = IPC/DEPC$$
$$IPCn3 = IPC/MLC/DEPC$$

6 Experiment

For each item, two human raters rated it separately with a score from 1 to 4. If these two scores are consistent (the difference between two scores is either zero or one), we put this item in an item-pool. Finally, a total of $1,257$ audio items were included in the pool. Following the score-handling protocol used in the TPO test, we used the first human rater's score as the item score. From the obtained item-pool, we selected speakers with more than three items so that the averaged score per speaker can be estimated on several items to achieve a robust score computation[3]. As a result, 175 speakers[4] were selected.

[3]The mean holistic score of these speakers is 2.786, which is close to the mean holistic score of the selected item-pool (2.785), indicating that score distribution was kept after focusing on speakers with more than three items.

[4]If a speaker was assigned in a Kappa set in the annotation as described in Section 4, this speaker would have as many as 12 annotated items. Therefore, the minimum number of speakers from the item-pool was about 105 ($1257/12$).

For each speaker, his or her annotations of words and structural events were used to extract the features described in Section 5. Then, we computed the Pearson correlation among the obtained features with the averaged holistic scores per speaker.

Feature	r
MLC	0.211
DEPC	0.284
IPC	-0.344
IPCn1	-0.386
IPCn2	-0.429
IPCn3	-0.462

Table 3: Correlation coefficients (rs) between the features derived from structural events with human scores averaged on test takers

Table 3 reports on the correlation coefficient (r) between the proposed features derived from structural events with holistic scores. Relying on three simple structural event annotations, i.e., clause boundaries, dependent clauses, and interruption points in speech disfluencies, some promising correlations between features with holistic scores were found. Between the two syntactic complexity features, the DEPC has a higher correlation with holistic scores than the MLC ($0.284 > 0.211$). It appears that a measurement about clauses' embedding profile is more informative about a speaker's proficiency level. Second, compared to features measuring syntactic complexity, the feature measuring the disfluency profile is better to predict human holistic scores on this non-native data set. For example, IPC has a r of -0.344, which is better than the features about clause lengths or embedding. Finally, by jointly using the structural events related to clauses and disfluencies, we can further achieve a further improved r. Compared to IPC, IPCn3 has a relative 34.30% correlation increase. This is consistent with our idea of reducing utterance-complexity's impact on disfluency-related features.

7 Discussion

In most current automatic speech assessment systems, features derived from recognized words, such as delivery features about speaking rate, pause information, and accuracy related to word identities, have been widely used to assess non-native speech from fluency and accuracy points of view. However, information beyond recognized words, e.g., the structure of clauses and disfluencies, has only received limited attention. Although several previous SLA studies used features derived from structural events to measure speaking proficiency, these studies were limited and the findings from them were difficult to directly apply to on large-scale standard tests.

In this paper, using a large-sized data set collected in the TPO speaking test, we conducted an sophisticated annotation of structural events, including boundaries and types of clauses and disfluencies, from transcriptions of spontaneous speech test responses. A series of features were derived from these structural event annotations and were evaluated according to their correlations with holistic scores. We found that disfluency-related features have higher correlations to human holistic scores than features about syntactic complexity, which confirms the result reported in (Mizera, 2006). In spontaneous speech utterances, simple syntactic structure tends to be utilized by speakers. This is in contrast to sophisticated syntactic structure appearing in writing. This may cause that complexity-related features are poor at predicting fluency scores. On the other hand, disfluencies, a pattern unique to spontaneous speech, were found to play a more important role in indicating speaking proficiency levels.

Although syntactic complexity features were not highly indicative of holistic scores, they were useful to further improve disfluency-related features' correlation with holistic scores. By normalizing IPC using measurements representing syntactic complexity, we can highlight contributions from speakers' proficiency levels. Therefore, in our experiment, IPCn3 shows a 34.30% relative improvement in its correlation coefficient with human holistic scores over the original IPC.

The study reported in this paper suggests promise that structural events beyond speech recognition results can be utilized to measure non-native speaker proficiency levels. Recently, in the NLP research field, an increasing amount of effort has been made on structural event detection in spontaneous speech (Ostendorf et al., 2008). Therefore, such progress can benefit the study of automatic estimation of structural events on non-native speech data.

For our future research plan, first, we will investigate automatically detecting these structural events from speech transcriptions and recognition hypotheses. Second, the features derived from the obtained structural events will be used to augment the features in automatic speech assessment research to provide a wider construct coverage than fluency and pronunciation features do.

References

B. Azar. 2003. *Fundamentals of English grammar*. Pearson Longman, White Plains, NY, 3rd edition.

P. Foster, A. Tonkyn, and G. Wigglesworth. 2000. Measuring spoken language: A unit for all reasons. *Applied Linguistics*, 21(3):354.

K. W. Hunt. 1970. Syntactic maturity in school children and adults. In *Monographs of the Society for Research in Child Development*. University of Chicago Press, Chicago, IL.

N. Iwashita. 2006. Syntactic complexity measures and their relation to oral proficiency in Japanese as a foreign language. *Language Assessment Quarterly: An International Journal*, 3(2):151–169.

P. Lennon. 1990. Investigating fluency in EFL: A quantitative approach. *Language Learning*, 40(3):387–417.

Y. Liu. 2004. *Structural Event Detection for Rich Transcription of Speech*. Ph.D. thesis, Purdue University.

G. J. Mizera. 2006. *Working memory and L2 oral fluency*. Ph.D. thesis, University of Pittsburgh.

L. Neumeyer, H. Franco, V. Digalakis, and M. Weintraub. 2000. Automatic Scoring of Pronunciation Quality. *Speech Communication*, 30:83–93.

L. Ortega. 2003. Syntactic complexity measures and their relationship to L2 proficiency: A research synthesis of college-level L2 writing. *Applied Linguistics*, 24(4):492.

M. Ostendorf et al. 2008. Speech segmentation and spoken document processing. *Signal Processing Magazine, IEEE*, 25(3):59–69, May.

M. Roll, J. Frid, and M. Horne. 2007. Measuring syntactic complexity in spontaneous spoken Swedish. *Language and Speech*, 50(2):227.

E. Shriberg, A. Stolcke, D. Hakkani-Tur, and G. Tur. 2000. Prosody-based automatic segmentation of speech into sentences and topics. *Speech Communication*, 32(1-2):127–154.

S. Yoon. 2009. *Automated assessment of speech fluency for L2 English learners*. Ph.D. thesis, University of Illinois at Urbana-Champaign.

K. Zechner, D. Higgins, and Xiaoming Xi. 2007. SpeechRater: A Construct-Driven Approach to Scoring Spontaneous Non-Native Speech. In *Proc. SLaTE*.

A Human-Computer Collaboration Approach to Improve Accuracy of an Automated English Scoring System

Jee Eun Kim
Hankuk University of Foreign Studies
Seoul, Korea
jeeeunk@hufs.ac.kr

Kong Joo Lee
Chungnam National University
Daejeon, Korea
kjoolee@cnu.ac.kr

Abstract

This paper explores an issue of redundant errors reported while automatically scoring English learners' sentences. We use a human-computer collaboration approach to eliminate redundant errors. The first step is to automatically select candidate redundant errors using PMI and RFC. Since those errors are detected with different IDs although they represent the same error, the candidacy cannot be confirmed automatically. The errors are then handed over to human experts to determine the candidacy. The final candidates are provided to the system and trained with a decision tree. With those redundant errors eliminated, the system accuracy has been improved.

1 Introduction

An automated English scoring system analyzes a student sentence and provides a score and feedback to students. The performance of a system is evaluated based on the accuracy of the score and the relevance of the feedback.

The system described in this paper scores English sentences composed by Korean students learning English. A detailed explanation of the system is given in (Kim et al., 2007). The scores are calculated from three different phases including word, syntax and mapping, each of which is designed to assign 0~2 points. Three scores are added up to generate the final score. A spelling error, a plural form error, and a confusable word error are considered as typical word errors. A subject verb agreement error, a word order error and relative clause error are typical examples of syntactic errors. Even when a student sentence is perfectly correct in lexical and syntactic level, it may fail to convey what is meant by the question. Such sentences are evaluated as grammatical, but cannot be a correct answer for the question. In this case, the errors can only be recognized by comparing a student sentence with its correct answers. The differences between a student answer and one of the answers can be considered as mapping errors.

These three phases are independent from one another since they use different processing method, and refer different information. Independency of three phases causes some problems.

(Ex1) *Correct answer*: The earth is bigger than the moon. *Student answer*: The earth is small than the Moon.	
Err1: MODIFIER_COMP_ERR|4-7|	syntactic
Err2: LEXICAL_ERROR|4|	mapping

(Ex1) is an example of error reports provided to a student. The following two lines in (Ex1) show the error information detected from the student answer by the system. Err1 in (Ex1) reports a comparative form error of an adjective 'small', which covers the 4 ~ 7th words of the student sentence. Err2 indicates that the 4th word 'small' of the student sentence is different from that of the answer sentence. The difference was identified by comparing the student sentence and the answer sentence. Err1 was detected at the syntactic phase whereas Err2 was at the mapping phase. These two errors points to the same word, but have been reported as different errors.

(Ex2) *Correct answer*: She is too weak to carry the bag. *Student answer*: She is too weak to carry the her bag.	
Err1: EXTRA_DET_ERR|7-9|	syntactic
Err2: UNNECESSARY_NODE_ERR|8|(her)	mapping

Similarly, Err1 in (Ex2) reports an incorrect use of an article at the 7~9th words. The syntactic analysis recognizes that 'the' and 'her' cannot occur consecutively, but it is not capable of determine which one to eliminate. Err2, on the other hand, pinpoints 'her' as an incorrectly used word by comparing the student sentence and the answer sentence.

(Ex1) and (Ex2) have presented the errors which are detected at different processing phases,

Proceedings of the NAACL HLT 2010 Fifth Workshop on Innovative Use of NLP for Building Educational Applications, pages 80–83,
Los Angeles, California, June 2010.

but represent the same error. Since these redundant errors are a hindering factor to calculate accurate scores, one of the errors has to be removed. The proposed system deals with 70 error types; 16 for word, 46 for syntax, and 14 for mapping. In this paper, we have adopted a human-computer collaboration approach by which linguistic experts assist the system to decide which one of the redundant errors should be removed.

2 Redundant Errors

The system-detected errors are reported in the following format:

Error_ ID | Error_ Position | Error_Correction_Info

Each error report is composed of three fields which are separated by '|'. The first field contains error identification. The second includes the numbers indicating where the error is detected in a student input sentence. For example, if the field has number "5-7", it can be interpreted as the input sentence has an error covering from the 5th word to 7th word. Since syntactic errors are usually detected at a phrasal level, the position of an error covers more than one word. The third field may or may not be filled with a value, depending on the type of an error. When it has a value, it is mostly a suggestion, i.e. a corrected string which is formed by comparing a student sentence with its corresponding correct answer.

2.1 Definition of Redundant Errors

(Condition 1) The errors should share an error position.

(Condition 2) The errors should be detected from different error process phases.

(Condition 3) The errors should represent linguistically the same phenomenon.

(Condition 1) implies that the two errors must deal with one or more common words. The position is indicated on the student sentence. However, there are some exceptions in displaying the position. An example of the exception is 'OBLIGATORY_NODE_MISSING_ERR' and 'OPTIONAL_NODE_MISSING_ERR' which are mapping errors. Since these errors are detected when a certain word is missing from a student input but included in the answer, the position is indicated on the answer sentence. Err5 and Err6 from (Ex3) represent the case. Error position '(7)' and '(8)' [1] means that the 7th and 8th word of the answer sentence, 'to' and 'our' are missing, respectively. When an error position points to an answer sentence not a student sentence, the error cannot be checked with whether it includes the words shared with the errors whose positions indicate the student sentence. In this case, the error is assumed to have shared words with all the other errors; Err5 and Err6 are considered containing shared words with Err 1~4 in (Ex3).

(Ex3) *Correct answer*: She is a teacher who came to our school last week. *Student answer*: She is a teacher who come school last week.	
Err1: CONFUSABLE_WORD_ERR|9|week	word
Err2: SUBJ_VERB_AGR_ERR|3-7|	syntactic
Err3: VERB_SUBCAT_ERR|6-7|	syntactic
Err4: TENSE_UNMATCHED_ERR|6|came[past]	mapping
Err5: OPTIONAL_NODE_MISSING_ERR|(7)|to	mapping
Err6: OPTIONAL_NODE_MISSING_ERR|(8)|our	mapping

Err1 and Err2 from (Ex3) cannot be redundant errors since they do not share an error position and accordingly do not satisfy Condition 1. Err2 and Err3 share error positions 6~7, but they are not also considered as redundant errors since both of them were detected at the same process phase, the syntactic phase. Err2 and Err4 satisfy both Condition 1 and 2, but fail to meet Condition 3. Err2 represents the subject-predicate agreement error whereas Err4 points out a tense error. In comparison, Err3 and Err5 are legitimate candidates of "redundant errors" since they satisfy all the conditions. They share error positions, but were detected from different error process phases, the syntactic phase and the mapping phase, respectively. They also deal with the same linguistic phenomenon that a verb "*come*" does not have a transitive sense but requires a prepositional phrase led by "*to*".

2.2 Detection of Redundant Errors

Two errors need to satisfy all the conditions mentioned in section 2.1 in order to be classified as redundant errors. The system's detecting process began with scoring 14,892 student answers. From the scoring result, the candidates which met Condition 1 and 2 were selected. In the following subsections, we have described how to determine the final redundant errors using the system in collaboration with human's efforts.

---

[1] Error positions in answer sentences are marked with a number surrounded by a pair of parenthesis.

2.2.1 Selection of the Candidates

The system selected candidate errors which satisfied Condition 1 and 2 among the student sentences. For example, Table 1 presents 8 candidates extracted from (Ex3).

1	CONFUSABLE_WORD_ERR|9|week OPTIONAL_NODE_MISSING_ERR|(7)|to
2	CONFUSABLE_WORD_ERR|9|week OPTIONAL_NODE_MISSING_ERR|(8)|our
3	SUBJ_VERB_AGR_ERR|3-7| TENSE_UNMATCHED_ERR|6|came[past]
4	SUBJ_VERB_AGR_ERR|3-7| OPTIONAL_NODE_MISSING_ERR|(7)|to
5	SUBJ_VERB_AGR_ERR|3-7| OPTIONAL_NODE_MISSING_ERR|(8)|our
6	VERB_SUBCAT_ERR|6-7| TENSE_UNMATCHED_ERR|6|came[past]
7	VERB_SUBCAT_ERR|6-7| OPTIONAL_NODE_MISSING_ERR|(7)|to
8	VERB_SUBCAT_ERR|6-7| OPTIONAL_NODE_MISSING_ERR|(8)|our

Table 1 **Candidate pairs of errors extracted from (Ex3).**

As a result of the selection process, the total of 150,419 candidate pairs was selected from 14,892 scoring results of the student sentences.

2.2.2 Filtering Candidate Errors

The candidates extracted through the process mentioned in 2.2.1 were classified based on their error identifications only, without considering error position and error correction information. 150,419 pairs of the errors were assorted into 657 types. The frequency of each type of the candidates was then calculated. These candidate errors were filtered by applying PMI (Pointwise Mutual Information) and RFC (Relative Frequency Count) (Su et al., 1994).

$$PMI(E_1, E_2) = \log \frac{P(E_1, E_2)}{P(E_1)P(E_2)} \qquad (1)$$

$$RFC(E_1, E_2) = \frac{freq(E_1, E_2)}{\overline{freq}} \qquad (2)$$

PMI is represented by a number indicating how frequently two errors E_1 and E_2 occur simultaneously. RFC refers to relative frequency against average frequency of the total candidates. The filtering equation is as follows:

$$PMI(E_1, E_2) \times RFC(E_1, E_2) \geq k \qquad (3)$$

Using this equation, the system filtered the candidates whose value was above the threshold k. For this experiment, 0.4 was assigned to k and 111 error types were selected.

2.2.3 Human Collaborated Filtering

Filtered 111 error types include 29,588 candidate errors; on the average 278 errors per type. These errors were then handed over to human experts[2] to confirm their candidacy. They checked Condition 3 against each candidate. The manually filtered result was categorized into three classes as shown in Table 2.

Class A: (number: 20)	(DET_NOUN_CV_ERR,DET_UNMATCHED_ERR) (EXTRA_DET_ERR, DET_UNMATCHED_ERR) (MODIFIER_COMP_ERR, FORM_UNMATCHED_ERR) (MISSPELLING_ERR, LEXICAL_ERR) ...
Class B: (number: 47)	(SUBJ_VERB_AGR_ERR,TENSE_UNMATCHED_ERR) (AUX_MISSING_ERR, UNNECESSARY_NODE_ERR) (CONJ_MISSING_ERR, DET_UNMATCHED_ERR) ...
Class C: (number: 44)	(VERB_FORM_ERR, ASPECT_UNMATCHED_ERR) (VERB_ING_FORM_ERR, TENSE_UNMATCHED_ERR) (EXTRA_PREP_ERR, UNNECESSARY_NODE_ERR) ...

Table 2 **Classes of Human Collaborated Filtering.**

Class A satisfies Condition 1 and 2 and is confirmed as redundant errors. When a pair of errors is a member of Class A, one of the errors can be removed. Class B also meets Condition 1 and 2, but is eliminated from the candidacy because human experts have determined they did not deal with the same linguistic phenomenon. Each error of Class B has to be treated as unique. With respect to Class C, the errors cannot be determined its candidacy with the information available at this stage. Additional information is required to determine the redundancy.

2.2.4 Final Automated Filtering Using Decision Rules

In order to confirm the errors of Class C as redundant, additional information is necessary.

(Ex4) <u>*Correct answer*</u>: I don't know why she went there. <u>*Student answer*</u>: I don't know why she go to their.	
Err1: CONFUSABLE_WORD_ERR|8|there	word
Err2: SUBJ_VERB_AGR_ERR|6|went[3S]	syntactic
Err3: **EXTRA_PREP_ERR|6-8|**	syntactic
Err4: **UNNECESSARY_NODE_ERR|7|(to)**	mapping
Err5: TENSE_UNMATCHED_ERR|6|went[past]	mapping

(Ex5) <u>*Correct answer*</u>: Would you like to come? <u>*Student answer*</u>: you go to home?	
Err1: FIRST_WORD_CASE_ERR|1|	word
Err2: **EXTRA_PREP_ERR|3-4|**	syntactic
Err3:OBLIGATORY_NODE_MISSING_ERR|(1,3)| Would _ like	mapping
Err4: **UNNECESSARY_NODE_ERR|4|(home)**	mapping
Err5: LEXICAL_ERR|2|come	mapping

[2] They are English teachers who have a linguistic background and teaching experiences of 10 years or more.

EXTRA_PREP_ERR' and 'UNNECESSARY_ NODE_ERR' were selected as a candidate from both (Ex4) and (Ex5) through the steps mentioned in section 2.2.1 ~ 2.2.3. The pair from (Ex4) is a redundant error, but the one from (Ex5) is a false alarm. (Ex4) points out a preposition '*to*' as an unnecessary element whereas (Ex5) indicates a noun '*home*' as incorrect.

To determine the finalist of redundant errors, we have adopted a decision tree. To train the decision tree, we have chosen a feature set for a pair of errors (E_1, E_2) as follows.

(1) The length of shared words in E1 and E2 divided by the length of a shorter sentence (*shared_length*)
(2) The length of non-shared words in E1 and E2 divided by the length of a shorter sentence. (*non_shared_length*)
(3) The Error_Correction_Info of E1 (*E1.Correction_Info*)
(4) The Error_Correction_Info of E2 (*E2.Correction_Info*)
(5) Edit distance value between correction string of E1 and E2 (*edit_distance*)
(6) Error Position of E1 (*E1.pos*)
(7) Error Position of E2 (*E2.pos*)
(8) Difference of Error positions of E1 and E2 (*diff_error_pos*)

12,178 pairs of errors for 44 types in Class C were used to train a decision tree. We used CART (Breiman et al., 1984) to extract decision rules. The followings show a part of the decision rules to eliminate redundant errors from Class C.

E1=CONJ_MISSING_ERR
E2=OPTIONAL_NODE_MISSING_ERR
If E2.Correction_Info='conj' ***and*** E2.pos=1 ***then*** redundant_error

E1=EXTRA_PREP_ERR, E2=UNNECESSARY_NODE_ERR
If E2.Correction_Info='prep' ***and*** E2.pos=1 ***then*** redundant_error

E1=VERB_SUBCAT_ERR,
E2=OPTIONAL_NODE_MISSING_ERR
If diff_error_pos <=3 ***and*** E2.Correction_Info={'prep' , 'adv'}
then redundant_error

E1=VERB_ING_FORM_ERR, E2=TENSE_UNMATCHED_ERR
If E2.Correction_Info='verb-ing' ***then*** redundant_error
...

The errors are removed according to a priority specified in the rules. The syntactic phase is assigned with the highest priority since syntactic errors have the most extensive coverage which is identified at a phrasal level. On the other hand, the lowest priority is given to the mapping phase because mapping errors are detected through a simple word-to-word comparison of a student input with the correct answer.

3 Evaluation

We evaluated the accuracy of determining redundant errors. Table 3 presents the results. The evaluation was performed on 200 sentences which were not included in the training data. Even though the redundancy of the pairs of errors in Class A and Class B are determined by the human expert, the accuracies of both classes did not reach 100% because the errors detected by the system were incorrect. The total accuracy including Class A, B, and C was 90.2%.

	Class A	Class B	Class C
Accuracy	94.1%	98.0%	82.3%

Table 3: **The accuracy**

The performance of our automated scoring system was measured using exact agreement (Attali and Burstein, 2006) of the final scores calculated by the system and human raters. The overall performance was improved by 2.6% after redundant errors were removed.

4 Conclusion

This paper has introduced a human collaborated filtering method to eliminate redundant errors reported during automated scoring. Since scoring processes are performed through three separate phases including word, syntax and mapping, some of the errors are redundantly reported with different IDs. In addition, it is almost impossible to predict every type of errors that could occur in student answers. Because of these issues, it is not easy for the system to automatically determine which errors are reported redundantly, or to estimate all the possible redundant errors. As a solution to these problems, we have adopted a human assisted approach. The performance has been improved after redundant errors were removed with the approach implemented in the system.

References

Jee Eun Kim, K. J. Lee and K. A. Jin. 2007. Building an Automated Scoring System for a Single Sentence. *Korea Information Processing Society* Vol.4, No.3 (in Korean).

Keh-Yih Su, Ming-Wen We and Jing-Shin Chang. 1994. A Corpus-based Approach to Automatic Compound Extraction, In *Proceedings of the ACL 94.*

Leo Breiman, Jerome Friedman, Charles J. Stone, and R.A. Olshen. 1984. *Classification and Regression Trees.* Monterey, Calif., U.S.A.: Wadsworth, Inc.

Yigal Attali and Jill Burstein. 2006. Automated Essay Scoring with e-rater® V.2.

Towards Identifying Unresolved Discussions in Student Online Forums

Jihie Kim, Jia Li, and Taehwan Kim
University of Southern California
Information Sciences Institute
4676 Admiralty Was, Marina del Rey, CA, U.S.A
{jihie, jiali, taehwan}@isi.edu

Abstract

Automatic tools for analyzing student online discussions are highly desirable for providing better assistance and promoting discussion participation. This paper presents an approach for identifying student discussions with unresolved issues or unanswered questions. In order to handle highly incoherent data, we perform several data processing steps. We then apply a two-phase classification algorithm. First, we classify "speech acts" of individual messages to identify the roles that the messages play, such as question, issue raising, and answers. We then use the resulting speech acts as features for classifying discussion threads with unanswered questions or unresolved issues. We performed a preliminary analysis of the classifiers and the system shows an average F score of 0.76 in discussion thread classification.

1 Introduction*

Online discussion boards have become a popular and important medium for distance education. Students use discussion forums to collaborate, to exchange information, and to seek answers to problems from their instructors and classmates. Making use of the dialog to assess student understanding is an open research problem. As the class size increases and online interaction becomes heavier, automatic tools for analyzing student discussions are highly desirable for providing better assistance and promoting discussion participation. In this paper, we present an approach for automatically identifying discussions that have unresolved issues or unanswered questions. The resulting discussions can be reported to instructors for further assistance.

We present a two-phase machine learning approach where the first phase identifies high level dialogue features (speech acts such as question, issue raising, answer, and acknowledgement) that are appropriate for assessing student interactions. The second phase uses speech acts as features in creating thread classifiers that identify discussions with unanswered questions or unresolved issues. We also describe an approach where thread classifiers are created directly from the features in discussion messages. The preliminary results indicate that although the direct learning approach can identify threads with unanswered questions well, SA based learning provide a little better results in identifying threads with issues and threads with unresolved issues.

2 Modeling Student Discussions

Our study takes place in the context of an undergraduate course discussion board that is an integral component of an Operating Systems course in the Computer Science Department at the University of Southern California. We obtain our data from an existing online discussion board that hosts student technical discussions. Total 291 discussion threads (219 for training and 72 for test) with 1135 messages (848 for training and 287 for test) from two semesters' discussions were used for this study. 168 students participated in the discussions.

2.1 Discussion Threads

Unlike prototypical collaborative argumentation where a limited number of members take part in the conversation with a strong focus on solving specific problems, student online discussions have much looser conversational structure, possibly involving multiple anonymous discussants. Student

*

Proceedings of the NAACL HLT 2010 Fifth Workshop on Innovative Use of NLP for Building Educational Applications, pages 84–91,
Los Angeles, California, June 2010.

discussions are very informal and noisy with respect to grammar, syntax and punctuation. There is a lot of variance in the way that students present similar information. Messages about programming assignments include various forms of references to programming code. Figure 1 shows an example discussion thread that is relatively technical and formal. The raw data include humorous messages and personal announcements as well as technical questions and answers.

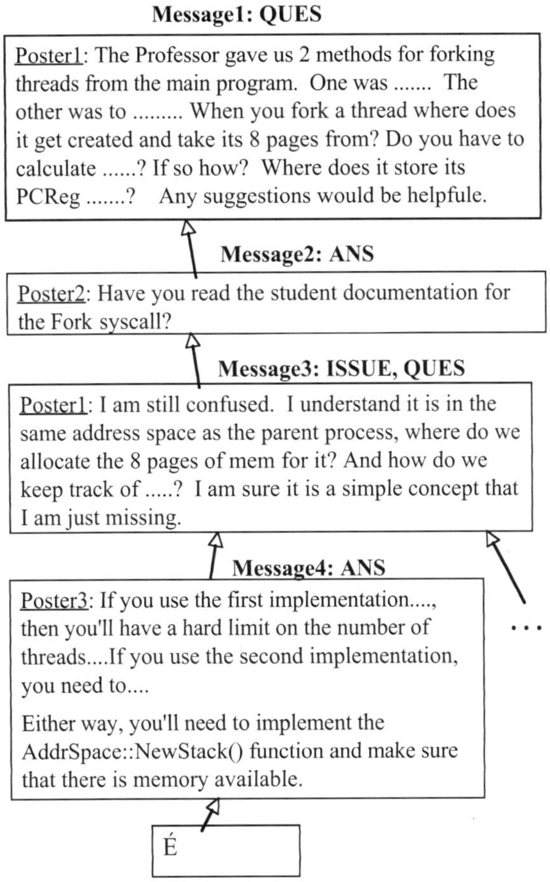

Figure 1. An example discussion thread

The average number of messages per discussion thread in our undergraduate course is 3.9, and many discussion threads contain only two or three messages. Discussions often start with a question from a student on a project or an assignment. In some cases, the discussion ends with an answer that follows the question. In some other cases, the original poster may raise additional issues or ask questions about the answer. The discussion can continue with the following answer from another student as in Figure 1. However, sometimes the discussion ends with hanging issues or questions without an answer.

2.2 Speech Acts in messages: Identifying roles that a message plays

For conversation analysis, we adopted the theory of Speech Acts (SAs) to capture relations between messages (Austin, 1962; Searle, 1969). Each message within a discussion thread may play a different role. A message could include a question for a particular problem, or it could contain an answer or suggestion with respect to a previous question in the thread. Messages can include question, answer, acknowledgement, and objection. Since SAs are useful in understanding contributions made by students in discussions, and are natural indicators for unanswered questions or unresolved issues, we use SAs as features for classifying discussion threads in a two phase learning as described below.

Table 1. Speech Act Categories and Kappa values

SA Category	Description	kappa
QUES	A question about a problem, including question about a previous message	0.94
ANS	A simple or complex answer to a previous question. Suggestion or advice	0.72
ISSUE	Report misunderstanding, unclear concepts or issues in solving problems	0.88
Pos-Ack	An acknowledgement, compliment or support in response to a prev. message	0.87
Neg-Ack	A correction or objection (or complaint) to/on a previous message	0.85

We divide message roles into several SA categories, extending the approaches presented in (Kim et al., 2006; Kim and Ravi 2007). We focus on the categories that are relevant to the problem of identifying discussion threads with unanswered question or unresolved issues.

The message might contain a question about a particular problem (QUES) or report a misunderstanding, unclear concepts or issues in solving a problem (ISSUE). It might propose an answer or suggestion with respect to a previous question in the thread (ANS). Finally, a message might acknowledge the previous message with support

(Pos-Ack) or show disagreement or objection (Neg-Ack). SAs relate a pair of messages that has a 'reply-to' relation. A pair of messages can be labeled with multiple SAs, and a message can have multiple SAs with more than one messages. This allows us to capture various relations among messages. Table 1 describes the categories we are focusing on and the kappa values from two annotators. Figure 1 shows SA relations between message pairs.

During annotation of the corpus, the annotators marked the cues that are relevant to a particular SA category as well as the SA categories themselves. Such information provides hints on the kinds of features that are useful. We also interviewed the annotators to capture additional cues or indicators that they used during the annotation. We iterated with several different annotation approaches until we reach enough agreement among the annotators on a new dataset that was not seen by the annotators before.

Table 2 shows the distribution statistics of each SA category among the whole training and test corpus. Since a message may have more than one SA, the percentage sum of all SAs doesn't equal to 1. As we can see, Pos-Ack and Neg-Ack are experiencing lacking data problem which is one of the challenges we are facing for SA classification.

Table 2. Statistics for each Speech Act Category

SA Category	Training set		Test set	
	# of msgs	Percentage	# of msgs	Percentage
QUES	469	55.31%	146	50.87%
ANS	508	59.91%	176	61.32%
ISSUE	136	16.03%	46	16.03%
Pos-Ack	78	9.20%	30	10.45%
Neg-Ack	23	2.71%	8	2.79%

3 Message Speech Act Classifiers

In this section, we first describe how raw discussion data is processed and show the features generated from the data, and we then present the current SA classifiers.

3.1 Discussion Data Pre-processing

Besides typical data preprocessing steps, such as stemming and filtering, which are taken by most NLP systems, our system performs additional steps to reduce noise and variance (Ravi and Kim 2007).

We first remove the text from previous messages that is automatically inserted by the discussion board system starting with righ angle braket (>) when the user clicks on a *"Reply to"* button. We also apply a simple stemming algorithm that removes *"s"* and *"es"* for plurals. Apostrophes are also converted to their original forms. E.g., "I'm" is converted to "I am". For discussions on programming assignment, the discussion included programming code fragments. Each section of programming code or code fragment is replaced with a single term called code. Similar substitution patterns were used for a number of categories like filetype extensions (*".html", ".c", ".c++", ".doc"*), URL links and others. Students also tend to use informal words (e.g. *"ya", "yeah", "yup"*). We substitute some of such words with one form ("yes"). For words like *"which", "where", "when", "who" and "how"*, we used the term categ_wh. We do not replace pronouns ("I", "we", "they",) since they may be useful for identifying some SAs. For example, "You can" may be a cue for ANS but "I can" may not.

We also apply a simple sentence divider with simple cues (punctuation and white spaces such as newline) in order to captures the locations of the features in the message, such as cue words in the first sentence vs. cues in the last sentence.

3.2 Features for Speech Act Classification

We have used six different types of features based on input from the annotators.

F1: cue phases and their positions: In addition to SAs (e.g. QUES), the human annotators marked the parts within the message (cue phrases or sentences), which helped them identify the SAs in the message. In order to overcome data sparseness, we generate features from the marked phrases. That is, from each phrase, we extract all the unigrams, bigrams, trigrams (sequence of 1/2/3 words) and add them to the feature set. We also added two separate unigrams, three separate unigrams and a unigram and a bigram combinations since the annotations in the training data indicated that they could be a useful pattern. All the cues including separate cues such as two unigrams are captured and used for a single sentence. Positions of the cues are included since in longer messages the cues in the beginning sentences and the ones in the end sentences can indicate different SAs. For example, THANK in the beginning indicates a positive answer but THANK in latter part of the message usually means politeness (thank in advance).

F2: Message Position: Position of current message within the discussion thread (e.g. the first message, the last message, or middle in the thread).

F3: Previous Message Information: SAs in the previous message that the current message is replying to.

F4: Poster Class: Student or Instructor.

F5: Poster Change: Was the current message posted by the same person who posted the message that the current message is replying to?

F6: Message Length: Values include Short(1-5words), Medium(6-30 words), and Long(>30 words).

F1 is a required feature since the annotators indicated cues as useful feature in most cases. All the others are optional.

3.3 Speech Act Classifiers

We applied SVM in creating binary classifiers for each SA category using Chang and Lin (2001). Also, Transformation-based Learning (TBL) was applied as it has been successfully used in spoken dialogue act classification (Samuel 2000; Brill 1995). It starts with the unlabeled corpus and learns the best sequence of admissible "transformation rules" that must be applied to the training corpus to minimize the error for the task. The generated rules are easy to understand and useful for debugging the features used. TBL results are also used in generating *dependencies* among SA categories for **F3**, i.e. which SAs tend to follow which other SAs[1], as describe below.

<u>SA Classification with TBL</u>

Each rule $Rule_i$ is composed of two parts - (1) $RuleLHS_i$ - A combination of features that should be checked for applicability to the current message (2) $RuleTAG_i$ - SA tag to apply, if the feature combination is applicable to the current message.

[1] It is possible to collect related clues from SVM with distribution of feature values and information gain although dependencies can be easily recognized in TBL rules.

$$Rule_i :: RuleLHS_i \Rightarrow RuleTAG_i$$

Where $RuleLHS_i = X_i$

$$X_i \in X; (X \subseteq F1 \times F2 \times F3 \times F4 \times F5 \times F6)$$

The $RuleLHS_i$ component can be instantiated from all the combination of the features F1, …,F6. $RuleTAG_i$ is any SA (single SA) chosen from a list of all the SA categories. An example rule used in Speech Act learning is shown below:

Rule1 :: IF cue-phrase = {"not", "work"}
& poster-info = Student
& post-length = Long
=> ISSUE

Rule1 means if the post contains two unigrams "not" and "work", the poster is a student, and the post length is long, then the Speech Act for the post is ISSUE.

We apply each rule in the potential rule set on all the posts in the training corpus and transform the post label if the post is applicable. The rule with highest improvement by F score is selected into the optimal rule set and moved from the potential rule set. The iteration continues until there is no significant improvement with any rule.

The training corpus was divided into 3 parts for 3-fold cross validation. The rules from 3 rule sets are merged and sorted by weighted Mean Reciprocal Rank (MRR) (Voorhees, 2001). For example, if we have 5 rules among 3 rule sets as follows,

Rule set 1 (0.85 on test): R1 R2 R3
Rule set 2 (0.88 on test): R2 R1 R4
Rule set 3 (0.79 on test): R1 R4 R5

For R1, we calculate the weighted MRR as (0.85*1 + 0.88*(1/2) + 0.79*1) / 3. After sorting, we get top N rules from the merged rule set. Table 3 shows some of the rules learned.

Table 3. TBL rule examples

IF cue-phrase = {"?"} => QUES
IF cue-phrase = {"yes you can"} & poster-info = Instructor & post-length = Medium => ANS
IF cue-phrase = {"yes"} & cue-position = CP_BEGIN & prev-SA = QUES => ANS
IF cue-phrase = {"not know"}

& poster-info = student
& poster-change = YES => ISSUE

Based on the rules generated from TBL, we analyze dependencies among the SA categories for **F3** (previous message SAs). In TBL rules, ANS depends on ISSUE and QUES, i.e. some ANS rules have QUES and ISSUE for **F3**. Also Pos-Ack and Neg-Ack tend to follow ANS. Both SVM and TBL classifiers use this information during testing. That is, we apply independent classifiers first and then use dependent classifiers according to the dependency order as following:

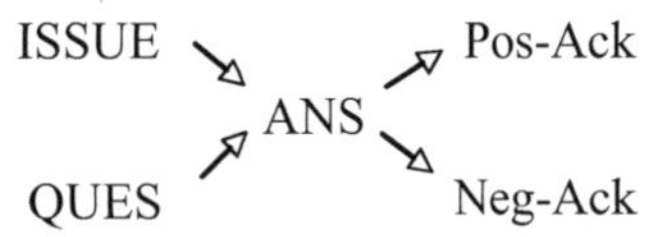

Currently there is no loop in the selected rules but we plan to address potential issues with loops in SA dependencies.

SA Classification with SVM

Table 4. Some of the top selected features by Information Gain

SA Category	Top features
QUES	"?" POST_POSITION "_category_wh_ … ?" PREV_SA_FIRST_NONE "to … ?"
ANS	POST_POSITION PREV_SA_QUESTION "?" POSTER_INFO
ISSUE	POSTER_INFO "not … sure" POST_POSITION FEATURE_LENGTH "error"
Pos-Ack	PREV_SA_ANSWER POST_POSITION PREV_SA_FIRST_NONE "thanks" & cue-position = CP_BEGIN "ok" & cue-position = CP_BEGIN
Neg-Ack	"yes, " ", but" POST_POSITION ", but" "are … wrong"

Given all the combination of the features F1,…, F6, we use Information Gain (Yang and Pederson 1997) for pruning the feature space and selecting features. For each Speech Act, we sort all the features (lexical and non-lexical) by Information Gain and use the top N (=200) features. Table 4 shows the top features selected by Information Gain. The resulting features are used in representing a message in a vector format.

We did 5-fold cross validation in the training. RBF (Radial Basis Function) is used as the kernel function. We performed grid search to get the best parameter (C and gamma) in training and applied them to the test corpus.

Table 5. SA classification results

SA Category	SVM			TBL		
	Prec.	Recall	F score	Prec.	Recall	F score
QUES	0.95	0.90	0.94	0.96	0.91	0.95
ANS	0.87	0.80	0.85	0.83	0.64	0.78
ISSUE	0.65	0.54	0.62	0.46	0.76	0.50
Pos-Ack	0.57	0.44	0.54	0.58	0.56	0.57
Neg-Ack	0	0	0	0.5	0.38	0.47

Table 5 shows the current classification accuracies with SVM and TBL. The main reason that ISSUE, Pos-Ack and Neg-Ack show low scores is that they have relatively small number of examples (see statistics in Table 2). We plan to add more examples as we collect more discussion annotations. For thread classification described below, we use features with QUES, ANS, ISSUE and Pos_Ack only.

4 Identifying Discussions with Unanswered or Unresolved Questions: Thread Classification

Figure 2 shows typical patterns of interactions in our corpus. Many threads follow pattern (a) where the first message includes a question and the subsequent message provides an answer. In (b), after an answer, the student presents an additional question or misunderstanding (ISSUE), which is followed by another answer. Often students provide positive acknowledgement when an answer is satisfying. Pattern (c) covers cases for when the question is unanswered.

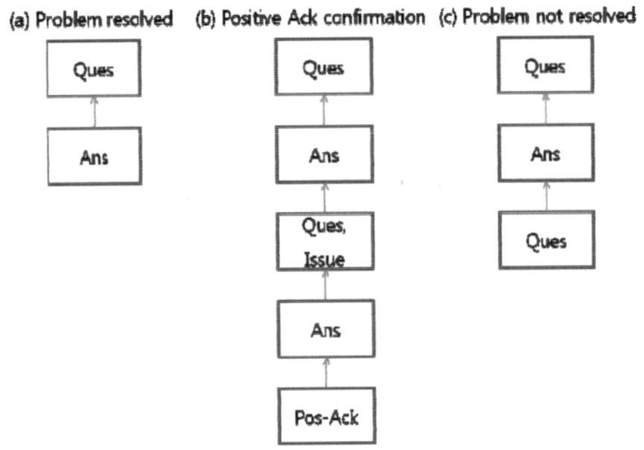

Figure 2. Example patterns in student discussion threads

We are interested in the following assessment questions.

(Q1) Were all questions answered? (Y/N)

(Q2) Were there any issues or confusion? (Y/N)

(Q3) Were those issues or confusions resolved? (Y/N)

There can be multiple questions, and Q1 is false if there is any question that does not have a corresponding answer. That is, even when some questions were resolved, it could still be False (not resolved) if some were not resolved. If Q2 is False (i.e. there is no issue or question), then Q3 is also False.

These questions are useful for distinguishing different interaction patterns, including threads with unanswered questions. In the second phase of learning, we use SA-based features. Our initial analysis of student interactions as above indicates that the following simple features can be useful in answering such questions:

(T-F1) Whether there was an [SA] in the thread

(T-F2) Whether the last message in the thread included [SA]

We used TBL rules for Pos-Ack and SVM classifiers for other SA categories because of relatively higher score of Pos-Ack from TBL and other categories from SVM. We use 8 (2 x 4) features created from T-F1 and T-F2. SVM settings are similar to the ones used in the SA classification.

Table 6 shows the thread classification results. We checked SVM classification results with human annotated SAs since they can show how useful SA-based features are (T-F1 and T-F2 in particular) in answering Q1—Q3. The results shown in Table 6-(a) indicate that the features (T-F1 and T-F2) are in fact useful for the questions.

When we used the SA classifiers and SVM in a pipeline, the system shows precisions (recalls) of 83%(84%), 77%(74%) and 68%(69%) for Q1, Q2, and Q3 respectively.

Table 6. Thread Classification Results

	Precision	Recall	F score
Q1	0.93	0.93	0.93
Q2	0.93	0.93	0.93
Q3	0.89	0.89	0.89

(a) Classification results with human annotated SAs

	Precision	Recall	F score
Q1	0.83	0.84	0.83
Q2	0.77	0.74	0.76
Q3	0.68	0.69	0.68

(b) SVM classification results with system generated SAs

The results with system generated SAs provide an average F score of 0.76. Although the ISSUE classifier has F score of 0.62, the score for Q2 is 0.76. Q2 checks one or more occurrences of ISSUE rather than identifying existence of ISSUE in a message, and it may become an easier problem when there are multiple occurrences of ISSUEs.

5 Direct Thread Classification without SAs

As an alternative to the SA-based two-phase learning, we crated thread classifiers directly from the features in discussion messages. We used SVM with the following features that we can capture directly from a discussion thread.

F1': cue phases and their positions in the thread: we use the same cue features in F1 but we use an optional thread level cue position: Last_message and Dont_Care. For example, for a given cue "ok", if it appears in the the last message of the thread, we generate two features, "ok"_Last_message and "ok"_Dont_Care.

Given a set of candidate features, we use Information Gain to select the top N (=200) features. The resulting features are used in creating vectors as described inS 3.3. Similar cross-validation and SVM settings are applied.

Table 7. Results from Direct Thread Classification

	Precision	Recall	F score
Q1	0.86	0.86	0.86
Q2	0.81	0.62	0.70
Q3	0.75	0.33	0.46

Table 7 shows the classification results. Although the direct learning approach can identify threads with unanswered questions well, SA based learning provides a little better results in identifying threads with issues (Q2) and unresolved issues (Q3). It seems that SA-based features may help performing more difficult tasks (e.g. assessment for ISSUEs in discussions) We need further investigation on different types of assessment tasks.

6 Related Work

Rhetorical Structure Theory (Mann and Thomson, 1988) based discourse processing has attracted much attention with successful applications in sentence compression and summarization. Most of the current work on discourse processing focuses on sentence-level text organization (Soricut and Marcu, 2003) or the intermediate step (Sporleder and Lapata, 2005). Analyzing and utilizing discourse information at a higher level, e.g., at the paragraph level, still remains a challenge to the natural language community. In our work, we utilize the discourse information at a message level.

There has been prior work on dialogue act analysis and associated surface cue words (Samuel 2000; Hirschberg and Litman 1993). There have also been Dialogue Acts modeling approaches for automatic tagging and recognition of conversational speech (Stolcke et al., 2000) and related work in corpus linguistics where machine learning techniques have been used to find conversational patterns in spoken transcripts of dialogue corpus (Shawar and Atwell, 2005). Although spoken dialogue is different from message-based conversation in online discussion boards, they are closely related to our thread analysis work, and we plan to investigate potential use of conversation patterns in spoken dialogue in threaded discussions.

Carvalho and Cohen (2005) present a dependency-network based collective classification method to classify email speech acts. However, estimated speech act labeling between messages is not sufficient for assessing contributor roles or identifying help needed by the participants. We included other features like participant profiles. Also our corpus consists of less informal student discussions rather than messages among project participants, which tend to be more technically coherent.

Requests and commitments of email exchange are analyzed in (Lampert et al., 2008). As in their analysis, we have a higher kappa value for questions than answers, and some sources of ambiguity in human annotations such as different forms of answers also appear in our data. However, student discussions tend to focus on problem solving rather than task request and commitment as in project management applications, and their data show different types of ambiguity due to different nature of participant interests.

There also has been work on non-traditional, qualitative assessment of instructional discourse (Graesser et al., 2005; McLaren et al., 2007; Boyer et al., 2008). The assessment results can be used in finding features for student thinking skills or level of understanding. Although the existing work has not been fully used for discussion thread analysis, we are investigating opportunities for using such features to cover additional discourse analysis capabilities. Similar approaches for classifying speech acts were investigated (Kim and Ravi 2007). Our work captures more features that are relevant to analyzing noisy student discussion threads and support a full automatic analysis of student discussions instead of manual generation of thread analysis rules.

7 Summary and Future Work

We have presented an approach for automatically classifying student discussions to identify discussions that have unanswered questions and need instructor attention. We applied a multi-phase learning approach, where the first phase classifies individual messages with SAs and the second phase classifies discussion threads with SA-based features. We also created thread classifiers directly from features in discussion messages. The preliminary results indicate that SA-based features may help difficult classification tasks. We plan to perform more analysis on different types of thread classification tasks.

We found that automatic classification of undergraduate student discussions is very challenging due to incoherence and noise in the data. Especially messages that contain long sentences, informal statements with uncommon words, answers in form of question, are difficult to classify. In order to use other SA categories such as Neg-Ack and analyze various types of student interactions, we plan to use more annotated discussion data.

A deeper assessment of online discussions requires a combination with other information such as discussion topics (Feng et al., 2006). For example, classification of discussion topics can be used in identifying topics that participants have more confusion about. Furthermore, such information can also be used in profiling participants such as identifying mentors or help seekers on a particular topic as in (Kim and Shaw 2009). We are investigating several extensions in order to generate more useful instructional tools.

Acknowledgments

This work was supported by National Science Foundation, CCLI Phase II grant (#0618859).

References

Austin, J., *How to do things with words*. 1962. Cambridge, Massachusetts: Harvard Univ. Press.

Boyer, K., Phillips, R., Wallis M., Vouk M., Lester, J., Learner Characteristics and Feedback in Tutorial Dialogue. 2008. *ACL workshop on Innovative Use of NLP for Building Educational Applications*.

Brill, E. 1962. Transformation-based error-driven learning and natural language processing: a case study in part-of-speech tagging. *Comput. Linguist.*, 21(4).

Carvalho, V.R. and Cohen, W.W. 2005. On the collective classification of email speech acts. *Proceedings of SIGIR*.

Chang, C.-C. and Lin, C.-J. 2001. *LIBSVM: a library for support vector machines*.

Feng, D., Kim, J., Shaw, E., Hovy E., 2006. Towards Modeling Threaded Discussions through Ontology-based Analysis. *Proceedings of National Conference on Artificial Intelligence*.

Graesser, A. C., Olney, A., Ventura, M., Jackson, G. T. 2005. AutoTutor's Coverage of Expectations during Tutorial Dialogue. *Proceedings of the FLAIRS Conference*.

Hirschberg, J. and Litman, D. 1993. Empirical Studies on the Disambiguation of Cue Phrases", *Computational Linguistics*, 19 (3).

Kim, J., Chern, G., Feng, D., Shaw, E., and Hovy, E. 2006. Mining and Assessing Discussions on the Web through Speech Act Analysis. *Proceedings of the ISWC'06 Workshop on Web Content Miningwith Human Language Technologies* (2006).

Kim J. and Shaw E. 2009. Pedagogical Discourse: Connecting Students to Past Discussions and Peer Mentors within an Online Discussion Board, *Innovative Applications of Artificial Intelligence Conference.*

Lampert, A., Dale, R., and Paris, C. 2008. The Nature of Requests and Commitments in Email Messages, *AAAI workshop on Enhanced Messaging*.

Mann, W.C. and Thompson, S.A. 1988. Rhetorical structure theory: towards a functional theory of text organization. Text: *An Interdisciplinary Journal for the Study of Text*, 8 (3).

McLaren, B. et al.,2007. Using Machine Learning Techniques to Analyze and Support Mediation of Student E - Discussions, *Proc. of AIED 2007.*

Ravi, S., Kim, J., 2007. Profiling Student Interactions in Threaded Discussions with Speech Act Classifiers. *Proceedings of AI in Education.*

Samuel, K. 2000.*An Investigation of Dialogue Act Tagging using Transformation-Based Learning*, PhD Thesis, University of Delaware.

Searle, J. 1969. *Speech Acts*. Cambridge: Cambridge Univ. Press.

Soricut, R. and Marcu, D. 2003. Sentence level discourse parsing using syntactic and lexical information. *Proceedings of HLT/NAACL-2003.*

Sporleder, C. and Lapata, M., 2005. Discourse chunking and its application to sentence compression. In *Proceedings of Human Language Technology conference – EMNLP.*

Stolcke, A. , Coccaro, N. , Bates, R. , Taylor, P. , et al., 2000. Dialogue act modeling for automatic tagging and recognition of conversational speech, *Computational Linguistics*, v.26 n.3.

Shawar, B. A. and Atwell, E. 2005. Using corpora in machine-learning chatbot systems." *International Journal of Corpus Linguistics*, vol. 10.

Witten, I. H., and Frank, E. 2005. *Data Mining: Practical machine learning tools and techniques,* 2nd Edition, Morgan Kaufmann, San Francisco.

Yang, Y. and Pedersen, J. 1997. A Comparative Study on Feature Selection in Text Categorization. *Proc. International Conference on Machine Learning*.

Off-topic essay detection using short prompt texts

Annie Louis
University of Pennsylvania
Philadelphia, PA 19104, USA
lannie@seas.upenn.edu

Derrick Higgins
Educational Testing Service
Princeton, NJ 08541, USA
dhiggins@ets.org

Abstract

Our work addresses the problem of predicting whether an essay is off-topic to a given prompt or question *without* any previously-seen essays as training data. Prior work has used similarity between essay vocabulary and prompt words to estimate the degree of on-topic content. In our corpus of opinion essays, prompts are very short, and using similarity with such prompts to detect off-topic essays yields error rates of about 10%. We propose two methods to enable better comparison of prompt and essay text. We automatically expand short prompts before comparison, with words likely to appear in an essay to that prompt. We also apply spelling correction to the essay texts. Both methods reduce the error rates during off-topic essay detection and turn out to be complementary, leading to even better performance when used in unison.

1 Introduction

It is important to limit the opportunity to submit uncooperative responses to educational software (Baker et al., 2009). We address the task of detecting essays that are irrelevant to a given prompt (essay question) when training data is *not* available and the prompt text is *very short*.

When example essays for a prompt are available, they can be used to learn word patterns to distinguish on-topic from off-topic essays. Alternatively, prior work (Higgins et al., 2006) has motivated using similarity between essay and prompt vocabularies to detect off-topic essays. In Section 2, we examine the performance of prompt-essay comparison for four different essay types. We show that in the case of prompts with 9 or 13 content words on average, the error rates are higher compared to those with 60 or more content words. In addition, more errors are observed when the method is used on essays written by English language learners compared to more advanced test takers. An example short prompt from our opinion essays' corpus is shown below. Test-takers provided arguments for/or against the opinion expressed by the prompt.

[1] "In the past, people were more friendly than they are today."

To address this problem, we propose two enhancements. We use unsupervised methods to expand the prompt text with words likely to appear in essays to that prompt. Our approach is based on the intuition that regularities exist in the words which appear in essays, beyond the prevalence of actual prompt words. In a similar vein, misspellings in the essays, particulary of the prompt words, are also problematic for prompt-based methods. Therefore we apply spelling correction to the essay text before comparison. Our results show that both methods lower the error rates. The relative performance of the two methods varies depending on the essay type; however, their combination gives the overall best results regardless of essay type.

2 Effect of prompt and essay properties

In this section, we analyze the off-topic essay prediction accuracies resulting from direct comparison of original prompt and essay texts. We use four different corpora of essays collected and scored during high stakes tests with an English writing component. They differ in task type and average prompt length, as well as the skill level expected from the test taker.

Proceedings of the NAACL HLT 2010 Fifth Workshop on Innovative Use of NLP for Building Educational Applications, pages 92–95,
Los Angeles, California, June 2010.

In one of the tasks, the test taker reads a passage and listens to a lecture and then writes a summary of the main points. For such essays, the prompt text (reading passage plus lecture transcript) available for comparison is quite long (about 276 content words). In the other 3 tasks, the test taker has to provide an argument for or against some opinion expressed in the prompt. One of these has long prompts (60 content words). The other two involve only single sentence prompts as in example [1] and have 13 and 9 content words on average. Two of these tasks focused on English language learners and the other two involved advanced users (applicants to graduate study programs in the U.S.). See Table 1 for a summary of the essay types.[1]

2.1 Data

For each of the task types described above, our corpus contains essays written to 10 different prompts. We used essays to 3 prompts as development data. To build an evaluation test set, we randomly sampled 350 essays for each of the 7 remaining prompts to use as positive examples. It is difficult to assemble a sufficient number of naturally-occurring off-topic essays for testing. However, an essay on-topic to a particular prompt can be considered as *pseudo off-topic* to a different prompt. Hence, to complement the positive examples for each prompt, an equal number of negative examples were chosen at random from essays to the remaining 6 prompts.

2.2 Experimental setup

We use the approach for off-topic essay detection suggested in prior work by Higgins et al. (2006). The method uses cosine overlap between tf*idf vectors of prompt and essay content words to measure the similarity between a prompt-essay pair.

$$sim(prompt, essay) = \frac{v_{essay} \cdot v_{prompt}}{\|v_{essay}\| \|v_{prompt}\|} \quad (1)$$

An essay is compared with the *target* prompt (prompt with which topicality must be checked) together with a set of *reference* prompts, different from the target. The reference prompts are also chosen to be different from the actual prompts of the negative examples in our dataset. If the target prompt is ranked as *most similar*[2] in the list of compared prompts, the essay is classified as on-topic. 9 reference prompts were used in our experiments.

Type	Skill	Prompt len.	Avg FP	Avg FN
1	Learners	276	0.73	11.79
2	Advanced	60	0.20	6.20
3	Advanced	13	2.94	8.90
4	Learners	9	9.73	11.07

Table 1: Effect of essay types: average prompt length, false positive and false negative rates

We compute two error rates.

FALSE POSITIVE - percentage of on-topic essays incorrectly flagged as off-topic.

FALSE NEGATIVE - percentage of off-topic essays which the system failed to flag.

In this task, it is of utmost importance to maintain very low false positive rates, as incorrect labeling of an on-topic essay as off-topic is undesirable.

2.3 Observations

In Table 1, we report the average false positive and false negative rates for the 7 prompts in the test set for each essay type. For long prompts, both *Types 1* and *2*, the false positive rates are very low. The classification of *Type 2* essays which were also written by advanced test takers is the most accurate.

However, for essays with shorter prompts (*Types 3 and 4*), the false positive rates are higher. In fact, in the case of *Type 4* essays written by English language learners, the false positive rates are as high as 10%. Therefore we focus on improving the results in these two cases which involve short prompts.

Both prompt length and the English proficiency of the test taker seem to influence the prediction accuracies for off-topic essay detection. In our work, we address these two challenges by: a) automatic expansion of short prompts (Section 3) and b) correction of spelling errors in essay texts (Section 4).

3 Prompt expansion

We designed four automatic methods to add relevant words to the prompt text.

[1]Essay sources: Type 1-TOEFL integrated writing task, Type 4-TOEFL independent writing task, Types 2 & 3-argument and issue tasks in Analytical Writing section of GRE

[2]Less strict cutoffs may be used, for example, on-topic if target prompt is within rank 3 or 5, etc. However even a cutoff of 2 incorrectly classifies 25% of off-topic essays as on-topic.

3.1 Unsupervised methods

Inflected forms: Given a prompt word, *"friendly"*, its morphological variants—*"friend"*, *"friendlier"*, *"friendliness"*—are also likely to be used in essays to that prompt. Inflected forms are the simplest and most restrictive class in our set of expansions. They were obtained by a rule-based approach (Leacock and Chodorow, 2003) which adds/modifies prefixes and suffixes of words to obtain inflected forms. These rules were adapted from WordNet rules designed to get the base forms of inflected words.

Synonyms: Words with the same meaning as prompt words might also be mentioned over the course of an essay. For example, *"favorable"* and *"well-disposed"* are synonyms for the word *"friendly"* and likely to be good expansions. We used an in-house tool to obtain synonyms from WordNet for each of the prompt words. The lookup involves a word sense disambiguation step to choose the most relevant sense for polysemous words. All the synonyms for the chosen sense of the prompt word are added as expansions.

Distributionally similar words: We also consider as expansions words that appear in similar contexts as the prompt words. For example, *"cordial"*, *"polite"*, *"cheerful"*, *"hostile"*, *"calm"*, *"lively"* and *"affable"* often appear in the same contexts as the word *"friendly"*. Such related words form part of a concept like *'behavioral characteristics of people'* and are likely to appear in a discussion of any one aspect. These expansions could comprise antonyms and other related words too. This idea of word similarity was implemented in work by Lin (1998). Similarity between two words is estimated by examining the degree of overlap of their contexts in a large corpus. We access Lin's similarity estimates using a tool from Leacock and Chodorow (2003) that returns words with similarity values above a cutoff.

Word association norms: Word associations have been of great interest in psycholinguistic research. Participants are given a *target* word and asked to mention words that readily come to mind. The most frequent among these are recorded as *free associations* for that target. They form another interesting category of expansions for our purpose because they are known to be frequently recalled by human subjects for a particular stimulus word. We added the associations for prompt words from a collection of 5000 target words with their associations produced by about 6000 participants (Nelson et al., 1998). Sample associations for the word *"friendly"* include *"smile"*, *"amiable"*, *"greet"* and *"mean"*.

3.2 Weighting of prompt words and expansions

After expansion, the prompt lengths vary between 87 (word associations) and 229 (distributionally similar words) content words, considerably higher than the original average length of 9 and 13 content words. We use a simple weighting scheme[3] to mitigate the influence of noisy expansions. We assign a weight of 20 to original prompt words and 1 to all the expansions. While computing similarity, we use these weight values as the assumed frequency of the word in the prompt. In this case, the term frequency of original words is set as 20 and all expansion terms are considered to appear once in the new prompt.

4 Spelling correction of essay text

Essays written by learners of a language are prone to spelling errors. When such errors occur in the use of the prompt words, prompt-based techniques will fail to identify the essay as on-topic even if it actually is. The usefulness of expansion could also be limited if there are several spelling errors in the essay text. Hence we explored the correction of spelling errors in the essay before off-topic detection.

We use a tool from Leacock and Chodorow (2003) to perform *directed* spelling correction, ie., focusing on correcting the spellings of words most likely to match a given *target* list. We use the prompt words as the targets. We also explore the simultaneous use of spelling correction and expansion. We first obtain expansion words from one of our unsupervised methods. We then use these along with the prompt words for spelling correction followed by matching of the expanded prompt and essay text.

5 Results and discussion

We used our proposed methods on the two essay collections with very short prompts, *Type 3* written by

[3]Without any weighting there was an increase in error rates during development tests. We also experimented with a graph-based approach to term weighting which gave similar results.

advanced test takers and *Type 4* written by learners of English. Table 2 compares the suggested enhancements with the previously proposed method by Higgins et al. (2006). As discussed in Section 2.3, using only the original prompt words, error rates are around 10% for both essay types. For advanced test takers, the false positive rates are lower, around 3%.

Usefulness of expanded prompts All the expansion methods lower the false positive error rates on essays written by learners with almost no increase in the rate of false negatives. On average, the false positive errors are reduced by about 3%. Inflected forms constitute the best individual expansion category. The overall best performance on this type of essays is obtained by combining inflected forms with word associations.

In contrast, for essays written by advanced test takers, inflected forms is the worst expansion category. Here word associations give the best results reducing both false positive and false negative errors; the reduction in false positives is almost 50%. These results suggest that advanced users of English use more diverse vocabulary in their essays which are best matched by word associations.

Effect of spelling correction For essays written by learners, spell-correcting the essay text before comparison (*Spell*) leads to huge reductions in error rates. Using only the original prompt, the false positive rate is 4% lower with spelling correction than without. Note that this result is even better than the best expansion technique–inflected forms. However, for essays written by advanced users, spelling correction does not provide any benefits. This result is expected since these test-takers are less likely to produce many spelling errors.

Combination of methods The benefits of the two methods appear to be population dependent. For learners of English, a spelling correction module is necessary while for advanced users, the benefits are minimal. On the other hand, prompt expansion works extremely well for essays written by advanced users. The expansions are also useful for essays written by learners but the benefits are lower compared to spelling correction. However, for both essay types, the combination of spelling correction and best prompt expansion method (*Spell + best expn.*) is better compared to either of them individually.

	Learners		**Advanced**	
Method	**FP**	**FN**	**FP**	**FN**
Prompt only	9.73	11.07	2.94	9.06
Synonyms	7.03	12.01	1.39	9.76
Dist.	6.45	11.77	1.63	8.98
WAN	6.33	11.97	**1.59**	**8.74**
Infl. forms	6.25	11.65	2.53	9.06
Infl. forms + WAN	**6.04**	**11.48**	-	-
Spell	5.43	12.71	2.53	9.27
Spell + best expn.	***4.66***	***11.97***	***1.47***	***9.02***

Table 2: Average error rates after prompt expansion and spelling correction

Therefore the best policy would be to use both enhancements together for prompt-based methods.

6 Conclusion

We have described methods for improving the accuracy of off-topic essay detection for short prompts. We showed that it is possible to predict words that are likely to be used in an essay based on words that appear in its prompt. By adding such words to the prompt automatically, we built a better representation of prompt content to compare with the essay text. The best combination included inflected forms and word associations, reducing the false positives by almost 4%. We also showed that spelling correction is a very useful preprocessing step before off-topic essay detection.

References

R.S.J.d. Baker, A.M.J.B. de Carvalho, J. Raspat, V. Aleven, A.T. Corbett, and K.R. Koedinger. 2009. Educational software features that encourage and discourage "gaming the system". In *Proceedings of the International Conference on Artificial Intelligence in Education*.

D. Higgins, J. Burstein, and Y. Attali. 2006. Identifying off-topic student essays without topic-specific training data. *Natural Language Engineering*, 12(2):145–159.

C. Leacock and M. Chodorow. 2003. C-rater: Automated scoring of short-answer questions. *Computers and the Humanities*, 37(4):389–405.

D. Lin. 1998. Automatic retrieval and clustering of similar words. In *COLING-ACL*, pages 768–774.

D. L Nelson, C. L. McEvoy, and T. A. Schreiber. 1998. The University of South Florida word association, rhyme, and word fragment norms, http://www.usf.edu/FreeAssociation/.

Author Index

Aluisio, Sandra, 1
Amaral, Luiz, 10

Boullosa, Beto, 19
Boyd, Adriane, 10
Boyer, Kristy, 66

Chen, Lei, 74
Chodorow, Martin, 45

Dimitrov, Aleksandar, 10

Eskenazi, Maxine, 49

Filatova, Elena, 45

Gamon, Michael, 37
García-Narbona, David, 19
Gasperin, Caroline, 1

Ha, Eun Young, 66
Higgins, Derrick, 92

Kim, Jee Eun, 80
Kim, Jihie, 84
Kim, Taehwan, 84

Leacock, Claudia, 37
Lee, Kong Joo, 80
Lester, James, 66
Li, Jia, 84
Louis, Annie, 92

Metcalf, Vanessa, 10
Meurers, Detmar, 10

Ott, Niels, 10

Perry, Jason, 57
Phillips, Rob, 66
Preuß, Susanne, 19

Quixal, Martí, 19

Roth, Dan, 28
Rozovskaya, Alla, 28

Scarton, Carolina, 1
Shan, Chung-chieh, 57
Skory, Adam, 49
Specia, Lucia, 1

Tetreault, Joel, 45, 74

Vouk, Mladen, 66

Wallis, Michael, 66

Xi, Xiaoming, 74

Ziai, Ramon, 10